Flying High

Flying High

How JetBlue Founder and CEO
David Neeleman
Beats the Competition . . .

Even in the World's
Most Turbulent Industry

James Wynbrandt

WILEY

John Wiley & Sons, Inc.

Published by John Wiley & Sons, Inc., Hoboken, New Jersey.
Published simultaneously in Canada.

For general information on our other products and services, or technical support, please contact our Customer Care Department within the United States at 800-762-2974, outside the United States at 317-572-3993 or fax 317-572-4002.

Wiley also publishes its books in a variety of electronic formats. Some content that appears in print may not be available in electronic books.

For more information about Wiley products, visit our web site at www.wiley.com.

Library of Congress Cataloging-in-Publication Data:
Wynbrandt, James.
    Flying high : How JetBlue founder and CEO David Neeleman beats the competition—even in the world's most turbulent industry / James Wynbrandt.
      p. cm.
    Includes bibliographical references and index.
    ISBN 0-471-65544-9 (cloth)
    1. JetBlue Airways—History. 2. Neeleman, David, 1959–
3. Airlines—United States—History. I. Title.
HE9803.J48W96 2004
387.7'0973—dc22   2004003670

Printed in the United States of America.

10 9 8 7 6 5 4 3 2 1

Contents

Introduction

New York's John F. Kennedy International Airport was long past the days when it served as a chic gateway to the Jet Age. Often resembling an overcrowded immigration detention facility more than an airport, it was the last choice among travelers in the know looking to get in or out of the city by air. But on this February morning in 2000, one gate area in the otherwise dormant and deserted Terminal 6 was filled with some of New York's most prominent and powerful figures, all appearing thrilled at having made the trek out to JFK. Among the attendees: Mayor Rudolph Giuliani, Senator Charles Schumer, and Governor George Pataki. There were also members of Congress, representatives of the Federal Aviation Administration, and a host of other local, state, and national officials.

But, all eyes were on the tall, lanky man at the podium who had just received the key to New York City. His boyish features and gee-whiz earnestness were offset by a full head of prematurely gray hair. Wearing his trademark khaki pants, striped tie, and blue blazer, David Neeleman paused while delivering a litany of thank-yous to the assembled guests and colleagues. Perhaps he was taking a rare moment to savor the achievement this event marked. After all, this ceremony heralded the beginning of what he was confident would be a new era in air travel. Yet it also signified an end of his own unique journey—one that stretched some 20 years. It was an incredibly successful and satisfying period by any reckoning. Neeleman had already launched two successful airlines, had a heartbreaking relationship with a third, brought e-ticketing to the airline industry, and created the world's first virtual call center. But this was all just a prelude, a preamble to the statement he was about to make with the unveiling of his latest venture, which he called JetBlue.

In preparing for this day, Neeleman had raised a record amount of money for a start-up airline, assembled one of the greatest management teams in the industry, worked his way through numerous logistical hoops, and stirred up incredible media buzz. He had pledged to bring "humanity" back to air travel, with a fleet of brand-new aircraft fitted with leather seats and individual live television that passengers could watch throughout the entire flight. What's more, he insisted that JetBlue would be customer-focused, while offering fares that would be about two-thirds lower than what the competition previously charged.

He further promised that his company would demonstrate the right way to treat customers and employees, deliver service in an industry that had forgotten the meaning of the word, use technology to streamline operations, and cut costs in a way that would yield a competitive advantage. It was no wonder that with all of these promises, some members of the press reported on events leading up to the launch with an air of skepticism. But Neeleman had never been deterred by the doubts of others before, and this time was no different. He was about to make all of New York, and soon the rest of the country, pay attention—not necessarily to him, but to the right way of doing business.

At precisely 8:55 A.M. on February 11, 2001, cheered by celebrity dignitaries and all of the company's initial crewmembers (the airline's term for *employees*), JetBlue Flight 1 pushed back from the gate, bound for Fort Lauderdale, Florida, its cabin filled with invited guests. Less than three hours later the brand-new airplane, the smell of its leather seats still fresh, landed at its destination to the sounds of applause and celebration. Not a bad accomplishment for a soft-spoken Mormon whose attention deficit disorder affliction once made him doubt he'd ever be able to find a job of any kind; whose first business went bankrupt; and who rubbed so many people the wrong way at a previous job that he was fired in less than six months.

The airline industry has had more than its share of larger-than-life figures since World War I ace Eddie Rickenbacker helped launch Eastern Airlines. From Howard Hughes and Juan Trippe to Neeleman's own hero, Herb Kelleher of Southwest Airlines, the aviation industry has been driven by colorful and innovative characters. While Neeleman holds true to this mold, he's cut from a decidedly different cloth. Unassuming, caring, low-keyed, and outwardly egoless, he's managed to thrive in one of the world's most cutthroat businesses.

Indeed, JetBlue is not Neeleman's first airline success. After healing the wounds suffered from the collapse of his initial entrepreneurial venture in college, Neeleman helped to launch Morris Air while still in his 20s. Starting as a charter operator, under Neeleman's leadership Morris grew into a force so impressive that Southwest Airlines bought it out. After a failed stint as a Southwest employee, Neeleman went on to start a company that introduced e-ticketing, thus revolutionizing the airline industry. He then helped to create WestJet, a thriving low-fare airline in Canada, before setting the wheels in motion for the founding of JetBlue. And he accomplished all this before the age of 40.

How has Neeleman managed to prosper multiple times in an industry littered with failures? What is he doing right that so many others have done wrong? And how can you apply the lessons from his incredible achievements to your own business and life? These are among the issues we'll explore in *Flying High*.

While *Flying High* tells the tale of JetBlue—from how it was founded to the way in which it operates today—this book is the story of David Neeleman. The events of his life leading up to that triumphant flight to Fort Lauderdale paint a fascinating portrait of arguably the most innovative figure in modern-day aviation. They also provide many insights into how he developed the groundbreaking strategies that propelled JetBlue to its fast start.

In the opening chapters of this book, you'll learn more about Neeleman's background—from his childhood and service as a Mormon missionary to the start of his first business, its ultimate failure, and his rise back to the top as president of Morris Air. Then, you'll get the inside story of how Neeleman sold Morris Air to Herb Kelleher at Southwest Airlines, while learning about his brief career there and why he was fired in a matter of months. The book will next detail how Neeleman triumphed over this adversity, and show how he discovered and dealt with a mental disorder that contributed to both his tribulations and successes. It will continue with his co-founding of the company that introduced electronic ticketing, and his pivotal role in getting the successful Canadian airline WestJet airborne. And, of course, it will provide a comprehensive account of how Neeleman planned, created, and now operates one of the most successful airlines in history.

Throughout this fascinating journey, you'll discover the management techniques that Neeleman has developed and used over the years, which most observers credit for JetBlue's unparalleled accomplishments. The book concludes with a list of Neeleman's

14 rules for success, as evidenced and shaped by the events and challenges faced throughout his life. While he applies these rules to running JetBlue, they are truly applicable to every business in every industry.

David Neeleman's vision and passion have transformed the travel experience for not only the millions who have flown on JetBlue, but also those who fly on virtually every other airline. His innovations have changed the playing field and forced all other carriers to reevaluate the way they do business. Yet his life and career provide lessons for us all in how creativity, dedication, and teamwork can turn almost any enterprise into a winner, no matter what the industry or the obstacles in the way. I hope you will come away from this book confident that you, too, now know how to bring a greater degree of humanity, customer service, profitability, fun, and satisfaction to your own chosen field.

CHAPTER 1

The Journey Begins

David Neeleman claims he still recalls the moment from his second birthday. Whether he remembers the actual event, or only the ingrained impressions of early viewings of it captured in a family photograph, as his father, Gary, suggests with a chuckle, no one knows. But anyone looking for clues to the future course of this airline innovator's life can't ignore the significance of his recollection, imagined or otherwise. When the birthday cake was brought out, it wasn't the glowing candles that caught David's attention. There atop the confection sat a small red airplane. Something about the ornamental craft transfixed him, he says. This fascination followed him into adulthood, leading to a series of successful aviation businesses and eventually the founding of an airline that is transforming the airline industry, sparking copycat competitors, and forcing the old-line carriers that historically dominated the domestic skies to rethink their operating principles and practices.

The birthday was celebrated in São Paulo, Brazil, where Neeleman was born in October of 1959. He was the second son and child in a brood of seven, four boys and three girls. His father,

Gary, a Salt Lake City native, was the Latin America bureau chief for United Press International (UPI), a high-profile position in the sophisticated city. His mother, Rose, had been Gary's assistant before becoming his wife.

The Neeleman family (they pronounce their name in three syllables, Nee-le-man) had immigrated to the United States from Holland, where they'd been members of the Mormon church, around the turn of the last century. Gary's father, John, was born a few months after the Neelemans arrived in Salt Lake City.

Gary graduated with a degree in fine arts from the University of Utah, but took up journalism because it offered more of a future. His fluency in several languages, including Portuguese, had served him well in his theater studies and helped him win the choice posting in Brazil. UPI's Latin American desk—also known as Latam or the Chester desk (referring to either a radio transmitter in Chester, Pennsylvania, or a long-forgotten telex operator by that name, according to UPI lore)—was the heart of UPI's Spanish-language wire news service. For much of the last century it was the preeminent international news organization in Central and South America. Latin America was also one of UPI's most successful and lucrative markets.

Reporting the news was only one of the challenges of Gary Neeleman's job. Just getting the hardware the bureau needed to operate was a monumental task. "It was a torment," Gary recalls. "You couldn't import anything. We'd go to the foreign ministry and say, 'Look, we've got to have another seven teletype machines because Eisenhower is coming,' and they might (occasionally) give us a break."

Young David Neeleman was clearly a precocious boy. Early on he exhibited his own unique talents in a family of high-achieving children. "David was one that was full of ideas, very, very active, and thinking outside the box all the time," says Gary Neeleman.

Brazil in the early 1960s was a time and place of rigid class distinctions, doubly so for the U.S. citizens who worked for American companies with operations in Brazil. The country's upper class, to which the foreign-born executives of multinational companies belonged de facto, and the teeming masses of the poor were in permanent conflict. Yet upper- and lower-class Brazilians were united in their antipathy for what was seen as heavy-handed American influence over the country's business and culture.

Anti-Americanism was a driving force in the country's body politic. "One group put out a booklet entitled 'A Day in the Life of a Brazilian,' in which a cartoon character wakes up, brushes his teeth with Colgate toothpaste, eats his Kellogg's cereal with orange juice packaged by General Mills, then drives his Ford to work, where he takes an Otis elevator to his office," says Gary Neeleman, recalling the prevailing attitude of the time.

Gary Neeleman exhibited none of the colonialist attitudes common to foreign-born managers of the era, who often displayed a condescending and patronizing manner to the locals. While many U.S.-born news executives in Latin America questioned the abilities and sympathies of Latin-born reporters, Neeleman fiercely defended their professionalism during his 27 years at the news organization.

"Just because wages are lower in those countries does not mean the talent is less," he maintained. "I know journalists in those countries who can write rings around most U.S. journalists. . . . I want to debunk the 'fact' that just because somebody is a local hire he's inferior."

When David Neeleman was five, his father was transferred back to the United States and returned to Salt Lake City with his family. David was enrolled in the Peruvian Park Elementary School. Though the name may have provided some link to his early years in South America, the transition to primary school wasn't an easy one. "It was an adjustment," Gary admits. "The kids spoke better Portuguese than they did English." Gary recalls that David was "a handful," a child who was "clearly bright but a window gazer who constantly fell behind on his lessons" and who "was always looking out the window, thinking of something else."

David Neeleman's third grade teacher prophetically told his mother that he could be "tremendously successful when he grows up—if he hires himself an assistant." But the teacher was more sanguine than others about young David's chances for eventual achievement. In fact, Neeleman recalls he was almost left behind that year. "They wanted me to repeat the third grade, but my parents said, 'He's a smart kid. You don't know what you're talking about.'" In the end, Neeleman was permitted to move up to the fourth grade.

An inability to focus and a short attention span dogged Neeleman outside the classroom as well. "David hated fishing," his father remembers. "He didn't have the patience. He would start fishing, and two minutes later, he is throwing rocks in the pond."

FIRST LESSONS IN CUSTOMER SERVICE

It was during this time of educational turmoil that Neeleman acquired his initial lesson in the ingredients of business success, through the example of the family patriarch—his grandfather, John Neeleman. John, the first of the Neelemans born in the United States, started what has been purported to be the first convenience store in the country. Called the Miniature Market, on South Street in Salt Lake City, it was in business before the first 7-Eleven opened its doors. From the start, John Neeleman had strong ideas about customer service, according to Gary, his son.

"Dad's main idea was that you don't tell the customer you can't do it or you don't have it," Gary Neeleman explains. "You do everything humanly possible to make it happen."

In fact, though it was open around the clock, John Neeleman didn't consider his establishment to be a convenience store, but rather a "service store." It served a collection of customers that included split-shifters, truck drivers, college students, late-working waitresses, and entertainers. As local reporter Fred Ball recalls, John "cashed their checks when nobody else would, delivered groceries to nearby apartment houses, shut-ins, and to anyone who needed something, even if he didn't carry it.

"If someone asked for a product the store didn't have, John would stall the customer with a doughnut and a cup of coffee or a cold drink while Gary was sent to the back room with a wink to 'look' for the item," Ball continues. "Gary would then bolt out the back door to the Safeway store a few blocks away to bring back the needed item."

As Gary Neeleman notes, "Dad hated to tell anyone he didn't have what was needed."

Everyone in the family helped out at the store. John depended on his children and later his grandchildren to pitch in. All are said to remember checking out items at the cash register while standing on a milk crate, so they'd be tall enough to see over the counter. David Neeleman gained his first work experience when he started working at his grandfather's store at age nine. This focus on customer service had a lasting impact on the boy.

"If there wasn't an item in the store that somebody wanted, he'd actually run out and buy it somewhere else and bring it back, because he [my grandfather] hated disappointing customers," Neeleman says. "He knew the value of a valued customer, and I think that was instilled in me."

John Neeleman's ideas about delivering the best possible product were also absorbed by young David. "We had these great sand-wiches that he'd make, using the best bread and making sure that he had the best quality meat, and knowing that if he made the best product, that people would come back and [keep] buying those sandwiches," David Neeleman says. "And, before long, he was sell-ing 500 of those things a day."

Who knows what might have happened had the grandfather coupled his drive for customer service and the concept of around-the-clock convenience with his grandson's vision and creativity? Likewise, who can say whether David Neeleman would have recognized customer service as a key to the busi-ness success he would eventually achieve were he not exposed to his grandfather's tutelage? Fortunately, John "Grandpa" Neele-man was able to see at least some of the fruits of his lessons. By the time he died in 1990, his grandson was president of a suc-cessful Salt Lake City–based airline. In his eulogy at the funeral, David Neeleman related that much of his creative business sense was owed to his grandfather.

Whatever lessons nine-year-old David Neeleman was learning behind the counter of his grandfather's Miniature Market weren't following him into the classroom. His difficulty with reading and writing continued throughout his school years. He took easy courses just to maintain respectable grades. "I felt like I was al-ways behind," he remembers. Neeleman cites his parents' support through these times as being instrumental in helping him to over-come his doubts about himself. Says his father, "We didn't say, 'Oh, you dumb cluck. What on earth's going on with you? Can't you get better grades?' And all that kind of thing. We just sort of went along with him and said, 'No, you're going to be okay.'"

Whatever the endeavor, it seemed Neeleman's scattered atten-tion interfered. Both of his parents remember a band concert at his elementary school in which Neeleman played drums. Providing a steady beat was difficult enough for the hyperactive young-ster, but Neeleman complicated the task by acting as the pseudo leader of the band, according to his parents. "He couldn't hardly concentrate on what he was supposed to be doing," Gary says about the performance, "because he wanted to make sure every-one else was doing the right thing."

Gary Neeleman maintained his connection with Brazil and South America, frequently traveling there both on business and for the educational and cultural exchange programs he was in-volved with. He often took David and his other children along on these journeys. David accompanied his father, for example, on exhibition tours Gary arranged for U.S. college basketball teams. As he did at his grandfather's store, David pitched in to help.

"If they wanted a drink, he'd get them a drink," Gary Neele-man says of his son's assistance. "If they wanted a ball, he'd get them a ball. If they wanted more dessert, he'd get them more dessert."

But in the classroom, problems persisted throughout his four years at Salt Lake City's Brighton High School, leaving the ado-lescent Neeleman concerned about his future.

"When I got out of high school, I didn't feel I could read or write that well," he says. "I couldn't sit down and read a whole book. I thought, 'How am I ever going to be successful in any-thing if I can't read and write?'"

In 1977, after graduating from high school, Neeleman enrolled at the University of Utah, choosing accounting as his area of spe-cialization. The work with numbers wasn't as intimidating to him as other majors that required more reading and writing. He also became a manager of the school's basketball team, something he'd gained experience in on exhibition trips to Latin America with his father. Schoolwork continued to be a chore, but Neeleman absorbed other lessons that transcended reading and writing, and even business acumen, from both his parents and the Mormon faith he held so dear.

"I was raised in a great family," Neeleman says. "I had great examples in my parents. I'm a deeply religious person."

That religious conviction led him to leave college after his freshman year to serve the church as a missionary. Members of the Church of Jesus Christ of Latter Day Saints believe it is their duty to act as emissaries in spreading the word of God in the same way Jesus urged his disciples to proselytize in Matthew 28:19: "Go ye therefore, and teach all nations, baptizing them in the name of the Father, and of the Son, and of the Holy Ghost." Initially, married men served as the church's missionaries, leaving their wives and families for an unspecified period. Today the majority of missionaries are single men who serve for about two years. Following an interview with the prospective missionary, church officials recommend where the candidate will be posted. For David Neeleman, the church's assignment was to serve as a missionary in the country of his birth: Brazil.

The life of a Mormon missionary is demanding and ascetic. They live simply and aren't permitted to watch television, listen to the radio, or go to places of entertainment. Rising at 6:30 in the morning, they spend their days in religious study and spreading the Mormon message. This life transition was no doubt especially dramatic for Neeleman, who was assigned to spread the word in Rio de Janeiro's *favelas*, the notorious slums of the city.

"When I was [first] living in Brazil, I ran with all the rich and famous and hung out at all the fancy clubs," Neeleman reflects. "Then when I went back as a missionary, I hung out with the poor and the humble." He describes his service as "a life-changing experience," one that forever altered his outlook on life and, for that matter, business.

"I felt a contrast there and I saw that the poor and humble were the most wonderful, sweet people. . . . Then I realized that everybody is equal and you should treat people the same [and] with respect."

Neeleman not only became fluent in Portuguese, he discovered he had a gift for salesmanship: He baptized more than 200 converts. "It was really the first time I felt like I had some talent," he says. He also demonstrated the frugality he would practice throughout his career. A missionary's family is primarily responsible for providing his financial support. During his two years in the country, Neeleman's family sent him a total of $3,000. He saved $1,300 of it.

The lessons he learned, and the things he saw in the *favelas*, continue to resonate with Neeleman more than two decades later. "I found a lot of greed, and a lot of people that were being taken advantage of. Even today, when I see executives of companies that have stock worth umpteen [millions] and they're taking down, you know, $10 million salaries, or another $80 million . . . I can't understand that. You know, how much money do you need?"

NEELEMAN'S FIRST BUSINESS

Neeleman returned to Utah in 1980 and married his college sweetheart, Vicki Vranes. Their first child, Ashley, was born a year later. Neeleman also reenrolled at the University of Utah, where he continued his studies in accounting.

Whatever future awaited Neeleman as an accountant, the business opportunities of the present seemed limited. The recession of the early 1980s made the economic environment more difficult for almost everyone. During his sophomore year, a coed in Neeleman's accounting class told him that her mother knew someone in Hawaii who was having trouble selling timeshares in a hotel he had converted into condominiums. While Neeleman often alters the terms of the financial transaction he engineered with the property owner in various retellings, the basic story remains the same:

"I called him and said I'd pay him $100 plus the condo maintenance fees for each week he couldn't rent them," Neeleman offers. The owner agreed, and Neeleman started advertising the condos in a local newspaper, soon finding a market for the units. "I was paying $125 a week, and was collecting $500 a week," Neeleman says. "And before you knew it, I was doing three or four of these a day in college, thinking, 'Wow, this is a pretty good business.'"

As demand picked up, Neeleman negotiated with other properties to take on more rooms. At the same time, he began packaging the condos with seats on charter flights to Hawaii. Despite the problems he had in school, the lack of attention he struggled with, and the fears about his abilities, Neeleman had finally found something he could focus on and be successful at. He was as creative and energetic in his marketing as he was shameless. Neeleman was even known to approach newlyweds at their nuptials and hawk his Hawaii package as an ideal honeymoon.

Neeleman soon expanded his business, starting a full-fledged travel agency. He used his growing marketing muscle to buy discount tickets from a couple of upstart airlines—The Hawaii Express and, to a lesser extent, Pacific East Air. Both airlines offered fares to the islands from the West Coast that were far below the major carriers. That way, Neeleman was able to further reduce his prices and make his package deals to Hawaii even more attractive.

The Hawaii Express was founded by Michael Hartley, a long-time Hawaii resident. Hartley was a young airline entrepreneur, and elements of his operations would later be echoed in Neeleman's. A large, athletic man with exotic good looks, a perpetual grin, and well-groomed thick mustache, Hartley started Island Pacific Air, a small discount interisland carrier, in late 1973 while in his early 20s. He sold that business for a small profit in 1977 and moved to Oahu, where he ran an aviation services company. As a condition of the sale, Hartley signed a five-year noncompete agreement. He came up with the idea for The Hawaii Express one day while sitting on the beach.

The Hawaii Express began non-stop service from Los Angeles to Honolulu on August 26, 1982, flying a single leased Boeing 747. Formerly owned by Alitalia, the plane was one of the oldest 747s in the world. Hartley configured the all-coach cabin to hold an amazing 491 passengers. There were so many seats squeezed in, there was even one stuffed deep in the nose of the plane.

The airline's pilots were mostly former employees of Braniff Airways, which had folded a few months earlier. Many of the flight attendants hired by The Hawaii Express were on furlough from other carriers and joined the promising new upstart with great anticipation.

"This was just like a dream come true, because the Hawaii routes are so senior. Here we were, young and energetic, flying a great route that only required us to work about seven days a month," says Rebecca Reeder Hunt, one of the airline's original 50 flight attendants. "The other days we were on the beach having a good time."

The original mission of The Hawaii Express was to make getting to the islands fun and affordable. For the first year, the airline's only flight was a daily run from Los Angeles to Honolulu and back, often with the same cabin crew. The plane would leave LAX around 11 A.M., spend a couple of hours on the ground in Honolulu, and get back to California by midnight. "We thought we were on the ground floor of something really big, maybe even the next Southwest-type success story, except serving Hawaii with wide-body aircraft," Reeder Hunt says, adding that many crew members turned down offers from other carriers to stay on board.

The Hawaii Express eventually added two DC-10s to its fleet, though it still only flew the Los Angeles–Honolulu route. Every plane was packed. Passengers were attracted by the airline's low fares, which went as high as $128 and as low as $79 each way—significantly less than before The Hawaii Express arrived on the scene.

"We had movies and food—a hockey-puck sandwich, little bag of chips, and a brownie—and everyone had a great time," Reeder Hunt remembers. "It seemed like everyone in California had taken at least one flight on The Hawaii Express."

The airline was so popular for cost-conscious vacationers looking for an economical trip to the islands that the major carriers started to notice—and they responded aggressively. United among others began matching—and often beating—fares offered by The Hawaii Express. Still, the carrier dubbed "the big pineapple" continued to thrive—or so it seemed.

CHOOSING BUSINESS OVER
A COLLEGE DEGREE

By his junior year of college, Neeleman's small travel company had 20 employees and recorded $8 million in annual sales. Neeleman wanted to drop out of school and run his fledgling operation full-time. His parents, who'd helped him start his business by letting him work on it from their kitchen table, weren't pleased. After all, his mother had a master's degree, and his older brother had a law degree from Georgetown. "We're education minded," his father says. "We thought maybe he should stick around and go to school, but he was a rambunctious and active kid, and he wanted to get on with his life, so we didn't discourage or encourage him."

It wasn't a hard decision for David Neeleman. He hated every minute of his three years at the University of Utah. With his business flourishing, he felt he wouldn't need a degree in accounting to be a success after all.

"I couldn't focus," he later said of his college career. "I'm not ashamed that I don't have a degree."

Neeleman's success began drawing the attention of more than just the happy vacationers who felt they were getting a good bargain. "He was really doing things with Hawaii," says Rick Frendt, who at the time was president of a large Salt Lake City travel agency called Morris Travel. "He was doing the things we tried to do, things that couldn't be done. He was putting lots of people in rooms at prices half of anyone else. He just had a lot of charm."

Neeleman's travel company was debt-free. Bookings were growing. And by paying cash in advance for the rooms and seats on The Hawaii Express, he was able to negotiate even better rates. It seemed everything was going perfectly. Then the unexpected happened: The Hawaii Express ran into turbulence.

By the airline's first anniversary, insiders say, they noticed a mood change. New faces were beginning to appear in the executive suite, including an attorney who specialized in bankruptcies. Observant outsiders could see other indications of the company's ill financial health. For instance, aboard the planes, all the magazines stocked for passengers (other than the carrier's own thin inflight guide) came from the homes of flights crews, who carefully removed any personal address labels from the covers before handing them out. According to some, The Hawaii Express's operating expenses were higher than what the airline was charging its passengers. The price wars grew so brutal, the airline was forced to cut its already low fares even further to remain competitive. While the major carriers could absorb any temporary losses by hiking fares on other routes, The Hawaii Express flew to only one destination. And while there were plans to begin service to Honolulu from San Francisco and perhaps other cities down the line, they never materialized. Eventually the fight got too tough for the upstart carrier to handle. In December 1983, The Hawaii Express filed for bankruptcy and stopped flying.

"All of a sudden, the airline went out of business—and basically put us out of business," Neeleman says. "When the hotels we had paid in advance wouldn't give the money back, we were done." Neeleman lost not only his own money, but also the money from customers who had paid for their trips in advance.

If he'd had more cash, Neeleman's business could have been salvaged, he later surmised. Other seats to Hawaii could have been found. Inconvenienced vacationers could have been compensated. But he had little reserves, and without financial backing, there was no way to stave off his own company's bankruptcy. Neeleman's business and the dreams that went with it were lost.

Hartley ultimately landed on his feet. Three years after the demise of The Hawaii Express, he started a travel agency called Cheap Tickets. The company contracted with major carriers to sell excess seats to destinations around the world at discount prices. One of the hot companies of the Internet boom, Hartley sold it in 1999, pocketing $50 million for his share of the business.

David Neeleman, too, would rebound from the failure of his company. And his recovery was only weeks away.

CHAPTER 2

Have I Got a Deal for You

With Salt Lake City being the close-knit, small community it was in the early 1980s, the failure of 24-year-old David Neeleman's business didn't go unnoticed.

"I just happened to be meeting with his uncle that day over some business," remembers June Morris, proprietor of the state's largest travel agency at that time, Morris Travel. Neeleman's uncle was her tax attorney. "He said, 'Oh, did you hear, my nephew's lost his business?' I said, 'Well, good, give me his phone number.'"

Morris, a shrewd businesswoman who's part Aunt Bea and part Mary Kay, had met Neeleman once before. She recalls that his father, Gary, came in with him a couple of years earlier to discuss an idea for a travel business with her. What she hadn't grasped then was that it was *David's* idea, and that he'd asked his father to accompany him to the meeting. David Neeleman's fledgling Hawaiian condo rental business was growing. The idea he and his dad brought to Morris involved packaging bulk airline seats to Hawaii that could be put together with cheap accommodations on the island. But at that time, this concept, which would play such a large role in the future success of both Neeleman and Morris, somehow didn't strike a responsive chord with her.

Though nothing came of that first meeting, David Neeleman made an indelible impression. "When he walked into a room, the energy level went up," Morris says. But there was a more immediate reason she was aware of Neeleman: "He was taking away some of my Hawaiian clientele," she notes. Since she'd passed on his idea, he'd done quite well putting together discount travel packages on his own.

Morris wasn't one whose clients were easily poached. While Utah's Mormon culture is strongly patriarchal, June Morris had blissfully ignored this throughout her life, always exhibiting the energy, self-reliance, and confidence she had learned from her mother.

"My mother was certainly a stand-up-and-be-counted female," Morris says. "I just figured that's the way it was. I didn't give a thought about male- or female-oriented."

Morris began her career at American Express, handling corporate travel for the company's clients. A single mom, the former June Frendt became a top producer in the western states and was one of the few women American Express sent through its management training program. But after marrying Mitch Morris, a successful businessman, she quit her job to take up the life of a housewife, as her new husband requested. The new lifestyle didn't agree with her.

"I stayed home for a few months and I said, 'Hey, I'm not doing this. I'm going back to work.'" Mitch Morris, who was himself an entrepreneur, encouraged his bride to start her own travel business. He even offered to guarantee a loan if she needed financing. At first June demurred, claiming she was incapable of starting a business. Finally she decided to plunge ahead. She sat down, ordered the requisite brochures and forms, and established a one-person agency, which was aptly named Morris Travel.

While her husband invested no money in the company, he provided what would be a doubly valuable contribution: a Univac computer—the fabled and, at the time, state-of-the-art mainframe. The only other mainframe in the state as large was at the University of Utah. Mitch Morris also owned, among other businesses, one of the largest photo finishing companies in the country. The Univac kept track of billing and served as a central database for all of the company's locations. He offered to let June use the Univac for any purpose that would help her business. She sat down with his programmer to develop applications for the agency.

"At that time travel agencies didn't have any back-room systems," June Morris explains. "So I could go out and offer everybody in town reports of who traveled, what they paid, what their departments' travel costs were, and what we saved them." This was a service no other agency could offer to corporations at the time and was an extremely effective marketing tool.

Adds Rick Frendt, Morris's son and president of the agency, "We really used that to go after commercial accounts."

June brought Frendt aboard around 1976. He was a freshly minted MBA who had inherited his mother's interest in travel. At the time, Morris Travel was a $3 to 4 million agency with eight employees.

"I had to hire him because he had the business smarts," Morris says. Frendt took over day-to-day operations, while Morris gave herself responsibility for "the schmoozing and the ideas."

With Frendt's help, the advantage provided by the Univac, and Morris's own business savvy, the agency, in her words, "took off." She boasts, "We had every major account in town."

One of the biggest was the travel account of Sperry Univac itself, maker of the mainframe she used. Her husband, Mitch, asked Sperry executives—in light of his being a Univac customer—why his wife's agency wasn't getting their travel business.

He pointed out that her company also used a Univac computer. After he provided an introduction for his wife, Morris Travel won the Sperry Univac account.

By the time June Morris heard about the demise of David Neeleman's business in 1984, Morris Travel was a $50 million agency with 100 employees and several locations throughout Utah. But Morris Travel was at a crossroads. June Morris was trying to reposition the company to avoid becoming a victim of her own success. "The travel agency was very successful, but it was heavily corporate," she says. "With [airline] deregulation, I was afraid the airlines were going to do just what they're doing now: cutting out the commissions. So that's when I decided I needed to expand into the leisure market."

Back then, airlines generally paid agencies a 10 percent commission on the base fare of tickets. For complete travel packages or cruises, the commissions could be even higher. Morris knew if her business was totally dependent on what the airlines alone paid, and the commission rate was dropped, her revenues would plummet.

"The goal was to change the mix, so we'd be 50-50," Frendt recalls—in other words, half business and half leisure. "We just didn't think that things could continue in business travel, so we specifically went after leisure business."

That's when Neeleman came along.

"Of course, we knew of his reputation of being incredibly creative," Frendt says. In terms of marketing and negotiating deals, "David was the most creative person we'd seen."

June Morris took Neeleman's phone number from his uncle and gave him a ring.

"June called me up and said, 'Hey, why don't you come work for us and do what you're doing, you know, on your own?'"

Neeleman recounts. "And I said, 'No, I hate this business. Stay away from me.'"

"He was really down," Morris says, "just devastated. He had no interest."

After some cajoling, Neeleman agreed to drop by her office, where he met with Morris and her son.

"He was convinced he wanted to have absolutely nothing to do with the travel business," Frendt remembers. "He was going to go down to Phoenix and start a drapery business," the business his wife's family had in Salt Lake City. Neeleman did, however, offer to pass along insights into what he'd been doing at his agency if Morris and Frendt felt it would be helpful in their agency's pursuit of the leisure end of the travel business.

But Morris recognized that Neeleman had something very special, and she wanted *him*, not just a brain dump of ideas.

"I said, 'Now, David, why don't we do this: You come to work—work as many hours as you want to, do whatever works out for you—and then in a few weeks you tell me how much you're worth,'" Morris says. Neeleman agreed and in June 1984 came to work at Morris Travel. "After about a week, he decided it [the travel business] was kind of fun again," Frendt says.

"He was the perfect person at the time, and Morris Travel was the perfect springboard for his creativity," Morris adds. "And it was great. So that's how we started."

At Morris, Neeleman tried to pick up from where he'd been grounded, by arranging vacation packages to Hawaii. But with the airlines that carried the bulk of his customers out of business, finding seats this time around wasn't easy. Getting good pricing on the air transportation component was crucial to making the packages work. That way agencies could offer passengers an all-inclusive price with airfare, transfers, and hotel accommodations for the same or less than the cost of a flight alone bought directly from a major carrier. Western Airlines was the major carrier serving Salt Lake City at the time. It refused to offer Neeleman and the Morris team much in the way of deals. A few discount seats were available on Northwest Airlines, but not enough to base a business on. So Neeleman and Frendt flew to Hawaii to meet with Al Wells, a vice president of Hawaiian Airlines, to see if they could arrange a deal with him. They reached a unique agreement.

"He had an old DC-8 sitting around one day a week, so on Thursday night he'd fly it to Salt Lake, and Friday morning, back to Honolulu for us," Frendt recalls.

The goal was to start the 204-seat flights in May and run them through the summer, until the peak travel season ended in September. But as difficult as finding seats in the first place had been, filling them would prove to be a bigger challenge.

"David made the commitment that he'd somehow put butts in all those seats," Frendt says. "He always had an idea a minute."

Neeleman and Frendt went back to Hawaii and got both the time-share condo property Neeleman had used before and some additional hotel rooms lined up. Once back in Salt Lake City, they put together a brochure and were on their way.

The entry-level vacation package Morris Travel offered was a couple of hundred dollars cheaper than any other on the market, but it wasn't generating much interest as the launch of their first flight approached. Neeleman and Frendt went back to see Wells, the Hawaiian Airlines executive. The message they brought was simple, according to Frendt: "Hey, it's not working." They needed a better price on the seats. With the credibility and commitment of Morris Travel behind him, Neeleman was able to negotiate a bigger discount on the first 20 seats. Neeleman used the discounted seats to convince June Morris, who kept close tabs on her precocious protégé, to let them lower the price on the vacation packages.

She agreed, and they began offering the first 20 to 40 seats each week for a much lower cost. While Delta Airlines charged about $800 for a round-trip ticket from Salt Lake City to Honolulu, Morris Travel offered fares as low as $399, with rooms for a five-night stay going for just $20 per night. With the new price structure, business picked up. When price alone couldn't drive enough traffic to fill the planes, Neeleman's initiative carried the day.

"Whatever it took, we'd fill the seats," Frendt says. "Again, that's where David's creativity came in like you can't believe. David would be out at the malls, recruiting people: 'Hey you want to go to Hawaii? $100? Day after tomorrow?' Somehow we'd find those last 20 to 30 seats, top this thing off, every week."

If they couldn't find enough paying customers, they'd trade seats for whatever they could, from office furniture to food.

"We even had a guy, a grocery guru, and he'd buy groceries with coupons (and trade them with us for seats), so then we'd have like a grocery store at the office," Frendt says. "If it wasn't a 100 percent load factor (in terms of the percentage of seats filled on the planes), it was 99 percent all summer long, and we went through the fall and were able to fill that, too."

That year, Hawaiian Airlines determined that beginning in the fall, it would have no further need for the DC-8 Morris used for its weekly flights. The airline offered to base the plane in Salt Lake City and give Morris Travel more use of the aircraft. The extra use allowed Morris to offer red-eye return flights from Hawaii, making the packages more appealing to customers. Neeleman, Frendt, and Morris also decided to use the extra flying time allotted to them to offer charter service between Salt Lake City and Los Angeles three times a week, in large part to help reposition the aircraft for the Hawaii flights. Western Airlines charged $200 one way for the Salt Lake to Los Angeles trip. Morris Travel planned to sell tickets for $59, plus federal excise tax, a pricing ploy they later found out was illegal. The law required that all taxes be included in the advertised fare so that the price consumers saw was all-inclusive. "We didn't know that was illegal," Frendt says, laughing as he looks back on what they thought was a clever marketing effort. "We were a bunch of stupid kids."

To handle the volume of calls they expected for their flights to Los Angeles, Morris Travel hired six agents, got some card tables to seat them at, and gave them booking sheets to write down the reservations. The agency then placed a small advertisement in the weekend edition of the *Salt Lake Tribune*, announcing the impending inauguration of Salt Lake City to Los Angeles service aboard Morris Air.

"We thought we were all set," Frendt recalls. "Monday morning, the phones went crazy." Frendt estimates the agents could only handle 6 percent of the call volume that day. "It was just a magical thing between Salt Lake and Los Angeles. There was so much pent-up demand."

With the charter bookings bringing in sales much more quickly than anticipated, the Morris team needed help dealing with the agency's finances. One of Morris's employees, Cindy Dunham Evans, recommended her husband, Gordon ("Gordy") Evans, who had just earned a master's degree in business, for the position of comptroller. Conservative and cautious, Gordy would become a key part of the Morris Air team, and a great complement to Neeleman's exuberant shotgun style.

TECHNOLOGY HELPS THE RAPIDLY EXPANDING MORRIS TEAM

Just as June Morris had used her husband's Univac to track travel data for her corporate clients, so was the computer put to work tracking information for Morris Air. Again, the quick expansion of business caused growing pains. Transferring data from the paper booking sheets alone was daunting. And the program that worked so well for tracking the travel of corporate clients wasn't ideally suited for managing the charter passengers Morris Air was serving.

"We were growing too fast," Morris says. "We were out of room. We had folding tables and chairs and we kept adding people. It was really kind of a funny operation."

Four months after Gordy Evans joined the company, his brother, David, returned from missionary service in San Antonio.

"I was 20 years old," David Evans recalls. "I heard of this Neeleman guy and I asked my brother to introduce me to this Mr. Neeleman. My brother looked at me like, 'Mister? He's only 23 or 24!' David was just this kid."

Planning to reenroll in college, where he had studied finance, David Evans was looking for part-time work. With the company's okay, Gordy offered him a job doing data entry and backing up the computer system. David Evans went to work in the garage in the back of the funky Morris Air Service office on the west side of Salt Lake City. Though he wasn't studying computer science at school, he turned out to be "a whiz," according to June Morris. "He was so smart."

David Evans soon wrote and implemented a program that tracked all of Morris Air's booking and ticketing information. Unfortunately, the initial program had what Rick Frendt calls "a fly" in it: It only recorded the outbound flights, not the returns. As a result, during the second week of the program's operation, returns were overbooked by about 50 percent on every flight.

"We were out there at the airport selling [tickets] for $59 and we'd be writing out tickets on Delta for $200 and giving them to [our overbooked passengers]," Frendt remembers. "It was so depressing there at that time that week. But we stuck to it, and at some point, we thought we were going to Los Angeles just to get the plane to Hawaii, and realized Los Angeles was a gold mine."

Meanwhile, David Evans quickly corrected his program, which would ultimately morph into the backbone of the e-ticketing system used by most airlines around the world today. Eventually, Neeleman appointed Evans as vice president of information systems at Morris Air.

"We got along well I think because I was able to put into computer code the things that he could imagine," Evans says. "It took a while for me to figure out that he comes up with three or four ideas and one of them is good. You have to figure out which one is good, which one to stick to. Maybe let him tell you about it a couple of times. If he tells you about it the third time, he hasn't lost interest in it, and you gotta do it. He gets very, very focused on things that he really believes in. Other things come and go pretty quickly."

MORRIS EARNS WHILE IT LEARNS

At the end of 1984, noise restrictions grounded Hawaiian Airlines' DC-8, but Neeleman and his team saw there was enough business to enable Morris Air to lease other aircraft for its charter flights.

The secret to their success was simple, according to June Morris: "The price. It was around $600 (round-trip) to Los Angeles [on the scheduled airlines] and we were doing it for $120. And that's not a hard decision when you're in Utah with a bunch of kids."

Destinations were added. Vacation packages were expanded. Seats were filled. The business grew quickly. Morris Travel also bought seats in bulk on other charters to Hawaii and Mexico, which Neeleman filled by arranging still more irresistible deals on accommodations.

"We did fantastic," Morris admits. "We even would bring people in from Los Angeles for plastic surgery because the surgeons [in Salt Lake City] do charge much less than they do on the West Coast. So we had everything you can imagine going. It was wild."

David Neeleman was everywhere: on the phone, on the tarmac, and bouncing basketballs down the hallways of the Morris offices. A friend of his father's watched in amazement one day as the young Neeleman dashed all over Salt Lake City International Airport on a typical day, doing everything from overseeing boarding to sweeping the floor. Said the friend, "If that . . . kid is sitting in the pilot seat, I'm going home."

"David is like a sponge," Morris explains, summing up his unique talents. "He listens, he reads, he talks to people, he just soaks everything up. He's very creative coming up with all his ideas." And Neeleman had found in the Morris team a group that believed in and backed him in implementing his ideas. "We'd say 'Let's do it,' and figure out what we have to do. He was just an amazing young fellow at age 24."

Finding the aircraft to use for the charter flights they operated was an ongoing challenge. So was keeping costs down.

"We thought we had low costs," Frendt says, "but when we actually figured them out and added them up, they were among the highest in the industry. What made it work was because we had a 95 percent load factor. You can be marketing geniuses when your prices are half of everybody else's."

Meanwhile, Hawaii became less of the company's focus. Because of operating costs, making money on long-haul routes was difficult. Neeleman began studying the operations of People Express, the low-cost carrier started by Donald Burr in 1984 that was proving to be a big success in offering short-haul service throughout the Northeast. Using the lessons he gleaned from his studies,

Neeleman developed plans for expanding Morris Air's service to selected short-haul destinations, Boise and Spokane among them.

It was a heady time, as Morris Air rapidly expanded. "We were kind of an exciting little business for Utah," observes Frendt. Meanwhile, the company's esprit de corps grew as well, as Neeleman's creativity, ability, and genuine concern for his colleagues helped to cement the bond of loyalty all felt for the company, and for him personally.

"He was really open," Frendt says. "People would come in and they'd have ideas, and he was always open to listen. He'd often take suggestions and move in those directions."

"He's the big shot, and he's dribbling basketballs down the hall," a former colleague chuckles in recollection. "He's just like this little kid. Really kind of hyperactive. The kind of kid you want to give Valium and say 'Go be quiet.' He's got an idea like every two minutes."

But all the creative ideas Neeleman came up with, and those he supported, were based on one overriding concern, says Frendt: "He always came about everything with the bottom line. He wasn't the type to fly off the handle. He was just a real natural at it. I'd always say, 'Watch out! You're going to see this guy on the cover of *Fortune* magazine, mark my words.'"

Neeleman was wont to stand on desks and do pirouettes or perform cartwheels down the hall on particularly good days. "Whenever we had a bit of good news, David would jump up and touch the ceiling," Morris says. Given his penchant for such exuberant physical displays, Morris hired a ballet instructor to teach Neeleman and three other executives a dance from Swan Lake to perform in tutus at the office Christmas party one year. "He was very enthusiastic, jumping and doing his pirouettes," Morris recalls. "He could really do those dances."

In addition to the bonds forged by the business, given the tight-knit Salt Lake City community, many of the employees and their families were close even before coming to work at Morris. As June Morris said of the workforce, "These people are not employees, they are our friends. We know all their kids and what they do. It's more of a family situation."

Morris herself was instrumental in the success of the venture, according to Carla Meine, who would take charge of customer service at Morris Air. "June has great vision, and I also think she was great for David. David's real aggressive, a very big risk taker. I think June was a good balance for him. It's always nice to have someone else who has great vision, too, but who can say, 'Okay, let's take a step back.' She, as the owner, would say, 'Let's not do that quite so quick,' or 'Let's do this,' or 'Let's change that a little.' She was a great motivator, a very big inspiration to all of us."

HIGHER STANDARDS, LOWER COSTS

"We thought we were pretty good," Frendt remembers. But Neeleman was always looking for ways to operate more efficiently and profitably. "At some point Neeleman started pushing, 'We gotta get our costs down.'"

But reducing costs was difficult for a charter operation. All the equipment was leased and even many of the crews were subcontracted, adding a premium to costs. And there was another, perhaps more important, result of the outsourcing: Because its charters were operated by other carriers, Morris Air had little control over the majority of the people representing its operation. If a complaint about rude service or some other problem was made, Morris could do little to rectify the situation since these crews technically worked for someone else.

Neeleman's thoughts about the kind of operation he'd like to have were further sparked through an unlikely source for him: a book. Neeleman always had difficulty reading. It was hard for him to focus long enough to finish a book. But he had no problem racing through *Moments of Truth*, by Jan Carlzon, then the CEO of Scandinavian Airlines (SAS). Published in 1987, the book told how Carlzon turned the declining carrier around by transforming the operation into a customer-focused organization, reducing layers of management, and giving employees more say in how they did their jobs—even how the company was run. Today these are accepted, if not always practiced, procedures, but it was a bold approach at the time.

Carlzon's central premise, which was applicable to most businesses, caught Neeleman's attention: that the limited interactions between passengers and frontline airline employees constituted "moments of truth" which, in large measure, determined the customers' experience. From this came Neeleman's credo of every employee being an ambassador for the brand. Tellingly, Carlzon wrote that he encountered the most resistance to his ideas and his efforts to reshape the company in the United States.

In 1989, Morris Air moved into a new headquarters building constructed especially for the company. It included room for a telephone reservations center that employed 400 people. Dave Evans was put in charge of overseeing the move to this new facility.

"It was pretty neat," Evans says. "We came from card tables and junky little rooms scattered about for our reservation agents to a really nice, open facility. I think people were all excited to move. Executives moved into the big office area. We'd finally made it! We came out from being this little charter operation that thought we may be bankrupt the next day to a charter airline that people were very concerned about in the industry."

In part because the charter business was doing so well, June Morris decided to sell her retail travel agency.

"That came about because all the travel agents in town who used to work with me now hated me," Morris laughs. The reason: Since so many travelers were booking their flights directly with Morris Air, agents in the area were being cut out of getting their commissions. "They were not about to buy [vacation packages] from Morris Travel," she says of her travel agent peers. So selling that part of the business made logical sense.

FROM CHARTER COMPANY
TO SCHEDULED AIRLINE

By the end of the decade Morris Air was operating some 300 flights per week, ultimately extending its service into Alaska. Alaska Airlines, to say the least, was unhappy about the incursion.

"[Alaska Airlines] went to the government and said, 'Hey, it's not fair for Morris Air—which walks like a duck, quacks like a duck, and looks like a real airline—to obey the charter rules, while we have to obey the airline rules,'" Evans says.

Whether Alaska Airlines formally complained to the Department of Transportation (DOT), which licenses and regulates commercial aviation, as some at Morris contend, is unknown. Alaska Airlines has no comment about the events in question, and the DOT doesn't make public the source of its actions. Nevertheless, after an investigation, the DOT concluded that Morris Air was indeed a de facto airline, operating as a scheduled air service, and not a charter carrier, which is governed by less stringent rules than a scheduled airline.

On October 28, 1992, the DOT issued Consent Order 92-10-44 concerning violations by Morris Air Service, finding that the company had, in part, deceptively given customers the impression that it was a scheduled carrier.

However, in mitigating comments, the consent order noted several facts: The DOT had received a total of seven complaints about the company over the previous five years; Morris Air had immediately rectified all technical violations when brought to the company's attention; and Morris Air had gone above and beyond the requirements of statutes enacted to protect the financial interests of the traveling public, to ensure they received the transportation they paid for.

"We thought we were compliant," Frendt says. "[The DOT] admitted that, although we were following the spirit, we weren't following the letter of the law."

Morris Air agreed to cease and desist the contested practices, and the DOT levied a fine of $200,000, with half of the sum to be forgiven if the company complied with the order. Frendt notes that while the fine was "a lot of money for a little company," that previous August "we made $1 million out of Utah, so it was a kind of a slap on the hand." But it was enough to convince them to do business the proper way going forward. "We said 'Okay, we can't do this as a charter. We've got to do it right.'"

As for those who sought the DOT's intercession, "They figured if they complained about us then maybe we'd go away," June Morris says. "Instead, they forced us into becoming an airline." And they roused a force that even the nation's most successful airline would have to reckon with.

CHAPTER 3

Morris Air Spreads Its Wings

By the beginning of the 1990s, the leisure travel business David Neeleman helped to build at Morris Travel had evolved into a thriving air charter operation, flying to locations around the western United States. But the limitations of operating as a charter company, along with the government regulatory action, made it imperative for Morris Air to transform itself into a real airline, and soon.

Neeleman also recognized that becoming a scheduled carrier was the only way to implement the improvements in customer service he sought. The point was driven home during a chance Valentine's Day encounter in 1990 with a woman affectionately known as "the Cookie Lady."

Carla Meine (at the time, Carla Gustman) was a director of operations for Mrs. Fields Cookies. She had been relocated to Salt Lake City from Seattle with her family a year earlier. Her territory included California, and Meine flew there weekly on Morris Air, becoming friendly with many of the carrier's flight attendants in the process. That February 14, she boarded a flight for Los Angeles armed with heart-shaped chocolate cookies she'd picked up at one of her company's stores for the flight attendants.

"When I saw the flight attendants," Meine recalls, "I said, 'Since we all have to work on Valentine's Day, and we can't be with our sweeties, here's some chocolate for you.'" The cabin crew was delighted.

At the time, Morris Air had both first class and economy cabins. Novell, the software development company, had prepurchased all the first class tickets on the flight, but few of its employees were aboard, leaving most of the forward cabin empty. Sitting in one of the first class seats that day was David Neeleman.

Flight attendants approached Neeleman and explained that their friend the Cookie Lady, a regular customer, was on board. They asked if she could be given a seat in the forward section, since it was almost empty. Neeleman readily assented. The attendants came back to Meine and told her the president of the company wanted her to join him in first class.

"I said, 'Oh, okay, cool,'" Meine remembers. She proceeded to the first class cabin and introduced herself to Neeleman.

"You must be the Cookie Lady," he said. "I understand you fly us every week."

Meine admitted she did.

"So, how do we do?" Neeleman asked.

"Do you want the diplomatic answer," she responded, "or do you want the honest answer?"

"Well, I want you to be honest," Neeleman insisted.

Meine didn't mince words. "Well, for the business traveler, you suck," she said. "Your service is terrible. You have great fares, and the reason I'm on you is because I have a budget, and I can fly to California four times on you or two times on Delta. I need to be in my region more often, so I fly on you every week versus every other week on Delta."

"What will make us better?" Neeleman asked.

For the rest of the flight, Meine told him in no uncertain terms. She ran down all the things Morris Air should do to improve customer service, while Neeleman listened intently. Near the end of the flight, Neeleman asked Meine if she'd read the book *Moments of Truth*, about how Jan Carlzon transformed SAS into a customer-focused carrier and turned around the airline's fortunes in the process. That, Neeleman told her, is what he wanted to do with Morris Air.

Meine, unfamiliar with the book but intrigued by Neeleman's description, told him she'd take a look at it. At the end of the flight Neeleman turned to her and said, "You know what you should do? You should come to work for me and head up the customer service department."

"Yeah, right," Meine laughed. "I have a great job. No thanks."

Truth is, there was one major problem Meine had with her work: the constant travel that kept her on the road and separated from her family four or five days a week. It was a drawback Neeleman had perceived during their conversation.

"The last comment he made to me at the airport was, 'When you want to get off the road and spend more time with your family, you call me,'" Meine recalls.

A couple of days later a copy of *Moments of Truth* arrived at Meine's home with a letter from Neeleman saying "I want to talk to you, give me a call." Meine read the book and, impressed with its message, called Neeleman to thank him for sending it.

"Are you really serious about doing this with your company?" she asked on the phone. Neeleman answered that he was. "I said, 'Well, I'll come and talk to you then.'"

Meine interviewed with Neeleman and June Morris. Soon thereafter, she was offered, and accepted, the position of Morris Air's director of operations.

"Initially, David was the one who trained me on exactly what he wanted to have happen," Meine says. "I'd give him suggestions and ideas of things I'd done in the past and he would say, 'Yeah, go make that happen.'

"He has an incredible skill for selecting very talented people that do things way better than he does. I think that's a really great leader, somebody who can say, 'I don't do this extremely well. I have an idea or a vision of where I want it to go, but I need someone to make that happen, and I need them to do it full-time, and I need them to do it way better than I would ever do it.' And he would hire someone, spend a little time with them, get them off the ground, and then let them go do it. There were roughly 12 of us that ran Morris Air, and David selected almost all of us. It was a great team of people."

TRAINING AND MOTIVATING STAFF

Under Neeleman's direction, Meine began by working with the company's reservations agents, training them on the proper way of treating customers on the phone. She also worked with the charter companies that supplied the outsourced employees, improving customer service among these contracted workers. Little by little Morris Air also started hiring its own people to run operations at the airports Morris Air served.

Neeleman ultimately put Meine in charge of all departments that had any direct contact with customers. That included customer service, reservations, flight attendants, airport operations, ticketing, tour groups, and human resources. But Meine soon discovered that assuring top-quality customer service wasn't the only task she faced.

"The one thing you learn very quickly is that he [Neeleman] is a genius at marketing," she says. "He was able to make the phone ring like nobody I had ever worked for. And since my job was to staff the call center and answer those calls, it became very apparent that my challenge was going to be keeping up with his ability to market the company, because he is incredible at that."

Neeleman also worked with Meine to create a reward and commission structure that would keep the reservationists motivated. Neeleman made sure the budget for incentives was adequate. More importantly, he kept the ideas coming on the best ways to deploy funds. "You always have to use ingenuity," Meine says about incentive programs. The company had one contest related to conversion rates, for example. Winners got a paid day off, while supervisors worked their shifts. In addition, the commissions generated by the supervisors were paid out to contest winners.

"It cost us relatively little," Meine notes, "and yet to the employee it was a huge benefit."

Nevertheless, since so many of the people working at Morris Air were still outsourced labor, Neeleman remained stymied in his efforts to make the changes he wanted throughout the company.

"It became apparent that if we really wanted the kind of customer service that we were talking about, we really needed them to work for Morris Air," Meine says. "That was one of the driving forces in becoming an airline."

Other factors—financial, legal, and operational—were also clearly involved. But, by several accounts, Neeleman's determination to create an organization dedicated to providing superior customer service was a major, if not the primary, consideration. The DOT fine against Morris Air for blurring the lines between charter airline and scheduled carrier triggered the transformation and proved to be a blessing in disguise. Neeleman got to work on assembling a team to handle the necessary paperwork and regulatory filings.

"David appreciates people who do jobs well, so we knew we had a good bunch," Rick Frendt says of the transition team. "We did it very quickly. I remember being told we were doing it in record time."

"David was very, very instrumental in all of this," June Morris adds. "He was a very innovative and restless soul, and I kept saying, 'Go for it!'"

CAPITAL IDEAS

Remembering how his first business went bankrupt because of a lack of sufficient capital once the charter air carrier he used went out of business, Neeleman convinced the Morris family to put more money than seemed necessary into the revamped operation. "I wasn't going out of business again," Neeleman vowed.

But even the Morris family's growing fortune wouldn't be enough. Neeleman wanted another $14 million available for contingencies. Mitch Morris, June's husband, approached a friend, Martin Hart from Denver, to see if he could suggest anyone the company might approach for investment capital. Hart was one of the original investors in Pizza Hut. He had done several successful deals with Morris, but he knew an airline wasn't the kind of investment just anyone could understand or support. Hart figured one investor he knew—Michael Lazarus, a founder of Weston Presidio, a venture capital firm headquartered in San Francisco—had the right temperament and attitude to be interested.

The firm was named for the adopted hometowns of its two founding partners. Lazarus resides in the Presidio, the rugged yet tony San Francisco neighborhood overlooking the Pacific ocean. Michael Cronin, his partner, lives in Weston, Massachusetts, one of Boston's most upscale suburbs. Both had come a long way, having grown up in tough, working-class neighborhoods—Lazarus in Pittsburgh, Cronin in Dorchester, Massachusetts. Cronin won a full scholarship to Harvard, while Lazarus got his education at Grove College, playing drums in bands to help pay for his education. Both studied business.

They met in the late 1970s when Lazarus was at Montgomery Securities in Boston and Cronin headed the Boston office of Security Pacific Capital. They worked together on several deals for their firms. The first involved a small Manhattan-based company that made a prebrushing mouthwash called Plax. Annual sales were about $15 million. After investing some $9 million for half the company, Lazarus and Cronin helped boost sales to $120 million within a year. In less than 18 months, they sold the company to Pfizer for $270 million. Other investment deals followed. After several years of making millions for others, the pair started their own investment firm in 1991 with $80 million raised from backers. This has since grown to some $2.3 billion.

The fact that a capital-intensive enterprise wasn't exactly in favor at the time Neeleman approached him didn't faze Lazarus or his firm. Even though the technology boom of the 1990s was just getting under way, shifting investor interest away from hard asset businesses, he was interested. "Our mantra here has always been, we don't think there are good or bad industries, just good or bad managers," Lazarus says. But Weston Presidio typically invested only in going concerns. Despite Morris Air's history as a charter operator, this technically was a start-up.

Nonetheless, Lazarus was intrigued enough to make the trip out to Salt Lake City to meet with Neeleman and Morris in 1991. In the two of them, Lazarus believed he'd found managers who were much better than good. He thought June, whose home he visited during his time in Salt Lake City, was "a wonderful, wonderful soul." He spent the evening walking around Temple

Square with Neeleman, listening to his vision for what he wanted to do with the airline.

"You knew this guy had to win," Lazarus says. "He had character, passion, intelligence." Lazarus and Neeleman quickly bonded. They were about the same age, and there was something of the outsider in both of them. Neeleman was a foreigner in the place of his birth and something of an alien in the land of his nationality. The big, broad-shouldered Lazarus, meanwhile, had working-class roots that were quite at odds with the world of venture capital in which he'd become a player. By the end of his visit, Lazarus was feeling fortunate about being asked to help the fledgling enterprise. Working with some of his firm's limited partners, Weston Presidio raised the entire $14 million Morris Air sought. Lazarus joined the airline's board and began a long association that would continue through his service as the chairman of JetBlue Airways a decade later.

"You know, David never used any of our money," Lazarus reveals about the investment. "The company was very profitable and beautifully run."

GOING TO MARS

Morris Air completed the requisite paperwork and received approvals in little time, becoming an official airline in 1992. David Neeleman was the company's president, Rick Frendt was the chairman, and June Morris the CEO. By January of 1993, Morris Air was operating flights across the West with a fleet of 23 leased Boeing 737 aircraft. Hawaii was no longer among its list of destinations.

But, as with the change at Morris from a vacation packager to a charter operator, the expanded business brought growing pains. The computer program David Evans had created for Morris

Travel almost a decade before was designed for a core operator-charter type airline. It facilitated booking hotels, cars, and other vacation package components, yet was unsuited for the demands of what all hoped would become a major airline. Seeking a solution for the technology squeeze, Neeleman and Evans went to see a demonstration of American Airline's proprietary system, referred to as SAAS (Sabre Airline Automated System), at the company's headquarters in Dallas.

"We saw this big presentation," Evans recalls, "and the American Airlines guys showed us how they thought it was really good. We're looking up there and there are these ugly dumb terminals, with green screens and an ugly command line. They're telling us how we had to buy all these terminals and it would be millions of dollars to really get our little airline set up."

Disappointment is a mild description of Neeleman's feelings by the time a break in the presentation was called.

"During the break, I was in the bathroom washing my hands and I heard in the stall some cussing—moaning and groaning, and just cuss words coming out," Evans says. The door opened and Neeleman emerged.

"I looked at him like, 'What's the matter?'"

"I can't believe it!" Neeleman said. "I don't want to put down $3 or $4 million on this. It's really not as good as the system we're using now. What are we gonna do?"

Neither man had an answer. But Evans kept thinking about the question as the presentation continued. Later that day he told Neeleman, "If all you want is a system that can do what SAAS does, I'll bet you I can get that done for you in three or four months."

Neeleman, still in bad spirits from the presentation, regarded him coolly. "Oh yeah, sure," he said. They boarded their flight and returned to Salt Lake City.

The next day Neeleman appeared in Evans' office, squirming a bit in his not atypical hyperactive manner. "You know what you told me?" he asked Evans, who immediately recognized exactly what Neeleman was alluding to. "Could you really do this in three or four months?"

Evans didn't doubt that he could. But he had a young family, and devoting that much time to the project would be a hardship. "Yeah," he assured Neeleman, though he added, "that would put a lot of extra burden on me. I could do it, but it's gonna stretch me out." Evans had an incentive plan in mind: His wife needed a new car. "Okay, I'll make you a deal," he told Neeleman. "I'll do this in three or four months if you buy my wife a new Grand Cherokee."

Neeleman's herky-jerky shuffling stopped. He turned around and ran out the door. Five minutes later, he came back and threw a check for $25,000, handwritten by the accounting department, on Evans' desk. "Here, do it," he said.

"David's always been one to make a decision fast when he knows what he really wants to get done," Evans observes.

Within four months Evans had developed the Morris Air Reservation System, referred to as MARS. It was installed that July. Not more than a month later, Neeleman and his team came up with an idea that would forever revolutionize airline bookings: a ticketless reservation system.

THE BIRTH OF E-TICKETING

As with Morris Air's evolution from a charter to a scheduled service carrier, the transition from paper tickets to ticketless reservations was driven by several factors. Among them: the savings on the costs associated with creating physical tickets, efforts by competitor airlines to squash the new carrier, and improved control over cash flow.

At the time, Morris Air used traditional tickets like all the other carriers. Some passengers arranged to pick up their tickets at their departure airport. These were referred to then as "will-call" tickets. The company physically flew these tickets to airports where they were needed for passenger pick-up. The vulnerability of the system became clear one day when a packet of will-call tickets missed their flight to Phoenix.

"There were about 50 or 60 people that had will-call tickets," Evans remembers. "The flight was delayed for an hour and a half while our gate agents handwrote 50 or 60 tickets. They handed [the handwritten tickets] to the passenger, the passenger then handed them back to the gate agent, and that was it. David was like, 'This doesn't make any sense at all. Why did we do the tickets at all?'"

Major carriers ridiculed the thought of a ticketless system, feeling passengers needed a physical voucher of some sort to feel secure that a seat on the airplane awaited them. Ironically, the hardball tactics played by these competitors were an added incentive for Neeleman to go ticketless at Morris. "All the major airlines were giving travel agencies incentive rebates for giving them market share," Frendt explains. These rebates, or "overrides," were paid to travel agencies that exceeded market share levels established by the airlines. These overrides could be a significant revenue source for many agents, especially in a market like Salt Lake City, where one airline (in this case Delta) had a major presence. Morris Air veterans claim that Delta threatened to end override payments to any travel agency that sold tickets on Morris Air. According to the American Society of Travel Agents, this is not illegal. But how could Delta, or any airline for that matter, know how its ticket sales volumes compared with those of other carriers, or what airline tickets a given travel agency had sold?

The answer was that at the time, all tickets collected from passengers at airline gates across the country were sent to a central clearinghouse in Juarez, Mexico, for a weekly tabulation. The results of this count were readily available throughout the travel industry. If a ticket had been sold and used, an airline could easily know what agency handled the sale—at least as long as there was a physical ticket to tabulate. The Morris Air brain trust concluded that ticketless reservations and sales would allow these transactions to go undetected.

"By doing e-tickets and not having tickets going through the ARC [Airlines Reporting Corporation] clearinghouse, the other airlines wouldn't know about it," Frendt notes. "At least that made it neutral rather than hurting their [the travel agent's] bonus. Another part," he said of the reasons favoring direct payments to Morris for ticketless reservations, was that "it was a horrible thing trying to get these agencies to pay us."

Ticketless reservations made directly with Morris would also eliminate another weapon Delta used against Morris that it also wielded through travel agents. "If we had a $79 flight to Los Angeles, [Delta] normally would have a $500 flight. All of a sudden they would have a $79 flight," Evans says. "We had real problems with distributing [tickets] ourselves. When someone called us and said, 'Hey, I want to buy a ticket to Los Angeles,' we were actually referring them to a travel agency to go get a ticket. They would get to the travel agent and the agent would say, 'Listen, you don't really want to fly Morris Air. I can get you the Delta ticket for the same price.' So they would end up buying Delta. When we went to ticketless travel, we avoided that whole thing. They'd call us, book the ticket, and be done."

One last factor made e-ticketing the obvious choice, according to Frendt: "Mostly it was the ease and quickness of it," created by Evans' innovative computer program.

But how did Evans, whose background was in finance, come to create an airline computer system that was, and remains, consistently ahead of competitors employing rooms full of information technology professionals? "It was just working with David from 1984 on," Evans insists. "I had eight years of inventing with David."

The e-ticketing system, combined with a program Evans developed called ADD (for reasons we'll see in a moment), provided the upstart airline with another competitive advantage over its much larger rivals: real-time data.

"Morris Air was real successful because we did have a lot of information that airlines just weren't used to at the time," Evans says. "With the ticketless system, you could immediately know your revenue. With an airline system like SAAS or Sabre, you had to wait weeks for the tickets to come back from Mexico and punch [the data] through some accounting system."

Now Neeleman could instantly get updates on operations at any time of the day. "He loved having information at his fingertips," Evans says. "Everything that happened to that point of the day for sales, the routings that were sold, the fares that were sold—he could look at that and see how sales were going, how promotions were going. He could run down to the reservation center and say, 'Hey, we want to make this flight a promotional sale' because it wasn't selling well, and that kind of thing."

The ADD program's name was chosen as a lighthearted double entendre: Besides harkening to the software's tabulation function, it also referred to Neeleman's peculiar combination of hyperactivity and eccentric behavior, which some likened to attention deficit disorder, a disease not well understood or much talked about at the time.

CHANGING RESERVATIONS

Once again, keeping up with growth was a challenge. Carla
Meine was having a problem finding room for the increased
number of telephone reservationists needed to handle the increased call volumes. "We were having half-hour holds. We had
filled up a 20,000-square-foot call center. We had no place else
to put agents," she says. As the call center crisis festered in
1993, AT&T was in the midst of an effort to convince potential
corporate customers to switch to their telecom service. Meine
and Morris Air's director of reservations attended a conference
sponsored by AT&T. It was there, during a breakout session
called "Bringing the Work Home," that she had a revelation
that would shape the future of Morris Air's—and later Jet-
Blue's—reservations workforce.

"When I went to that session, I just caught this amazing vision," Meine says. "The vision was of an army of reservation
agents, all happily and efficiently working from their homes." It
was the perfect answer to all their call center problems.

"I came back and I said 'David, we've got to do this. This is
the answer!'"

Neeleman's response: "I don't think so. I don't think we want
people working from home."

Meine pressed her case. "This would be great," she assured
him. "We could have them all over the valley." Neeleman remained unswayed.

"Are you going to build me another call center?" she asked.
"How are we really going to handle these phone calls?"

Neeleman ultimately demonstrated his ability to listen and be
open to new ways of doing things. "Eventually he got excited
about the idea and decided, 'Yeah, we really need to make that
happen,'" Meine says.

With Neeleman providing ideas on how the home reservationists would operate, Evans designed the technology solutions to get the computers and phone systems in sync. The technology was given a test run with 20 agents selected for their eagerness to work at home.

The result? "Productivity went up 15 percent, and the agents loved it. We knew we had a winner," Meine says.

Having seen the light, Neeleman became a champion for at-home reservationists. "Everybody said, 'Why would you do that? They're just going to sit around and watch soaps, and [customers] will hear babies crying in the background," Evans recalls. "But David said Salt Lake is a very educated place. There are a lot of females that are lawyers or have Ph.D.'s and are very highly qualified who decided, 'I just had a baby, I'm not going to work anymore.' So now they're stay-at-home mothers, and during the middle of the day they have time to work."

For airline reservations, midday represents the golden hours. The majority of regional airline flights are booked between 10 A.M. and 3 P.M. Now, when Morris Air needed to bring on additional staff to handle the volume, the company could simply call its at-home part-time staff and tell them to go online and take calls. The reservationists made a decent hourly rate, earned commissions on bookings, and were done by the time the kids got home from school. Morris Air's at-home reservation force grew from the initial handful to 180 agents.

As Neeleman and his team surveyed their expanding empire, it became clear they needed more capital to achieve their goals.

"We were getting matched [on fares], our load factors were dropping, and although we were still bumping along, doing fine, and making some nice money for a little company like us, we could see the key was getting costs down," Frendt says. "One way to do that was to buy [airplanes] rather than lease."

Fulfilling plans like that would take much more than Morris had, or even the $14 million it had raised from Weston Presidio. Privately held Morris Air would have to go public. Morgan Stanley, Alex. Brown, and other financial firms were brought on board to handle the initial public offering (IPO). Excitement was in the air as Morris made plans to fly its way into the big time of Wall Street.

CHAPTER 4

Off to Southwest

By 1993 Morris Air, the former charter carrier that Neeleman had helped turn into a popular scheduled airline, was poised to go public. Annual sales had reached $250 million. At the time it was one of only two U.S. airlines showing a profit. The other profitable carrier was the one on which Neeleman had admittedly patterned Morris: Southwest Airlines, the innovative carrier cofounded by the chain-smoking and flamboyant former attorney Herb Kelleher.

"He was my idol," Neeleman says of the brash and charismatic Southwest CEO. "I studied what Kelleher was doing and I tried to do it a little better."

In 1967, Texas entrepreneur Rollin King was dismantling an unprofitable commuter airline that served some small towns in Texas when he got an idea for another airline that would serve the state. He called his attorney to set up a meeting to discuss the idea. Herb Kelleher, the lawyer, was a rangy, silver-haired six-footer and New York native who had settled in his wife's hometown of San Antonio earlier in the 1960s, where he established a lucrative practice. Airlines weren't something he knew much about, but he agreed to meet King at the city's tony St. Antony Club anyway.

There, on a napkin now framed at Southwest Airlines headquarters, King drew a triangle, labeling the points Houston, Dallas, and San Antonio. These were the cities—the largest in Texas—that King proposed serving. About 200 to 250 miles apart, the distance was great enough to make driving a hassle and flying a smart alternative. Kelleher wasn't initially impressed. But after doing some research, he saw that in California, an airline called Pacific Southwest Airlines (PSA) was doing well. Part of the reason PSA prospered was that its flights didn't cross state borders. Therefore, it was regulated by a state commission, not by the heavy-handed U.S. Civil Aeronautics Board (CAB).

"It occurred to us that there was an opportunity to bring to Texas what, in effect, PSA had done in California, and that it would probably be even easier in Texas, since the quality of competition wasn't as good as it was in California," Kelleher later explained.

Because their proposed Texas airline wouldn't cross state borders, either, they could set their own prices and significantly undercut other airlines, whose fares were set by the CAB. Competitors Texas International, Braniff, and Continental Airlines sued to stop the airline, which became known as Southwest, from ever taking flight. Herb Kelleher handled the case in court and won. With Lamar Muse as president, Southwest Airlines began service in 1971 with four Boeing 737s and less than 70 employees, offering flights between Dallas, Houston, and San Antonio.

Like most aviation startups, Southwest ran into financial trouble early on and was forced to make a critical decision: It either had to sell one of its planes or lay off some employees. In an unusual move, Southwest decided to get rid of the plane. As a concession, the carrier asked employees to reduce gate turnarounds to 15 minutes so the remaining jets in the fleet could fly more often. The workers agreed, and thus began the airline's reputation for having some of the friendliest relationships between management and labor in the industry.

By 1974, Southwest Airlines had welcomed aboard its millionth passenger. In 1978, Muse stepped down as president and Herb Kelleher began filling in as interim president, CEO, and chairman of the board. He would be named to these positions permanently in 1982, while remaining very involved in the airline's overall operations during the entire time.

Southwest began expanding outside of Texas in 1979, adding service to New Orleans. In subsequent years, it started flying to such cities as San Francisco, Los Angeles, San Diego, Las Vegas, Phoenix, and St. Louis. Operating only 737s, the airline became known for operating on time, for not losing baggage (largely because it didn't offer connecting service), and for consistently having the fewest customer complaints. All the while, Southwest became famous not only for its no-frills service, but also for its unconventional methods. From humorous commercials to flight attendants and pilots who told jokes over the intercom, Southwest tried to make the process of flying fun. It also instilled this spirit of enjoying their jobs into its workers.

Much of this culture originated with Kelleher, the maverick, bourbon-loving leader whose zany antics have made headlines over the years. One of his most notable acts was in 1992, when Kelleher challenged the CEO of Stevens Aviation to an arm wrestling showdown. Both airlines were using the tagline "Plane Smart" in commercials. Instead of battling over ownership rights in court, Kelleher proposed the arm wrestling competition. The winner would own all rights to the slogan. Kelleher wound up losing the match, but the event created such positive publicity that Stevens ultimately let Southwest continue to use the slogan anyway.

When speaking of his philosophy for success, Kelleher always credits his employees. His formula, he maintains, is simple: He hires the best, treats them with respect, gives them lots of freedom to make decisions, and lets them have fun. Although Kelleher stepped down as CEO and president in 2001, he remains on the airline's chairman of the board and is an undisputed legend in the industry.

Just like Southwest, Morris offered point-to-point service, instead of using the hub-and-spoke feeder networks operated by the majors. This allowed planes to spend more time flying, which is when they make money, and less time waiting on the ground for passengers from connecting flights. Morris's single-model fleet of Boeing 737s, just like Southwest's, reduced the costs and complexity of service and maintenance. And Morris copied Southwest's no-frills service approach, too. Before Morris introduced e-ticketing, it mimicked Southwest by not offering assigned seating. The plastic, reusable boarding passes Morris used were identical to its Dallas-based role model's.

Most important, Southwest had a strong culture, a management fiercely loyal to its employees, and workers dedicated to both their jobs and the company. What's more, Southwest was focused on customer service. Neeleman sought to instill this same spirit in workers at Morris Air. Southwest even allowed members of Morris's service staff to tour its headquarters to learn some of its personnel procedures.

"They were really generous with their ideas," June Morris says. "So we picked up some ideas from them."

SELLING MORRIS AIR

As Neeleman and Morris continued preparing for Morris Air Service's IPO, they also explored other options for raising capital, including an outright sale. If anyone would be interested in buying Morris Air, who better than the people who had built the airline it was modeled upon?

Colleen Barrett, the current president and chief operating officer of Southwest Airlines, was Kelleher's executive assistant at the time. She has vivid memories of Morris Air's operations back then: "There were just incredible similarities in terms of equipment," she says. "I remember being aware that they were using some of our training techniques. And from a cultural perspective, June, in particular, seemed to have a true love for her people, just like we encourage at Southwest."

A dinner meeting was arranged for the Morris team to pitch Kelleher on a potential sale at Dallas's Palm restaurant, one of Kelleher's favorite eateries. He and other Southwest executives frequented the Palm so often, it had a small, private room it called "The Southwest Airlines Room." In it hung a portrait of Kelleher, and the names of key Southwest executives were painted on the wall. Ironically, because it was the restaurant's only private room, it was also frequently used for celebratory sit-downs by the honchos of cross-town rival American Airlines.

The Morris team—David Neeleman, June Morris, Rick Frendt, and June's husband Mitch Morris—arrived early for the meeting. Perhaps suddenly realizing how far they'd come in emulating their role models, the effect on all four of them upon beholding Kelleher's portrait and the emblazoned names was almost overwhelming. "We were looking at the wall, and there they all were," Frendt says, recalling the moment. "They have their own room!" the Morris team gushed to one another.

In the midst of their awe-inspiring excitement, Kelleher and Barrett burst into the room.

"Herb Kelleher happens to be one of those rare people who are magic," Frendt says in describing the first time he met the legendary leader. "He comes into a room and he makes every single person feel like they have all of his attention. He charmed us to pieces. And he listened." But as for buying Morris Air, "I don't think he was interested," Frendt admits.

"It [the meeting] was almost more social than anything else," says Barrett, confirming that Southwest had little desire to purchase Morris at the time. However, she recalls, "It was very clear from that one social meeting that we shared a lot of core values and philosophies."

As for her impressions of Neeleman, "David is a very hyper human being, and I remember being very impressed by his energy level. I remember thinking that he was just a young whippersnapper," Barrett says. "I clearly saw him as an entrepreneurial spirit. I felt like June thought of him almost like a son, and surely considered him a protégé."

Before the evening was over, the issue of the price of Morris Air was raised, but it didn't get very far. Still, Kelleher hadn't slammed the door shut enough to keep Neeleman from trying to get in. Neeleman had always been known for his marketing genius. This time he planned to ply his skills on getting Kelleher to become an interested buyer. He made subsequent trips to meet with Kelleher in Dallas in an effort to win him over. All the while, Neeleman began imagining his own role at Southwest in the future.

In the end, everything fit for both companies. They operated the same airplanes. They had an independent but complementary route system. Most important, they shared a customer-focused culture.

Kelleher and Neeleman got together one final time to thrash out the details of the sale, meeting at a room in an airport hotel to avoid drawing scrutiny. Kelleher agreed to pay $129 million in Southwest Airlines stock for Morris Air, and June Morris was given a seat on Southwest's board of directors. Neeleman was promised a prominent role in the future of the airline he'd long tried to emulate. Keller proclaimed that he and Neeleman were "kindred spirits."

"I was 33 and had $25 million in stock in a company that I idolized," Neeleman later recalled. "Herb said, 'We need a guy like you.' The world was my oyster."

After anticipating becoming a public company, news of the sale to Southwest was greeted with sadness and disappointment by most at Morris Air. As Carla Meine noted, "Going public meant that we [in the executive suite] all still had a job. Selling to Southwest meant that at our level we *weren't* going to have a job."

But Neeleman wasn't about to leave his employees to fend for themselves. He made sure Morris Air and Southwest provided extensive outplacement services for those slated to lose their positions in the sale. The company sought jobs for as many displaced Morris workers as possible, though few were with Southwest.

"What happened was the same thing that happens with any purchase from one company to another," Evans points out. "The purchasing company goes in and tells the company they're purchasing, 'Hey, we all love you. The reason we're buying you is because of the people.' And then when it came down to it, the [only] people they hired were our pilots and some of our reservation agents. As for middle managers and above, [few] of them took on jobs."

Evans was one of the handful of Morris executives to move to Southwest with Neeleman. Frendt wasn't interested in relocating to Dallas, and June Morris was in no position to take on full-time responsibilities, due to an illness from which she later recovered.

"I was diagnosed with cancer very shortly after we had made our deal. A lot of people thought that was the reason that we closed with Southwest, but it was not," Morris insists. "This deal was already done when I was diagnosed."

TAKING A SOUTHWEST COURSE

With the purchase completed in January of 1994, Herb Kelleher sent his top human resources executive, Ann Rhoades, to lead a team to oversee the transition of operations and employees from Morris Air to Southwest. During the four days per month the team spent at Morris headquarters, Rhoades, an effervescent blonde with an open, friendly face and boundless energy, worked closely with Neeleman, and the two got along well. That's not surprising, given their mutual interest in team building.

Southwest was credited with having a creative workforce. Rhoades played a large role in fostering this creativity, though it began before she arrived. "It started when the airline started," according to Rhoades. Kelleher and Barrett had stressed customer service ever since the airline's inception. "They really had to make it with very little, and finding great people was the key," Rhoades says. "They needed to make up for what they didn't have in services and frills."

By the late 1980s, Southwest had been seeking a way to integrate its customer-oriented service more formally into the airline's culture. Rhoades was the vice president for human resources at M Bank (which later became BankOne) at the time, and Kelleher served on the bank's board. Impressed with her forward-thinking ideas, Kelleher brought Rhoades to Southwest in 1988 to overhaul the human resources department. She set about recasting the substance and image of human resources at the company, beginning with the department's name. "Herb had asked me what I wanted to call it," Rhoades recalls. Her answer: The People Department. "So many HR departments are the type that say no," Rhoades notes. She wanted the People Department to be the type that said yes to its people.

Southwest, like Morris, had experienced rapid expansion, and Rhoades had overseen an explosive growth in its workforce. But the addition of just one more member to its ranks—David Neeleman— would generate considerable turbulence in its wake.

Neeleman came to work at Southwest Airlines in January 1994 as an executive vice president and member of the Executive Steering Committee. He bought a house in Dallas, but for the time being commuted between Southwest's hometown and Salt Lake City. He'd been told he was in line for any job he wanted at Southwest. The one he coveted most was Herb Kelleher's. "It was a dream," Neeleman said of his new position. "I just assumed that when I got to Dallas it would be a love fest." "But," as Neeleman later noted, "it's never the way you think it will be."

June Morris knew the adjustment would be difficult. Neeleman had built a formidable operation from scratch, and Morris had surrounded him with supportive people who understood his idiosyncrasies. She'd given him free reign to develop ideas and use his creativity. Things would be different at his new job.

"I spent a day with Colleen and Herb when I was in Texas, talking about it," Morris says. "They both knew that David was really good, and I said, 'Keep him, he's really smart. Keep him if you can.' But David was used to a small operation where you could do it yesterday. And when you move into a type of culture that's established, in the first place, there's jealousy. Plus, he had Herb and Colleen's attention, and I think some of the people kind of resented that."

"He was actually going to report directly to me," Barrett says. "Of course, we had to have an office for him. We're very lean, and I clearly remember thinking, 'Well, we've got to find some place to put him.' I finally just put him in a small office that I had that was basically in our customer relations area. It was really intended to be a temporary thing. His passion at the time was pretty much technology, so he was already on the telephone . . . trying to get his arms around what he was doing."

For someone whose passion was technology, Southwest was hardly a promised land.

"When I first got to Southwest, you couldn't even make a reservation on the phone," Neeleman reflects. "You were instructed to go to the airport to buy your ticket. And they were still using the old mainframe system they had inherited from Braniff."

Everywhere he looked at Southwest, Neeleman saw things he felt needed to be drastically overhauled. And he wasn't shy about telling anyone and everyone about them. He insisted that Southwest needed to go to assigned seating, institute electronic ticketing, and reduce its sales through travel agencies because agencies would steer customers to other carriers at Southwest's expense, as they had with Morris Air.

"I tend to remember him wanting to make dramatic and immediate changes to our system. That's the thing that really sticks out in my mind," Barrett says. "We didn't want to be a leader [in terms of industry innovations]. We wanted other people to try things, and we wanted to learn from their mistakes. That's really where I remember the biggest concern, and the biggest turmoil if you will [with Neeleman. It was] all on the technology side."

June Morris tried to help Neeleman make the adjustment. "I saw him in the office and said, 'David, now, just sit back and keep quiet for a while. Then you can get your ideas across. But don't be too rambunctious.' Of course, that's impossible. He just wanted to be able to change things immediately, like you can in a small company. You just can't do it in a big company. So he kind of stepped on some toes."

Says Ann Rhoades, "By that point [Southwest] was 20-plus years old. So many people [there] had been original players, and frankly had been very successful. If David had waited until the third day, instead of on the second day, to start telling everyone what they were doing wrong and how they had to change it, things might have worked out differently."

"They basically wanted me to sit there and listen for two years," Neeleman recalls. "And I was always blurting, 'Why would you want to do it that way?'" He found the frequent management meetings "endless" and "pointless." "After two hours of talking about what to do about pregnant ramp agents, I'd blurt out, 'Can't we just decide and move on?'"

When he wasn't taking part in a scheduled meeting, Neeleman was just as apt to charge into one in progress and launch into a rant about what needed to be changed.

"He was very good at that, barging into meetings," Barrett recalls.

"David can be very vocal," Morris adds.

"He was used to being able to jump on ideas and try things," Frendt offers. "Usually he and I could butter the way to get through our tiny little organization. It just wasn't possible at Southwest. They were really quite fixed in their ways. So it was very frustrating for David, and I think it was frustrating for Herb and Colleen, too; they saw how much potential he had."

Neeleman's constant hectoring became more than just an annoyance. "He was rocking the boat of the management team they had taken a long time to establish," Rhoades says. "It was really being very destructive."

"I just thought it was a characteristic he couldn't control," Barrett observes of Neeleman's outbursts. "I remember thinking . . . you would probably have to sit down with him, like a young teenager, every three months and talk to him. Afterwards he'd be very good for a while, and then it would start all over again. I just thought it was a behavior that was characteristic of who he was."

Not all the changes Neeleman sought were technology-based. Among the other innovations he wanted to bring to the airline was a concept contained in a business plan he wrote called "Southwest Express." The plan called for flying to underserved markets with full-size 737-200s just once or twice a day, or even three times a week. These markets were currently being served by old turboprops, and Neeleman surmised there was a pool of untapped customers dying for jet service that would have made infrequent flights very profitable. Many of these ideas would echo in the future in JetBlue's business plan. But the idea for Southwest Express found no other supporters within the company.

NEELEMAN AND SOUTHWEST— NOT A HAPPY MARRIAGE

While trying to fit into the Southwest mold, Neeleman developed a habit of repeatedly scribbling "DSAW" on a notepad during meetings. This was his shorthand for "Don't Say a Word."

"I realized that I was an entrepreneur in a very successful business," Neeleman later said. "You know, kind of a revolutionary in a company that didn't need a revolution. And, after about five months, I was like driving myself crazy and them crazy."

One night, five and a half months into Neeleman's tenure, Kelleher invited Neeleman to dinner. He informed the newly arrived executive that the employment arrangement wasn't working out. Kelleher told Neeleman to go see Rhoades, who would arrange a transition out of the company, the next day.

"I went to say I quit and they said, 'No, you're fired,' so I said, 'Okay,'" he later joked. But there was no doubt to anyone how he felt at the time. "It was hard," he said of being dismissed after his high expectations and decade of success.

"He was hurt," Rhoades confirms of David's demeanor during their meeting. "He loved Southwest. But David being David, he actually started pitching his next company while he was getting fired." The idea Neeleman told Rhoades about: He wanted to start a chain of dental practices in Salt Lake City, where families would be placed in "a kind of oral hygiene assembly line."

As necessary as it was, the dismissal also bothered Kelleher and Barrett, according to Morris. "They were sad about it because they appreciated his creativity. But it just didn't fit with their particular operation."

To smooth the exit, Neeleman agreed to sign a noncompete agreement that banned him from involvement in the domestic airline business for five years. He tried to change the terms so it would only apply to markets in which Southwest operated, but when Kelleher refused to make any modifications, he signed anyway.

In the aftermath, many reasons were cited for Neeleman's failure to fit in. "It was a big company that needed process, not an entrepreneur," Neeleman surmises.

"There was a little bit of jealousy," adds Rhoades. "But David was also a little annoying back then."

"It's funny when you think about it in retrospect," Barrett shares. "David was so bright, and David was so eager, and David was such a quick, quick thinker. I think he was just a little too fast paced for us. I think we put him to sleep. He was a real change agent. The bigger the challenge, the more excited David would get. We're known for our very steady but conservative growth. He was light-years ahead of us when it came to technology. If David were to walk into Southwest today, he would have a totally different reaction to us."

Despite the buoyancy displayed in his exit interview with Rhoades, the firing deeply affected Neeleman. "He's a very sensitive and caring fellow, and has very tender feelings," June Morris says. "But he's not one to hold a grudge. He's just one to say, 'Well, that wasn't supposed to be, and now I'll go do my own thing.'"

Still moving on from Southwest wasn't to be quite so easy. Dormant feelings of inadequacy from his school years resurfaced. The sting of memories from teachers who labeled him "unable to catch on" returned. Of course, with more than $20 million banked from the Morris Air sale, Neeleman had no financial worries. His wife, Vicki, told him he didn't have to work at all, ever again. But Neeleman felt he had something to prove—to himself and to the team at Southwest that had banished him.

NEELEMAN'S ATTENTION DEFICIT DISORDER

It was during this time of introspection and reflection that Neeleman came to a critical discovery about himself. His youngest brother, Mark, still in high school, was doing poorly, smoking marijuana, and exhibiting cognitive problems. Ultimately Mark was diagnosed with attention deficit disorder, or ADD. This neurological disorder is characterized by symptoms that can include difficulty focusing mentally, rapid speech, impulsiveness, excessive irritability, a tendency to high-risk behavior, and organizational problems. Also known as attention deficit hyperactivity disorder (ADHD), it is estimated to affect 3 to 7 percent of children and 2 to 4 percent of all adults, representing some 8 million people in the United States alone. Affected adults have a higher incidence of switching jobs, substance abuse, and gambling problems. They also commit more crimes and have higher-than-average divorce rates. They often suffer from depression, anxiety, and low self-esteem as well.

To Neeleman, the symptoms were surprisingly familiar. Of those affected who attend college, as few as 5 percent ever graduate. Perhaps more tellingly, it's estimated that 30 percent of all affected adults are entrepreneurs. Moreover, the disorder is genetically linked, having a tendency to run in families. For Neeleman, the recognition that he had this condition was in many ways a huge relief.

"A lot of the impetuous behavior that I had at Southwest was explained by my attention deficit disorder," Neeleman says. The affliction explained why "I would blurt things out in the middle of meetings, and I couldn't keep my mouth shut sometimes when I needed to, when I saw something that needed to be addressed.

"You have no tolerance for boredom," Neeleman says of the condition. "When you find something you love, you apply 100 percent of your attention to it. But if you don't have that thing you love to focus on, you can't focus on anything. You just bounce around, and you're kind of miserable. That's the downside."

Still, according to Neeleman, there are many good sides to ADD. "On balance, ADD has been a positive," he contends. "People with it tend to be more creative, to think outside the box more. They take more risks."

A number of medications can help alleviate the condition and increase one's focus. Stimulants including Ritalin, Concerta, and Adderall have been used. The Food and Drug Administration recently approved Strattera, the first drug created to treat adults with ADHD. However, less than 10 percent of those affected seek treatment. Neeleman is among this majority.

"If I had a magic pill that would take it away, I wouldn't do it," Neeleman has said, "because I think with this distractibility and with this disorganization and the procrastination and the inability to focus and all the bad things that come with ADD, comes creativity and hyper-focus."

At a conference of educators at Harvard University where Neeleman discussed his ADD, a participant asked why he'd never taken any medication to control the condition.

"I'm afraid I'll take it once, blow a circuit, and then I'd be like the rest of you," Neeleman answered, only half jokingly.

Neeleman has, however, adopted strategies to bring order to his life. He develops routines—for example, always putting his wallet and keys in the same place when he's at home. He wears a Casio DataBank watch, typing reminders of ideas or appointments. Because he used to frequently lose his watch, he began the practice of buying a couple of watches at a time. "Since that fact was published a while ago in a magazine, I've had people from all over the country sending me watches in the mail," Neeleman says. "Now I have a closet full of them."

Neeleman also surrounds himself with people who are naturally organized. "Other people pay my bills. My assistant helps me write letters and keeps my calendar. I have no idea what I'm doing from one day to the next," he admits.

Barrett remarks that during his time at Southwest, Neeleman didn't recognize he needed the support of others to achieve his goals. "Some people do have trouble when they're used to running a show, being part of a team," she said. "That was a problem."

Realizing this fact may have been one of the greatest lessons Neeleman learned during his short tenure at the carrier.

"When I started Morris Air, I was involved in every single operational detail of the whole business," Neeleman explains. "If a plane was broken I knew about it . . . I was on the phone trying to get parts, and I was so burned out with the business. Then when I moved to Southwest, I was commuting back and forth and didn't really have anything to do at night, so I'd go down to dispatch and hang out down there. And there were all kinds of storms going on and really horrible things for the airline. Planes were diverting everywhere—ice storms in St. Louis, snowstorms here, thunderstorms there—and I was disturbed by it. I said, 'I wonder if Herb knows all this is going on?' I'd go upstairs and he'd just be completely focused on the future of the airline, and not worried about what was happening on that particular day. So I learned a valuable lesson there: If I ever started another airline again, I would do it with great cooperation from people that I could turn to and say, 'Run the airline and then we'll talk monthly about the performance of the airline and make sure that it's going the right direction.'"

Among the most critical members of Neeleman's current support team is his wife, Vicki, who finds herself constantly picking up after him, or trying to locate him after he's wandered off in the midst of household chores.

"She hopes that one day I'll just take a pill and see if she can get me to go help her clean the garage," Neeleman says. "Man, those types of things—I just can't fathom myself doing them. I'll do it for like a minute, and the next thing you know, I'm gone upstairs doing something else.

"It's hard to do the mundane things in life. I have an easier time planning a 20-aircraft fleet than I do paying the light bill. My wife is always saying, 'Why do you leave your socks all over the bedroom every single night everywhere but where they're supposed to go?' And I'm like, 'Do I do that?'"

Says Vicki: "You can't get mad at everything or you'd be mad at him all the time."

Neeleman had finally solved the riddle of his peculiar restlessness and fluctuating focus. But a more perplexing problem faced him: What to do with his future? The airline business was now deeply entrenched in his blood. But for the next five years, at least domestically, he'd have to sit on the sidelines because of the noncompete agreement he'd signed with Southwest. What would he do in the meantime? Neeleman went home to Salt Lake City to come up with an answer. As it turned out, remaining idle wasn't a viable option. There was a hunger in his soul that even $25 million couldn't satisfy.

CHAPTER 5

Opening Up New Skies

Casting about for his future and flush with cash from the Morris sale, Neeleman initially embarked on a career as a venture capitalist. It was brief and unsuccessful. He invested in a pretzel company, a health and fitness business, and a firm that made first-aid skin products, among others.

"He had no clue what he was doing, and I think he lost money on all of them," says David Evans, who had developed Morris's groundbreaking electronic reservation system and gone on to Southwest with Neeleman.

"It's a different skill set [being a venture capitalist]," says Michael Lazarus, Neeleman's friend and Morris Air's financier, contrasting the worlds of aviation and investment. That thesis was about to be put to the test by some investors on the northern side of the domestic airline market.

Clive J. Beddoe, an avuncular, rugged Englishman, immigrated to Canada in 1970, settling in Calgary, Alberta, at the foot of the rugged Canadian Rockies. A certified chartered land surveyor, he was also an industrious entrepreneur. In addition to his business interests, Beddoe was an aviation enthusiast and pilot who flew aerobatic airplanes and other aircraft.

By the early 1990s the Hanover Group of Companies, which Beddoe founded in 1978, had diversified beyond real estate development to include buying and selling businesses. Every 18 months or so, a Hanover division would buy a company in need of some TLC, fix it up, and sell it. Mark Hill, a young senior executive at Hanover Development, the group's real estate arm, wanted to earn a pilot's license. Beddoe promised if a building they were completing was 97 percent occupied by Christmas, Beddoe would pay for Hill's flying lessons. The occupancy rate was achieved, and Hill got his license.

Piloting a plane was as exhilarating as he'd dreamed it would be—the feeling of freedom, the sense of unlimited potential. Yet a private pilot's license didn't free Hill from the tyranny of being reliant on commercial aviation, especially for longer trips. Air Canada had a virtual monopoly in the region. At the time, Hill was overseeing real estate purchases for Hanover in the Phoenix area. That required frequent flights to and from Calgary.

"I was horrified at the airfares we were paying," Hill recalls, "so we were finding all kinds of funny ways to get down there to avoid a Saturday night stay. In doing so, we discovered two little airlines in the western part of the United States that had really been unheard of in Canada. One was Southwest; the other was Morris Air."

Hill occasionally saw an article about Southwest Airlines but never read anything about Morris Air. He hadn't heard of David Neeleman at the time, either, though he'd flown Morris several times for his trips to Arizona.

"I was surprised how they could fly a 400-mile flight and charge a $90 walk-up fare," Hill says. "In Canada the same flight would cost $250. So that got me curious about how that works."

The lack of reasonably priced air travel in the region became glaringly clear after Beddoe bought a chemical company in Vancouver. The purchase required Beddoe to take frequent flights from Calgary to the West Coast city. Airfares were so high and schedules so inconvenient, Beddoe concluded he'd be better off buying an airplane and flying himself to Vancouver and back. In the spring of 1994 he did just that, purchasing a Cessna C-421 twin-engine, eight-seat aircraft. To offset operating costs, Beddoe offered the few open seats on each flight to friends, who shared in the expenses. The high demand for the seats piqued Hill's interest.

"There were only three or four seats [available] but people were lined up," Hill says. "It got my imagination going and got me interested: How does this business work?"

Hill took the time to find out, intensively studying the airlines and the economics behind the industry. He concluded the Calgary market represented a business opportunity, especially if he could run an airline based on the models of the Southwest and Morris operations. Hill set off to write a business plan for just such an airline to serve Canada and took it to Beddoe.

"This is really cool," Beddoe said after reading Hill's plan. "But the reality is none of us know how to run an airline business."

The next logical step was to find someone who did. Through Canadian aviation contacts, their search initially led them to Lamar Muse, the man who was instrumental in starting and running Southwest Airlines. In 1982, after he'd left Southwest, Muse started his own discount airline based in Dallas, fittingly called Muse Air. It was notable for being the first domestic airline with nonsmoking-only flights. Southwest bought Muse Air out three years later. Muse himself was now retired and spending several months a year in British Columbia. Nothing came of his discussions, with Beddoe and his team, leaving them with a sound business plan for a low-cost Canadian regional carrier, but no one to execute it.

"We need to find somebody to run this thing," thought Hill, Beddoe, and the other two key executives involved in the planning—Tim Morgan and Donald Bell. After all, they surmised, "this is a specialized business."

At the time, a young man from Salt Lake City had come to Beddoe seeking venture capital for a chain of craft stores stocked with merchandise made by Mormon wives in their homes. The supplicant was at the Hanover headquarters and overheard Beddoe and the others talking about their need for a seasoned airline executive, along with their conclusion that none was available in Canada.

"Well, Morris Air has been sold to Southwest," the Utah native said, presenting a copy of the day's *Salt Lake Tribune* with an article about the transaction, which had actually been completed several months before.

"Really?" Hill asked with intrigue. He picked up the phone and made some calls to track down the David Neeleman mentioned in the article as having run Morris Air. He was soon connected to Cathy Davis, Neeleman's assistant at Morris. The company's offices were still open as the final transition to Southwest's ownership was being completed.

"Of course, we didn't realize who David was," Hill admits. "He was just a name. And I started getting screened by her, because obviously there were a lot of people calling David at the time." Davis told Hill that Neeleman would give him a call.

"I was expecting it would take a week or so, but an hour later David called and said 'What are you guys up to?'"

"Well here's the concept," Hill answered, giving him a thumbnail picture of the low-cost airline operation the Hanover team hoped to put together.

Neeleman was interested enough to want to hear more. "Why don't you come down for an hour?" he suggested to Hill. Beddoe had a previous commitment and couldn't go, but the other three hopped in the C-421 and flew down to Salt Lake City to meet Neeleman.

NEELEMAN CONQUERS CANADA

It was one of the last days before the Morris Air offices would officially belong to Southwest, a day punctuated by the embraces of departing employees, a time of melancholy endings and new beginnings. Unbeknownst to the Hanover team, Neeleman had just ended his tumultuous tenure at Southwest, and the toll was evident on his face.

"He looked like shit when we first met him," Hill says bluntly. "In hindsight he was tired, he really was tired."

The hour passed quickly. Neeleman, drawn and drained as he'd been, was energized by the enthusiasm and forethought of the three Canadians eagerly spinning out their vision and offering their numbers. The meeting continued. "We kind of hit it off," Hill says. Neeleman informed them he was no longer at Southwest, and that a noncompete agreement barred him from the domestic airline business.

"David, you've got to run this thing," they told him, realizing that not only didn't his agreement preclude him from working in Canada, but it made the prospect more appealing. David demurred. Been there, done that, he told them.

Still the Calgary clan pressed Neeleman to be a part of the venture. Attracting a name like Neeleman's—now that they realized who he was—was important for more than just his operational know-how and abilities. At the time, two other groups were trying to start a regional airline based in Calgary. One was Greyhound Air, an offshoot of the venerable U.S. bus company of the same name. All three groups had little but smoke, mirrors, and press releases to build themselves up in the media and try to gain some traction in the marketplace.

"We really hadn't gotten anywhere," Hill admits. "Greyhound was probably the furthest ahead, so we knew if we had a name like David Neeleman, it would be enough to probably kill one, or at least give credibility to what we were doing." After all, when it came to starting a successful no-frills carrier, "Only two guys had done it before: One was Herb Kelleher and one was David."

Neeleman finally agreed to help their venture as a consultant, and even signed a noncompete agreement that covered Canada, pledging he would work with no other aviation group in their country for a year.

Next, the Calgary crew brought him up to Canada to "see the lay of the land," as Hill puts it. "David rolled in and got his head around the marketplace and asked fascinating questions," Hill says, recounting meetings they arranged with civic leaders in Calgary and Vancouver. "In Vancouver he asked everybody, 'Who's from Vancouver?' and almost no one raised their hand. At that point he knew there was good potential for an airline because everybody was from somewhere else, and that meant they all went home to somewhere else. He got turned on to that."

Neeleman took a seat on the board of directors and joined Beddoe, Hill, Tim Morgan, and Donald Bell—the four founders of WestJet, as the new enterprise was called—in getting the airline off the ground. "We wanted to have him emotionally committed," Hill says, "so we extracted [from him] a grand total of $200,000 Canadian, about the same as we all paid." In return, Neeleman received 800,000 shares in the company, each valued at about 25 cents Canadian. For the next four years, Neeleman shuttled from Utah to Calgary to help plan the airline and attend meetings. The WestJet founders also often came to Salt Lake City to see him, "kind of Muhammad going to the mountain," in Hill's words. There, they'd brainstorm and discuss strategy.

"He's not into detail at all. He's a conceptual guy," Hill notes, echoing a comment many have made about Neeleman. "He turned us on to a lot of things, most so painfully obvious I've forgotten what they are. But no one else was doing them."

Hill also observed another of Neeleman's oft-noted traits. "I figured out he had ADD," Hill says. "You'd have a conversation with him, and he'd walk out of the room, have three conversations, and come back in and pick up right where he left off. You realize he's not being rude; he's just David."

There were several nonstop flights a day between Calgary and Salt Lake City. Being in the same time zone, it was easy to spend a day in either location and be back home at night. The founders and Neeleman spent a few months refining their business plan and designing the airline. But it was obvious to all that when it came to aviation, there was more on Neeleman's mind than WestJet.

"You could always sort of tell he had an idea to start an airline [of his own]," Hill says.

Though Neeleman couldn't work for or run an airline in the United States due to his noncompete agreement, that didn't stop him from consorting with known airline industry figures. Many sought his advice and opinion. He kept in touch with top executives at airlines around the world and with old colleagues like David Evans. By this time Evans had taken Southwest to a ticketless system, as Neeleman had urged the airline to do before his discharge. As Evans explains, "After David left, someone down there came up with this idea that, 'Hey, maybe we ought to do a ticketless airline!' So it was their idea now and they did it."

When Neeleman dropped by to see him in the fall of 1995,

Evans, though still in the employ of Southwest Airlines, had recently started his own company: Evans Airline Information Solutions, Inc. (EAIS). The firm marketed a simplified ticketless reservation system that he had developed. Evans had sold a couple of them over the past year and Neeleman, ever in contact with senior airline executives, had generated lots of referrals for his old friend. But, as often had been the case, what was clear to the often absent-minded Neeleman was more opaque to others. Neeleman soon got to the point. "I'd like to buy into your company," he said to Evans. "Let's staff it up. I've got the money." Chiding Evans for being too conservative in his approach, he said, "We can make this thing big."

Says Evans, "And so he did."

EAIS changed its name to Open Skies. Evans was spending most of his time at Southwest, so Neeleman primarily ran the business. In this capacity, he kept in touch with airline CEOs all over the world, while becoming intimately familiar with what the reservation system could and couldn't do. Neeleman was also able to help Evans improve the system to meet what he would hypothetically want if he were ever running an airline. He was "kind of building the reservation system for his future," according to Hill. But in the present, Neeleman had another customer for the new Open Skies reservation system: WestJet.

Once WestJet's business plan was complete, it took the founders all of 30 days to raise enough money from local investors to buy three used 737s for about $5 million each, $2.5 million in spare parts, and $750,000 in computer equipment.

Frugality was a hallmark of the company's operations. Beddoe proudly showed reporters the 18-foot-long mahogany table in the conference room at the two-story WestJet headquarters near the

Calgary International Airport. What he was most proud of was that the company bought the table, valued at $16,000 new, for a mere $1,500 used. The highest salary the company paid was $85,000, but profit sharing was available to all employees from the first day. Onboard the aircraft, snacks were served instead of meals. No baggage connection to other airlines was offered.

"If you've got to be responsible for baggage personnel in Bangkok as well as counter staff in Lethbridge [Canada], there's just the sheer administration involved," Beddoe explained. "We do not have to worry about long distance charges to Bangkok or dealing with other currencies."

By cutting operational costs, WestJet was able to offer inaugural fares as low as $29 one way between Calgary and Edmonton, a distance of some 175 miles. Beddoe, Neeleman, and the rest at WestJet were convinced those prices would expand the marketplace far beyond what the experts thought it could accommodate.

"The biggest myth in the industry is the myth of overcapacity," Beddoe said at the time of the idea that there was already too much service. What we're really doing is attracting people into our airplanes who otherwise might have driven, or might not have traveled at all."

WESTJET ENJOYS SUCCESS

WestJet inaugurated service in February 1996 and was immediately successful, flying packed planes from Calgary to Edmonton, Vancouver, Kelowna, Winnipeg, and Victoria. The short routes enabled pilots to return to Calgary at the end of each workday, saving overnighting costs, while the low fares drew many to the skies who otherwise would stay on the ground, as predicted.

Neeleman and the WestJet team continued commuting between

Salt Lake City and Calgary, as operational strategy was refined and evolving conditions were successfully confronted. Neeleman's trips were frequent enough that "he always joked he was going to name a daughter Calgary," Hill quips. But Neeleman only needed to overnight in Calgary about ten times in the four years he was a company director.

WestJet became a proving ground for the technologies and concepts Neeleman hoped to employ in his next airline venture, including the Open Skies reservation system.

"We were really the beta testing site for that system," Hill says. "He could explore all the aspects of the system with this little airline in Canada. If it went down, nobody would ever hear about it. They were such great theory guys in Salt Lake, but they needed to test it. So it really was a joint effort. They needed us as much as we needed them."

That's another way of saying it was a win-win situation. The airline's success also served as a validation of the low-cost, customer-service model it was admittedly based on, as an admiring transportation analyst who witnessed WestJet's rise later commented.

"That is something from Southwest's playbook," notes Ted Larkin, one of the first analysts to follow the airline. "No reason to apologize for copying what other folks do. The problem is, most people aren't clever, diligent, or hardworking enough to pull it off." He followed his trenchant analysis with a particularly Neelemanesque coda: "This is true of any service business, whether McDonald's or a shoe store. If you get people to truly provide a service, you're going to want to go back for more."

The ride was not without some bumps. In September 1996, less than seven months after its founding, WestJet's fleet was temporarily grounded, albeit on a maintenance technicality, due to a complaint by Air Canada that arose because of the age of the aircraft. But this, too, served as a lesson for Neeleman's future airline.

"We had some issues with our federal regulator. He learned a little bit from that," Hill says. "He [Neeleman] was always pushing us to get new airplanes. Probably, in hindsight, he was right."

As the decade progressed, so did WestJet. Soon the airline would be in the same position Morris Air Service had found itself in: ready to tap the investment community for the capital needed for the major expansion the market called for by becoming a publicly traded company.

Neeleman's other aviation venture, the Open Skies e-ticket reservation system, was also prospering Open Skies provided all the hardware and software and handled all the installation. The client airline simply paid a fee, perhaps 15 or 20 cents, for each passenger the system processed. The biggest expense for Open Skies was the cost of the Hewlett-Packard (HP) computers that ran the system. Neeleman and Evans went to HP to cut a deal: HP would provide the hardware for free, Open Skies would supply the software and do the installation, and revenue would be split 50-50. Since hardware wasn't a large-margin item for HP at the time given the highly competitive market and because the company was focused on service-oriented revenue growth, it agreed to the deal. Six months into this arrangement, Open Skies had second thoughts. Neeleman and Evans couldn't figure out if an even split was equitable. After all, which party was taking the greatest risk? And who was doing the most work? They proposed a solution: HP should buy Open Skies and make it a division of the giant corporation. And that's what HP did. In October 1998, Hewlett-Packard paid $20 million to buy out Open Skies.

Neeleman now had one less encumbrance. The five-year term of his noncompete agreement with Southwest Airlines was less than a year from ending. Much of the groundwork for that date had already been prepared. But in the meantime, WestJet, the upstart Canadian carrier he'd been instrumental in launching, was preparing to go public, a tremendous feat and a rousing testament to his talents. The IPO was scheduled for June of 1999—the same month his noncompete agreement evaporated. Then Neeleman would be free to plunge back into the airline business. His own airline business. The call was too strong to postpone.

"I was disappointed he didn't stick around for the IPO (at WestJet)," Hill says. "It would have been interesting."

The value of the 800,000 WestJet shares Neeleman owned had already risen considerably by the time he sold out shortly after the IPO. From his 25-cent cost basis, adjusted for splits, shares would go as high as $65 over the next decade. But Neeleman took most of his profits early to pursue a dream of his own making.

"I always told David he sold too early," Hill notes. "He says, 'Yeah, but the money from that, together with the money from Southwest, helped launch JetBlue.'"

JetBlue would become the next and biggest endeavor of Neeleman's aviation career. It had been years in the planning. Now it was about to be unveiled to the world.

CHAPTER 6

A Different Kind of Airline

If anyone could claim as much respect from Neeleman as Herb Kelleher, the founder of Southwest Airlines, it was Donald Burr. Burr was the first to seize the possibilities created by the Federal Airline Deregulation Act of 1978. Before then, airline routes and fares were controlled by the Department of Transportation (having inherited the responsibility from the Civil Aeronautics Board), creating virtual monopolies that defied efforts to end the stranglehold on air travel held by major carriers. Southwest had overcome these hurdles by confining its initial operations totally within Texas, making the federal laws that regulated interstate fares and slots for landings and takeoffs moot. Airline deregulation was one of President Jimmy Carter's first initiatives, as he sought to free industries from government control. The intent was to create more competition and encourage smaller airlines to enter the marketplace. In its aftermath, any company that was deemed "fit, willing, and able," in the words of the Department of Transportation, could schedule service to virtually any city, and at any fare it wanted.

In April 1981 Burr founded People Express Airlines. Little more than a year before, Burr, his secretary, and another executive resigned from Texas Air, intent on forming their own airline. Burr wanted to create a work environment where employees were motivated as owners, and where everyone was required to own company stock. He also opted for a flat hierarchy, where there were no assistants, and everyone was a manager.

Burr based People Express at Newark Airport, which leased him the entire abandoned North Terminal. An initial stock offering of 3 million shares raised millions more than expected. People Express arranged to acquire 17 737s from Lufthansa. The first plane arrived in March 1981. The following month the airline began service to Buffalo, New York; Columbus, Ohio; and Norfolk, Virginia.

People Express offered fares far below those of the established carriers. But the airline went one better than Southwest on the no-frills ethos: Not only were pilots pressed into duty tidying cabins, there were no baggage handlers. In fact, anyone who brought more than a carry-on bag was charged for checking aboard luggage.

The cheap seats offered by People Express were an instant hit with the public. Within two years it became America's fifth largest airline. The carrier offered service to London in a leased 747. Burr then bought 50 Boeing 727-200s, expanding his domestic route system to 22 cities. At its peak in 1983, the airline had 4,000 employees and more than 70 aircraft. Fueled by his success, Burr went on an acquisition spree, buying airlines, including Frontier and regional carrier Britt Airways.

But the more People Express flew, the more money the company lost. Passengers appreciated the low fares, but being treated like cattle in the process didn't create customer loyalty. The airline was also starting to lose the charm and uniqueness that made it famous in the first place. When the major carriers matched fares on popular routes, flyers abandoned People Express by the planeload. The airline was losing money and in mid-1986, Burr gave in to pressure from his board and announced that part or all of People Express was for sale. Both United Airlines and Burr's former boss at Texas Air, Frank Lorenzo, were interested. United only wanted Frontier, while Lorenzo coveted the entire operation. Burr preferred Lorenzo's offer, but the board voted in favor of United. The deal fell apart when United's pilots rejected the contract proposal extended to Frontier's pilots. As a result, Frontier ceased operations and declared bankruptcy.

Meantime, Lorenzo again offered to buy out People Express, this time for about $125 million, less than half of the original offer he'd made a few weeks earlier. Burr's only other choice was bankruptcy, so he agreed to the deal, which was formally approved on December 31, 1986.

Like Neeleman, Burr discovered that once the airline industry is in your blood, it stays there. He began planning a comeback in 1996, and went with his son, Cameron, to see Neeleman about the Open Skies reservation system. The technology seemed like a hearty backbone for any airline operation, and Burr wanted to know more about it. But the low-fare pioneer was surprised when he found *himself* answering questions, as Neeleman peppered Burr with queries about People Express and its operations. "David had studied People Express," Burr says. "He asked a lot of good questions."

When what became known as JetBlue finally launched four years later, with many operational strategies similar to those Burr talked about during their meeting, Burr and his son suspected Neeleman might have poached some ideas from their plan. But given Neeleman's earlier proposal for Southwest Express, the brainstorming he had been doing with others, and the similar concepts he was already putting to work at WestJet, the more obvious conclusion was that in the airline industry, as elsewhere, great minds think alike.

THE FUND-RAISING DRIVE BEGINS

Neeleman had become good friends with Michael Lazarus, one of the principals of Weston Presidio, the investment firm that backed Morris Air Service. They kept in close contact after the sale. Neeleman even brought Lazarus various business proposals, including an opportunity to invest in WestJet and Open Skies, both of which Weston Presidio passed on (as it did on the chance Neeleman previously presented to back his idea of the family dental clinics). Neeleman and Lazarus also had quarterly meetings where they'd get together to talk about investment ideas and catch up on each other's lives. Sometimes they'd be joined by Tom Kelly, who became Morris Air's counsel in 1991 and remained Neeleman's trusted adviser.

The coffee shop at Salt Lake City's Middle America Hotel, with its Formica counter and comfortable booths, hardly seems like a place where important business is conducted. But with its unhurried, down-home atmosphere, it had served as a popular meeting place for the Morris Air executive team. In 1997, when Lazarus came to Salt Lake City for another quarterly meeting with Neeleman, they once again convened at a booth in the hotel's coffee shop. Tom Kelly was also in attendance, which was a little unusual for the get-togethers. Without much lead-up, Neeleman suggested that they should join forces to start an airline. Lazarus couldn't suppress his reaction.

"I laughed," Lazarus recalls. "Who needs an airline?"

Despite Neeleman's low-keyed introduction, this was no spur-of-the-moment idea floated off the top of his head. "David's a planner, a strategist. He had me locked up," Lazarus recalls of the meeting.

Neeleman, of course, wasn't deterred by the initial skeptical response.

"He had all these deep thoughts," Lazarus remembers. "'Let's fly where all the people live!' I thought he was out of his mind."

But at the same time, Lazarus knew it was impossible to knock Neeleman over by shooting down his arguments. In situations like this, you could be sure Neeleman had already thought about every angle as much as anyone could. If there was a flaw in his reasoning or assumptions, he would have already found it, "because he has a good command over it," as Lazarus observes. "And the more he expanded on the why and where, the more sense it made."

"What if we had the airline overcapitalized? What if we had all new airplanes? Now what do you think?" Neeleman asked.

By the end of the meeting, Lazarus wasn't laughing anymore. "This was a very big idea," Lazarus says. While Lazarus had caught the fire, it wasn't your typical venture capital deal. "We had a lot of soul searching and research to do."

For the time being they called this proposed airline New Air. Over the next two years, Neeleman and his inner circle would refine their business plan, find financing, buy airplanes, staff an organization, and take all the other preparatory measures required to start an airline. But it had to start with the management team.

HIRING THE RIGHT PEOPLE

Mission statements with lofty visions of purpose are fine. But concrete goals that can be quantified and qualified are more important to getting through the day ahead. Neeleman's mission was straightforward: "Our goal was to build the best coach product in America with the lowest cost."

Neeleman needed a top-notch management team to do that. He recognized his limitations. How could he lure the level of talent he needed when executives of that caliber already held senior positions at established airlines?

"I just had to paint the picture for people and say, 'This is what this thing can become,' " Neeleman says. He also offered key executives more money than his competitors were paying and equity positions in the new company. In addition, the opportunity to build something from scratch with Neeleman was an inducement in its own right.

"There are people in your life that you just want to please, I don't know why," Lazarus says. "David is one of them. He will do anything to motivate, inspire, and lead these people, and he knows the industry inside out."

Tom Kelly, who had joined Morris Air as chief counsel in 1991, was already on board. Described as "David's right hand" in offering counsel and advice, he became the new venture's chief counsel. But some of the key people Neeleman wanted aboard his new airline were off-limits—anyone working at Southwest Airlines, for example. With his noncompete clause in effect, approaching Southwest employees would have been grounds for legal action. Besides, as Lazarus notes, "It's kind of hard to steal anyone from Herb [Kelleher]," who was still Southwest's CEO at the time.

But as Neeleman's plans progressed and word of his return began to percolate in the industry, recruitment became almost a nonissue.

As Lazarus relates, "All of a sudden all of these people just started coming to us."

The confidence of prospective team members was bolstered by the selection of the first key executive to join the crew. David Barger, now president and chief operating officer at JetBlue, had been exposed to the airline business from an early age. His father was a United Airlines captain. His brother, Mike, had been a military pilot and Top Gun instructor.

Barger began his career in 1982 at New York Air, a pioneering post-deregulation low-fare start-up that was formed by Texas Air. Barger worked his way up from customer service agent at New York Air to director of stations. Texas Air, which also owned Continental Airlines, eventually sold off New York Air to Donald Trump. Barger moved over to Continental (which by then had been merged into Texas Air as well), and went on to become director of customer service, director of operations control and international operations, and vice president of the Newark hub. Dark-haired, thin, and almost bookish looking, with glasses framing his intense gaze, Barger was also among those credited with helping to turn the airline around, following a turbulent period under Frank Lorenzo's leadership. With Lazarus helping with the wooing, Barger became receptive to the pitch to become part of New Air.

In August of 1998, Barger officially joined Neeleman's start-up team. "He was very important," says Lazarus. "He was really the balance. David had all the ideas and Dave Barger is the one who executes the ideas, flawlessly." Barger would handle day-to-day operations. "He's the kind of guy who wears three beepers and two pagers," Lazarus adds. "He has endless energy and is totally committed."

On August 24, 1998, New Air was officially registered as a corporation in Delaware.

Not withstanding observations by Lazarus about the difficulty of hiring anyone away from Kelleher, another key figure who expressed interest in joining the upstart was John Owen, the treasurer from Southwest Airlines. "There is no one else in the world who is better at buying airplanes and running a successful financial operation" than Owen, Neeleman says. He'd seen Owen in action during his brief tenure at Southwest. Owen's abilities made a lasting impression. Owen has been described by others as being "brilliant with a balance sheet." A treasurer at an airline, unlike in other industries, is the key financial officer, given the capital expenditures associated with airline operations, beginning with the act of buying airplanes. Owen had been responsible for the financing and purchase of every aircraft Southwest acquired since his arrival there from American Airlines. He was also heavily involved in operations planning and analysis.

Owen always had great respect for Neeleman. Yet, while he was interested, Owen was very conservative and cautious by nature. He'd been at Southwest for 17 years, and would have to give up the financial incentives that awaited him a few short years away if he left now. That would make his commitment to Neeleman's start-up especially meaningful. As one team member said, "You want people to take some risk."

Customer service was going to be a primary focus of the new airline. Since employees would be the most important part of the operation, their selection and training was critical to the company's success. Again Southwest would serve as its model. "If you've ever flown Southwest, you know people [employees] are really handpicked," says Lazarus. "They have a certain touch. They can make fun of themselves and use humor to defuse a bad situation."

The person responsible for that was Ann Rhoades, the head of Southwest's People Department, who had developed the airline's happy employee group and its programs. Rhoades was also the executive who had handled Neeleman's firing from the airline in 1994. But even through that trying situation, the two had remained friends.

"She's really very instrumental up front [in coming up with] ideas on training and culture building, [along with] recruiting techniques," Lazarus says. Rhoades had left Southwest after being recruited by Peter Ueberroth in 1995 to help him run the Doubletree

Hotels chain. In 1998 she was in the midst of overseeing the human resource component of Doubletree Hotels' merger with the Promus Hotel Corporation. That fall Neeleman called. He told her about his plans for his airline, and the role he wanted her to play in it.

"He said, 'I need you for at least three years, so you can do the people side,'" Rhoades recalls. At the time she was planning to start her own human resources consulting business from her hometown of Albuquerque and was reluctant to postone her endeavor. Neeleman told her she could commute, to alleviate any concerns she had about relocating. Still, Rhoades had other reservations. She knew David was smart and capable, but she also understood he needed a team to be successful. And she didn't know how much he'd matured from his days at Southwest.

"David always treated people well, but I still wanted to see if he was going to have the balance in the management team," Rhoades says. At Neeleman's urging, she went to Salt Lake City to talk to Tom Kelly about the new airline. Even after the meeting, she wasn't totally convinced she wanted to join up, given the commitment it would take to establish the people culture.

"I said no to David three or four times," she says. "I didn't want to commute from Albuquerque." Neeleman continued his sales pitch.

Early in 1999 Rhoades came to New York to talk with Neeleman and meet the other members of the New Air team. "Once I met Dave Barger, I knew he had the right combination" for a successful organization, she says. "First of all, as a person, when you meet him as a presence, you know the man is fanatical about discipline. He had a reputation for discipline at Newark and for being very honest with personnel. The minute you meet him, his demeanor, his style, he's very reflective in the way he listens."

It was enough to get Rhoades to commit to three years with the airline. She would commute between Albuquerque and New

York. In April of that year she officially joined the New Air team. "It is the best I've ever worked with," she later said of the group.

Lazarus calls Rhoades "the other secret weapon," and "part of the magic of hiring skills and techniques and training" at the airline. "One thing you learn," says Lazarus of starting a successful business, "it's all about hiring the right people, building the culture, the leader, and the process."

A POTENTIAL PARTNERSHIP WITH RICHARD BRANSON

In 1998, an opportunity appeared that might catapult New Air off the ground: a potential partnership with British tycoon Sir Richard Branson, founder of Virgin Atlantic Airways. Branson, the British music industry mogul who had started the successful Virgin record label, got into the airline business in 1984 after attorney Randolph Field proposed he become involved in a new carrier, British Atlantic, that sought to establish service between England and the United States. Branson had long been an admirer of Freddie Laker, who had established the low-fare Laker Airways, plying that same North Atlantic route. Once Laker's airline went bust, Branson became appalled at the level of service available. People Express took up some of the slack for no-frills travelers, but Branson figured there was room in the marketplace for another competitor, after calling the People Express reservations department and being left on hold for half an hour. He concluded there was either a huge demand or People Express was incompetent. In either case, that spelled an opportunity to him.

Instead of hooking up with British Atlantic, against the advice of his board, Branson decided to start his own airline, promising "to provide the highest quality innovative service at excellent value for [the] money for all classes of air travelers," in the words of the newly dubbed Virgin Atlantic Airways. In a little over three months, the airline was in operation. Virgin Atlantic was an immediate success.

By 1998 Branson wanted to start a low-cost carrier in the United States that he proposed calling Virgin America. Mark Hill, one of the founders of WestJet and Neeleman's good friend, did some number crunching for Branson on the U.S. market and went to London to present his findings.

Every March, the FAA Commercial Aviation Forecast Conference draws a "who's who" of airline industry figures to Washington, D.C., to discuss current and future policy, legal, regulatory, and technology issues, plus other matters critical to the air transportation system. Neeleman and Richard Branson first met at this conference in 1998, and got acquainted over breakfast at the Mayflower Hotel. Their discussion covered topics ranging from Branson's desire to get into the U.S. domestic airline market to Neeleman's much noted attention deficit disorder. Neeleman, immersed in assembling the pieces for his planned venture, delivered his pitch cum mantra to Branson about what the American airline industry needed, what he was going to do about it, and the financing he already had in place to achieve his objective. The British tycoon, in his typical fashion, tuned in and out while evincing enough attention to show his interest in Neeleman's plans. Half an hour into the lunch, observing Branson's distracted demeanor, a lightbulb went on in Neeleman's head.

"He's got it, too!" Neeleman exclaimed, recognizing signature characteristics of ADD in Branson's behavior.

They truly were kindred spirits, and they shared some of the same goals as well.

"There was a community of interest," says David Tait, one of the original members of the Virgin Atlantic executive team, and at the time executive vice president, North America, for the British carrier. Neeleman and Branson discovered enough common interests to carry their conversation forward.

"It developed into a discussion about how possibly the Virgin brand might enhance the idea that David had in mind," says Tait. "I think he liked the idea of coming in with a big brand as well as the capitalization."

Neeleman and Lazarus went to England to meet with Branson and the Virgin Group's board of directors. They had dinner with Branson in a pub in Surrey to get better acquainted. The next day they met Virgin's board, to brief them on the U.S. market and the stringent rules governing foreign ownership of American airlines. The laws stipulate that certificates to operate domestic air transportation be held by a U.S. citizen. Two-thirds of the board of directors and managing officers (including the president) must also be U.S. citizens. And at least 75 percent of the voting stock must be owned by U.S. citizens. That meant the Virgin Group would have a minority voice in the airline.

The Virgin Group's board considered the plan and continued its discussions with Neeleman. Gareth Edmondson-Jones, who headed Virgin America's public relations department, told trade publications that summer that Virgin Atlantic was "looking at starting a low-fare subsidiary in the United States, possibly to be named 'Virgin America,' similar to our Virgin Express all–Boeing 737 operation in Europe." Said Edmondson-Jones, "A new stand-alone company would have to be created, and to even move forward on this would require changes to current foreign ownership regulations in Congress."

But Congress wasn't about to rewrite the regulations. Ultimately Neeleman grew disenchanted with the potential partnership. "We got tired of negotiations with them because they had their hands in all the pockets," he later said of Virgin. These discussions ultimately ended.

"We couldn't come to terms," Lazarus states simply, noting that Branson "was very nice about it."

In the end, Neeleman didn't walk away empty-handed. During the talks, Neeleman met two of Branson's key marketing executives, the aforementioned Gareth Edmondson-Jones and Amy Curtis-McIntyre.

"Amy was this amazing, hysterical New Yorker," Lazarus says. "She was just an incredible brand person."

Curtis-McIntyre was responsible for establishing Virgin Atlantic's identity, look, and feel. Edmondson-Jones, an Australian, was credited with building the Virgin Atlantic name through his superior public relations savvy and contacts. Marketing and PR were the two key positions Neeleman still had to fill. Even if he couldn't have a partnership with the Virgin Group, Neeleman wasn't going to let that stop him from pursuing a relationship with the impressive Virgin marketing team. Alex Wilcox, a promising new Virgin hire who had been drafted from the operations department to assist with planning for the abortive partnership, was the first to accept an invitation from Neeleman to be part of the JetBlue team. Gareth Edmondson-Jones was next. Amy Curtis-McIntyre had left Virgin Atlantic just before Neeleman began his hunt, and soon she, too, was aboard. By all accounts the moves engendered no ill feelings. No one begrudged the talented marketers taking the opportunity of a lifetime. With Tom Kelly, John Owen, Ann Rhoades, and the Virgin veterans (all given equity positions in New Air) on board, Neeleman had assembled what he called "kind of the dream team of airline management."

Along with these key executives, senior maintenance and other personnel who had worked with Neeleman at Morris were brought on board. Al Spain, a respected pilot and safety executive, was recruited to head New Air's pilot training and certification program.

New York's Monkey Bar became an unofficial outpost of the planning effort. Lazarus and the fledgling team met there to brainstorm and bounce ideas off each other late into the night. Neeleman, a devout Mormon who doesn't drink and isn't a night owl by nature, wasn't involved in many of these impromptu sessions, but they helped bond team members and demonstrated the commitment each brought to their role. When the subject of creating the right identity for the airline was raised, Amy Curtis-McIntyre was known to scream, "I'll protect the brand, don't worry!"

INVESTORS FOR THE NEW VENTURE

David Neeleman had made millions of dollars for his investors and partners in the aviation industry over the years, first with Morris Air, then with Open Skies and WestJet. But despite this track record, in the venture capital world New Air was viewed as a start-up. Neeleman and his comrades would have to convince potential investors their plan would be successful, just like any other entrepreneur. And Neeleman wasn't only looking for enough money to start an airline, a hefty amount in its own right. He wanted more than enough. He recalled his experience at his first travel agency, which had gone bust on the cusp of success because of a cash crunch. Moreover, he knew that without sufficient reserves, other airlines would try to use predatory pricing to drive him out of business, matching low fares on competitive routes that were subsidized by raising fares in less contested markets. The only way to prevent this was for competitors to know in no uncertain terms that New Air had the resources to weather any such efforts.

The idea of putting money into an airline—any airline—had four strikes against it from the start, according to Lazarus: "It's not an intuitive investment [for venture capitalists]," in that it doesn't make sense to most people. Second, an airline is capital expense intensive, and therefore can quickly eat up large sums of cash. Third, air transportation is a commodity industry in the eyes of most: An airline seat is an airline seat, and few investors will bet that an airline can breed true loyalty and attract customers by name alone. And fourth, of all the people who have tried to start a successful airline since deregulation in 1978, "everyone's failed," observes Lazarus. "You have to be a brave soul" to invest in an airline, he says. Neeleman and Lazarus set out to find such courageous believers, hitting the road with a presentation pitched to a select number of potential investors.

Even for Lazarus and his firm, Weston Presidio—for which Neeleman had turned $14 million into $34 million in a year's time with the sale of Morris Air to Southwest—it was an unusual investment. "Our firm really funds established businesses that have a lot of the risk removed," Lazarus says. "The management team is in place and works together, and the proof of concept is good. Everything is [already] done." This obviously wasn't the case with New Air. "This was not without a lot of risk," he adds.

The group of investors approached was rather exclusive. Only five venture capital firms were pitched: Bank of America, Bank of Boston, Massachusetts Mutual, JP Morgan Chase Partners, and Soros Quantum Funds. Initially, Neeleman and Lazarus met with internal sponsors at the investment firms whom the pair already knew and had good relationships with. Pitch meetings would last a couple of hours. The sponsors would then spread the word to other members of the firm, and subsequent meetings would be scheduled so the pitch could be repeated. The reception was always positive, but with the need for all those follow-up presentations, the process dragged on. When the pair felt potential investors were drawing out the process too long, they let the firms know. "After a while people have to fish or cut bait," Lazarus says.

Neeleman also gave high-worth individuals who had invested with him before an opportunity to participate in the financing. The Morris family was among them. But since June Morris was serving on the Southwest Airlines board, Neeleman could only reveal a limited amount of information about his new carrier to keep her from being put in a compromising position.

As good an investment as its promoters promised New Air would be, the team made clear in their pitch they weren't out to create a gold mine for investors, but rather a dependable source of profits. Dave Barger told them the company sought "a margin of between 15 percent and 20 percent, but not more than 20 percent. If it's higher than that, we're either gouging customers or not paying our staff enough."

After hearing the presentation, some attendees asked how the airline would keep its smooth operations going, to which Barger retorted, "Who wants to keep it going? We want to improve it."

The last to be pitched and sign on was Soros Quantum Fund, the investment vehicle of famed investor George Soros. "I went in with enormous skepticism about investing in an airline," says Neal Moszkowski, a partner at Quantum. "But [Neeleman's] presence, coupled with the strength of the team, was staggering."

The Soros fund became New Air's largest investor, initially putting up $40 million and taking some 24 percent of the company. Asked how much input Soros has in the company in which the investor has such a large stake, the boyishly enthusiastic Neeleman simply notes that the two have had lunch a couple of times and that "he's a great guy. And I think he has a long-term view of the company. I think he really likes it."

"In the venture capital world you want to spend all your time matching talent to the task," Lazarus says. In Neeleman and the proposed airline, investors had the ultimate combination. "David is perfect for this job," Lazarus maintains. "He focuses solely on the needs of his customers. He's also a natural born leader."

Weston Presidio itself put up $35 million and Lazarus was named chairman, a position he occupied for five years. He jokes that during this time, "the only thing I was allowed to do was move the chair," because "David is just a brilliant operator."

It took two years to raise the capital, but in the end "no one turned us down," Lazarus boasts. "We secured our funding even before getting an airline certificate, airport gate slots, and aircraft."

New Air had raised a total of $130 million, making it the best-capitalized new airline in aviation history. Now just a few items remained to be taken care of—like getting the airline's certificate, finding somewhere to base it, determining where the carrier would fly to, hiring hundreds of employees, and finding the airplanes on which to put its customers.

CHAPTER 7

Preparing for Departure

Investment analysts called New Air "the mother of all start-up airlines." Neeleman had assembled an all-star team of executives and investors to fund and execute the airline's business plan. But a tremendous amount of work was yet to be done. The fledgling airline had no name, no home base, no routes, no airplanes, few employees beyond the core group of executives, and didn't even have a license to fly. It was also a time of unprecedented tumult in the airline industry. Vast numbers of flights were being canceled and horror stories abounded of jets sitting on tarmacs for hours, holding passengers as virtual hostages. Congress was even considering passage of a passengers' bill of rights, forcing carriers to be accountable for their lapses. Neeleman wasn't daunted. He had visions of launching a different kind of airline.

"We started with the concept that we were going to bring humanity back to air travel," Neeleman said. "For some reason, with all the regulations and all the things we had to accomplish as an industry, we started calling our customers 'passengers.' I think there were actually people in our industry that got up in the morning and said, 'Oh, good, it's Tuesday. We're only booked to 35 percent capacity. It should be a good day. I won't have to deal with any of those annoying passengers.' We decided that those annoying passengers were actually paying our way and should be called customers. We figured that we would do a lot of work and try to create a better mousetrap. Try to create a little better company."

Thus began the process of what Michael Lazarus, one of the major investors in the airline and its chairman, called "peeling the onion," attending to the layers of details that stood between the start-ups intentions and its first scheduled flight.

On April 30, 1999, the company, doing business as New Air, filed an application to become a certificated scheduled air carrier. It had already selected the kind of aircraft it would operate, and to many in the industry the choice was a shock.

All low-fare airlines had previously started service with used aircraft, because the acquisition cost made it affordable to go into business. Neeleman had seen the folly in that strategy. He witnessed how Canada's WestAir, which ignored his advice to buy new aircraft, had its fleet grounded because it didn't follow the stringent maintenance rules that applied to older aircraft. And he recognized how the maintenance costs associated with these "cheap" airplanes negated any savings on the front end, particularly when a customer's wariness of dilapidated fleets was brought into the mix. That's why Neeleman made sure he raised enough money to buy all new aircraft. But what kind of plane was best?

Neeleman had pretty much taken the choice of aircraft for granted. He'd be going with Boeing, and specifically the 737. The best-selling airliner in aviation history, he'd flown them at Morris Air, and his hero Herb Kelleher had profited handsomely by sticking to that one aircraft throughout Southwest Airlines' history. What's more, almost every key New Air executive had come from an airline that operated the 737.

"All these people were Boeing people," Lazarus notes. "They grew up in the Boeing culture and knew the planes."

Neeleman and his team, headed by John Owen (the former Southwest Airlines treasurer who had a lot of experience buying planes), went to meet with Boeing's sales representatives in Seattle to close the deal. "We said, 'If you can accept this price, we are ready to shake hands right now,'" Neeleman recalled. "But they resisted, so we left that meeting and set up one with Airbus, though we didn't know much about them and were kind of using them just as a foil."

Based in Toulouse, France, Airbus was created as a consortium of aerospace manufacturers from four countries: France, Germany, Spain, and the United Kingdom. When Airbus was established in Paris in 1970, the world market for airliners was dominated by U.S. manufacturers Boeing, Lockheed, and McDonnell Douglas. The Europeans saw this cooperative venture as the only way to compete against the American giants, and Airbus had waged an aggressive campaign to develop aircraft and wrest market share from U.S. aircraft manufacturers ever since. By the end of the century, Boeing was its only remaining competitor, and the two were locked in a bitter rivalry for dominance of the commercial skies.

The Airbus A320, introduced in 1984, was designed as a competitor to Boeing's 737. But Airbus executives were skeptical that New Air was really interested in buying the company's planes. Neeleman reassured them. "I said, 'Have you ever had a prospect that was in our situation, and you sold them on the superiority of your product?' They said they had, so I said, 'Give me your pitch.'"

During the pitch the Airbus team pointed out that the A320 cabin was seven inches wider than the 737, providing more passenger comfort. It had bigger overhead storage bins and more sophisticated cockpit technology than the 737. And the all-coach configuration, with 162 seats, held 24 more passengers.

"The more we took a look at that airplane the more we liked it," Neeleman says. "There was unanimity among our management team. The price got our attention, and the product put us over the edge. We became very convinced that this was the airplane for us regardless of the cost."

Another determining factor was the creative financing package Airbus presented. "The whole key to the aircraft business is in financing," says Lazarus. "And they were very creative in what they did for us. The leverage we got was unbelievable." With the deals on maintenance and other discounts, the overall costs of going with the A320 were significantly lower than the 737.

New Air placed orders for 25 jets with options and purchase rights for 50 more in the A320 family, including the smaller A319 and the larger A321. The total value of the deal, if all the planes optioned were ultimately purchased, was more than $3.6 billion.

The *New York Times* called the decision "a blow" to Boeing's 737 program. Meanwhile the fleet of new planes "created instant credibility among fliers" for the new airline, Neeleman notes.

"Had Boeing shaken hands on the day we were there," says Neeleman, recalling the negotiations, "they would have had this deal. In the end, we got a price from Airbus that was lower than we would have agreed to originally, and we were convinced of the quality of the Airbus product. It's a lot of money that Boeing walked away from."

You get the feeling Neeleman's still pleased he went against the grain and came out ahead. Commerce, if not justice, had been served.

SETTING UP IN THE BIG APPLE

By this time, New Air had also decided on its home base: New York City. The choice clearly fit with Neeleman's mantra of going where the people are. "It's number one in retail sales," Neeleman has noted. "You have this large population that makes a lot of money per capita, and everyone in New York would like to get out. At the same time, everyone outside New York would like to come in. It's truly the nirvana of all markets."

But the airport he chose as the carrier's home base, John F. Kennedy International, again went against the industry's accepted wisdom. It was considered to be overcrowded and was farther away from New York City's population center than either LaGuardia or Newark. Neeleman saw the situation differently.

"What we figured is there were 5 million people that live closer to Kennedy than any other airport in New York, and it was really their airport of choice," he says. "It's just that there was no service out of Kennedy Airport." Crunching the numbers, Neeleman concluded that even if no one beyond that pool of potential customers (which excluded everyone in Manhattan) ever used the airline, it would still be successful. "And then we said, 'Well, if we do a really good job, we may get some of those people that go outside that 5 million [person] bubble."

Neeleman noted that JFK was only eight miles beyond LaGuardia. While it can be a slow and congested journey along the Van Wyck Expressway, Neeleman felt it was mostly a psychological barrier, and JetBlue's fares and service would be enough to break through.

"I have driven that probably 100 times," Neeleman once said about the route from LaGuardia to JFK, "and the longest it's ever taken me is 25 minutes."

As for airport congestion, an examination of operations revealed that JFK was only busy in the evening when transatlantic flights stacked up to depart for overnight flights to Europe. For most of the day, the airport was actually underutilized. Before JetBlue established operations, between 8 A.M. and 9 A.M., there were only 15 departures.

"We're going to be able to taxi and take off in 8 minutes, whereas at Newark, in the morning, once you push off, it's 42 minutes before you're airborne," Neeleman said.

Additionally, JFK wasn't hampered by the short runways at LaGuardia, nor the effects of weather that played havoc with airline schedules at Newark. "The runways at Newark are too close together, and every time the wind blows or visibility goes down or it's snowing or it's raining, they have to go to a single runway, which has a tremendously negative effect on the operation," Neeleman says, contrasting it with Kennedy, where "there are long runways and they're very far apart from each other." In 1998 Neeleman got in touch with the Port Authority of New York and New Jersey, which controls the New York metropolitan area's airports, seeking to lease space at JFK.

"We laugh about it now," says Neeleman, recalling the process. "This guy shows up from Salt Lake City, Utah, and says, 'I want to have a meeting with you guys.' 'What do you want?' 'I want to start an airline.' 'Start an airline, what do you mean? About 87 have gone out of business!' I got very little respect from the folks there, and I said, 'You know, I found this terminal, it's empty, your runways are empty most of the day, LaGuardia's congested, we'd like to put an airline here.'"

JFK's Terminal 6 was built for National Airlines in 1937. Pan American took charge of it with its purchase of National, and TWA acquired the space from Pan Am for its domestic terminal. (This is not to be confused with TWA's Eero Saarinen–designed international terminal, which was the subject of international preservation efforts, and to which a new JetBlue terminal facility under construction at Kennedy will be connected.) TWA abandoned the terminal when its business declined before its bankruptcy, and it had been vacant since. When Neeleman finally got officials to take him seriously enough to show him the space, he found it would take more than a welcome mat to get the facility ready for prime time. "When I walked through that terminal with the Port Authority of New York and New Jersey, it was totally trash everywhere," he says.

But finding a terminal was actually the least of the problems related to operating at JFK. Despite airline deregulation, New Air still needed permission from the federal government to land and take off from there.

When air travel was deregulated in 1978 (cargo operations were deregulated the year before), four airports were exempted: Chicago's O'Hare, Washington, D.C.'s National (now Ronald Reagan) Airport, and both LaGuardia and JFK airports in New York. The reason? These facilities were deemed potentially too popular. Opening them to any and all carriers might result in more planned operations (that is, takeoffs and landings) than these airports could handle. Indeed, the high-density rule that mandated these restrictions was enacted in 1968. At Kennedy, all available slots, or takeoff and landing positions, were spoken for.

On February 5, 1999, New Air Corporation filed with the Department of Transportation for an exemption to the high density rule, which limits the number of takeoffs and landings allowed at Kennedy Airport between 3:00 P.M. and 7:59 P.M. Neeleman planned to take advantage of the airport's low use in the mornings and midday, but flights would also have to be scheduled in the afternoons and evenings to meet the needs of business travelers. New Air sought 75 slots during that daily time period—each slot representing one takeoff or landing—to be phased in at 25 slots per year over three years.

"This is going to be good for everybody," Neeleman insisted to reporters upon making the filing. At the same time, he announced his commitment to providing superior service along with low fares, and shaking up the airline industry. Other than these few general hints, Neeleman was coy with the press about what exactly this so-called New Air was all about. Not wanting to tip off competitors to his exact intentions, the filing listed 44 potential destinations, without committing to any one of them.

But if Neelman wanted to make JFK his airline's home base, he'd need powerful help. Fortunately, Neeleman could offer a strong incentive to attract those who could aid him in the cause: cheap fares on the notoriously overpriced routes to upstate New York, to cities like Buffalo, Rochester, and Syracuse. High fares on these routes had long been a source of irritation to area politicians. Neeleman invited New York's newly elected Senator Charles "Chuck" Schumer out to breakfast.

"Three weeks after I won the Senate race, one of the first meetings I had was with David," Schumer recalls. Neeleman told him about his idea for starting a low-fare airline and asked for his assistance. Schumer's reaction to Neeleman's pitch: "Immediately I said, 'This guy can do it. He's for real.' Basically, at that breakfast I said, 'I'll help you get slots at Kennedy, but only if you fly to upstate New York.'"

Soon Governor George Pataki threw his support behind awarding slots to New Air as well.

The only official opposition to the airline's application for the slots came from the International Association of Machinists and Aerospace Workers, AFL-CIO (IAM), which argued that the

DOT shouldn't grant exemptions to an airline that paid employees "substandard wages and benefits." The IAM also said the application should be rejected because the airline's projections of operating at a 65 percent load factor during its first year of operation was "unrealistic."

On April 30, New Air applied to the DOT for airline certification. The company claimed it would achieve operating costs "comparable or even lower than those of industry leader Southwest," whose operating cost per available seat mile at the time was only 7.39 cents, about 25 percent below the industry average.

A NAME FROM OUT OF THE BLUE

The new airline had found a home, selected its airplanes, and filed its paperwork with the government. But one major task still awaited completion: deciding what to call the company. "That was the most frustrating thing, coming up with a name," Neeleman recalls.

During its planning, the enterprise had been dubbed "New Air." But this was simply a flag of convenience, not its permanent identity. As savvy marketers, Neeleman and his executive team recognized the importance of a good name. They also understood its limitations.

"I knew the name wouldn't make us, but I wanted a name we would be proud of, and that's important," Neeleman says. "A name doesn't make a company, a company makes the name, by how you deliver on the promise every single day."

Still, the name game was anything but child's play. Merkley Newman Harty, a New York advertising agency that specializes in brand building and is known for its edgy work (the firm's motto is "Creating heresy in a world of dogma"), was engaged to come up with the perfect name. Among the first the agency unveiled for the company were "Egg" and "It." The graphic possibilities of Egg intrigued and excited Neeleman and his team, though the less sunny side of the name outweighed any pictorial considerations. As Gareth Edmondson-Jones explains, "It was like, 'Think about it, man. Crack an egg . . .' It just wouldn't sound right."

"It" also developed a following that lasted beyond the first hearing. "'It' really stuck. 'It' we loved," Neeleman says. "But we just didn't like how it would look in newsprint. There was just no way it would work."

Later suggestions that got serious consideration included "The Competition" and "Taxi," Neeleman demonstrated how he thought the former could become part of air travel parlance with a made-up exchange: "'So how are you flying to Florida?'" he asked himself. "'I'm going on The Competition.'"

The name "Taxi" was a big hit with some people Neeleman bounced it off of. To go along with the name, he planned to paint the planes yellow with black-and-white check trim, the colors of a New York hack. But "Taxi" was deemed a turnoff to the start-up's prospective hometown customers. "My people in Utah loved Taxi because they hadn't spent half their life in a New York taxi, without air conditioning," Neeleman says.

"Chocolate" was another name the agency proposed. "I like chocolate, but I'm not sure I want to fly at 39,000 feet on Chocolate," Neeleman quips. "Crazy, crazy names they came up with."

"Zoom," "Civilization," "Yes!," "Home Airlines," and "Flair" also received consideration. So did "Blue."

"I said, 'That's good!'" Neeleman recalled of his reaction to the colorful name. "They said, 'But you don't get it; everything's going to be yellow.'"

Meanwhile, the New Air team went through the dictionary "eight times through" over 10 months, according to Neeleman, while the company's attorneys checked out promising potential names for trademarks.

Neeleman kept coming back to "Blue." But the fact that it couldn't be trademarked, being a word in common use, made it unacceptable.

Seeking more ideas, the team flew to San Francisco and held a meeting with Landor Associates, specialists in developing product names. They came up with more suggestions for the hopper: "Air Avenue," "Air Hop," and "Scout," none of which created much heat. Then they tossed out another idea: "True Blue."

"I said, 'Oh, sounds sweet to me; too sweet—sounds like a good frequent flyer program,'" Neeleman said. (Indeed, the airline's frequent flyer program would eventually be christened with that name.)

Nonetheless, time was running out. The company was scheduled to unveil itself to the world soon. A temporary name wouldn't do. This would be the chance to make a big impression, to create something memorable. Announcing an airline "as yet to be named" wasn't an option at the moment they held the media's attention.

Curtis-McIntyre lobbied for True Blue, and finally it was selected. The only hitch: the trademark turned out to be owned by Thrifty Rent-A-Car. Negotiations to acquire the rights commenced, moving along rapidly as the day of the announcement approached.

The unveiling press conference was scheduled for Wednesday, July 14, 1999, in New York City. All of the team assumed True Blue would be the name they'd present to reporters. But on the Friday night before the unveiling, negotiations with Thrifty for the rights to the trademarked name came undone. There would be no True Blue. So what name would be announced to the world in its place?

Neeleman kept saying, "Why can't we just call it Blue?" Curtis-McIntyre later recalled, "And I'm like, 'For the nineteenth time, you can't trademark *blue!*' Finally I said, 'David, just make up a word with "Blue" in it, and I'll train the rest of the world to just call it Blue. Like 'FlyBlue.' Only, no one's going to want to say they're going to fly 'FlyBlue.' So how about "JetBlue"?

For Neeleman, it was a eureka moment.

"That's it!" he exclaimed. His next move: "I went out and dialed 1-800-JET-BLUE and I got some tractor distributor in the Midwest, so I knew we could buy the name. Then I went to the Internet and typed www.jetblue.com, and it wasn't taken."

To Neeleman, *Jet* suggested strength, while *Blue*, as always, represented the sky's wild yonder. It also worked as a play on *jet black*. The company immediately trademarked the name. The following Wednesday, JetBlue was introduced to the world and the company filed notice with the government that the carrier was changing its corporate name to JetBlue Airways Corporation.

GETTING JETBLUE OFF THE GROUND

Seemingly, all the pieces were now in place. The management team. The investment capital. The airplanes. The application for the base of operations. But in the real world, things don't work as smoothly as they do on paper. Though all were committed in principle, none among these critical constituencies wanted to make the first move. Investors wouldn't put up money until the management team was officially in place and a deal with Airbus for the aircraft was consummated. Members of the management team were reluctant to put their names on the dotted line until, in prudent "show me the money" fashion, the company had the cash. And Airbus wouldn't guarantee the terms of the aircraft sale without the investment money in place.

"It was a wild circle we kept working down to center," is how

Lazarus describes it. Neeleman finally provided the spark to move things forward with a personal financial commitment. "I'll put up $5 million to get things going," he told Lazarus. That was enough to prod the investors, the management team, and Airbus to all move together.

But in the minds of its founders, as necessary as they were, the planes, airport slots, and financing were of secondary importance. Their primary concern was the organization's values—the beliefs underpinning the airline's commitment to bring humanity back to air travel. These beliefs were defined and codified in a meeting convened once all the key personnel had joined JetBlue.

As Neeleman recounts, "We sat together in a room one day and we said, 'Do we want a mission statement? What is it we want?' And we determined that we wanted to just create five values. And the values were safety—because obviously if we weren't safe, we wouldn't have a business—caring, fun, integrity, and passion.

"We said, 'Okay, good.' Now our general counsel is probably the man most like Gandhi I've met. He said, 'These qualities would be good for Gandhi, but can we make a profit? That's the question. Should we have something related to profit in those five values?' And I said, 'If we live by these values we'll make a profit, because the most important thing that we can do is be good to our people.' And that was the whole thing. 'Let's hire the best people, let's figure out a way to do that.'"

This task would fall to Ann Rhoades, who today, recounting this meeting, calls it the "key to the success" of JetBlue.

"A lot of you will not end up in the airline business," Neeleman frequently tells audiences in his speeches, when addressing the subject of hiring practices. "These [values] are applicable to any business you want to be in. We're in a service economy, and a service economy means that you rely on people. If you're going to rely on people then you better select the best people and you better train them well, and you better stand by them. These are very important concepts that we started out with."

The late 1990s dot-com economy was in full bloom at the time JetBlue set about staffing the airline. That meant crowded flights and unpleasant experiences for travelers. For pilots, mechanics, and flight attendants, it meant their skills were in demand. Industry analysts talked of looming labor shortages. JetBlue didn't want to rely on high pay to attract a superior workforce. Indeed, though JetBlue would offer profit sharing and other generous benefits, Neeleman didn't intend to match the wages unionized workers earned at other carriers. So how would his airline attract the level of talent he was looking for? Assuring the company met this recruitment challenge has been a major focus of the company from its inception.

"Our business is 100 percent about people," Neeleman often says, referring to JetBlue crewmembers. "It gets a little bit annoying sometimes when people talk so much about the TV and leather seats and new airplanes because those things are cool and they're important. But they would be of little importance to our business if we didn't have the best people in the industry. And they're working really hard to take care of our customers on a daily basis."

When Neeleman first talked about his hiring goals, skeptics abounded.

"I came from Utah originally to start the airline in New York," Neeleman recounts. "Some people smiled and said, 'You're going to start a customer service business in New York? What a stupid idea. People are not nice in New York and New York isn't known for customer service.' And I'm just kind of a dumb kid coming from Utah and I didn't know any better. I said, 'We have a lot of people to choose from, about 17 million. I'm sure we'll find some good people.'"

Once again Neeleman's instincts proved more prescient than the collective knowledge of the experts. The search began by redefining the identity of the workforce.

"We decided that we didn't like the term *employee*, that *employee* was a somewhat demeaning term," Neeleman says. "It didn't really give ample credit to those that were actually doing all the work while I was just sitting here getting all the credit. So Dave Barger, our president, came up with this term, *crewmember*. Everyone at JetBlue would be a crewmember. And then if you referred to a JetBlue worker as an employee, it would cost you a buck."

JetBlue wanted crewmembers, particularly those who had contact with its customers, with gumption and backbone. That was much more important than previous airline experience or even a dream of a life in aviation. "We've always said we hope to get most of our frontline people out of college or out of some other industry," Neeleman says. "We want all the people who went to school at say, Tulane, who want to spend a couple of years in Manhattan, enjoy it, then go on to the next career or whatever. Career flight attendants aren't necessarily what we're after." Reflecting that ethos, JetBlue placed help wanted ads in the *Village Voice*, a New York City weekly newspaper with a strong counterculture readership. But while much of the airline was based on the Southwest model, JetBlue didn't want the wisecracking, performer-wannabe type flight attendants its paragon was known for. New Yorkers already dealt with enough actor-waiters, smart-alecky counter help, and others who brought what's been called "an excess of personality" to the job.

"The people we put out at the gates will encounter a skeptical, very inconvenienced, and angry public," said Curtis-McIntyre.

"The only way to break out of the box is to have our front line trained, and it's not so much trainable as it's finding people who are born with a spirit of 'can do' and 'I know where you live, I get you.'"

Along with the young and free-spirited, Neeleman found models for ideal crewmembers in the Bible, pointing to the Old Testament story of Job, the beleaguered figure who lost his wealth, family, friends, and health, yet who remained unwavering in his faith and in his positive attitude. "Job is a person we'd like to have working for us at JetBlue," he sometimes tells audiences in illustrating the company's hiring goals.

Ann Rhoades, in charge of the hiring policies and procedures, developed the methodology for screening applicants (explored in greater detail in Chapter 8).

"We figured out a way that we wanted to interview people to determine if they were a right fit or not-right fit for the company," Neeleman says. "We came up with this type of interview called 'targeted selection,' where we really wanted a certain type of person. We wanted people who like people."

JetBlue sought to hire the best pilots possible, with more experience and seniority than the average airline applicant. But Rhoades recognized a problem. At the time Neeleman sold Morris Air, some flight crewmembers thought he had sold out the airline's pilots by not working hard enough to get them hired elsewhere. As long as that view persisted, pilots, a notoriously clannish lot, would be less than enthusiastic about signing on, particularly at a time when the economy was booming and pilots "were calling the shots," as Rhoades later said. She devised a simple but effective solution: "I had them meet David." When the first prospective pilots had a chance to talk to Neeleman face-to-face (as many pilots being considered for employment have subsequently done), his passion and commitment to crewmembers came through. The airline hasn't had a problem attracting pilots since. At last count, the airline had applications on file from more than 9,000 prospective pilots desiring to join the airline.

Looking back, with JetBlue drawing closer to its launch, Neeleman realized how beneficial the five years he'd been forced to wait to start his new airline because of his noncompete agreement with Southwest had been.

"I think that was really a blessing for me and for our whole team," Neeleman says, "because we really had time to think about what JetBlue was going to be like. We really spent a lot of time thinking about the types of people that we would hire. How would we train them? How would we motivate them? How would we incentivize? And how would we build this company? We thought a lot about it."

All this careful thinking was about to pay off for Neeleman, for his people, and for millions of air travelers.

CHAPTER 8

JetBlue Takes Flight

Idlewild, a trendy lounge on Houston Street in lower Manhattan, crackled with the electric current usually associated with a press event staged for a hot new film star or fashion mogul on the morning of July 14, 1999. Some might have thought it an unlikely setting for the introduction of a major business in a conservative industry. But it made perfect sense to the team at JetBlue.

Appropriating John F. Kennedy International Airport's original name, Idlewild's long, narrow interior is configured to resemble the first-class cabin of a Boeing 747. The club's furnishings underscored for the audience the aircraft-oriented business at hand, from the booths made out of airline seats right down to the cramped modular lavatories. The interior of Idlewild suggests an era when there was a certain panache to the entire enterprise of air travel, imbuing all inside with a patina of glamour. And the fun, slightly subversive atmosphere reflected JetBlue's own ethos. Even before it had a name or an airplane, JetBlue enjoyed the cachet usually associated with a hip underground club, thanks to the savvy marketing work of Amy Curtis-McIntyre and Gareth

Edmondson-Jones. That made Idlewild an ideal venue for unveiling the new airline to an eager media.

At the podium that morning, the grinning and youthful CEO looked like a kid let loose in a candy store. Yet despite his credentials and boyish charm, local reporters weren't going to roll over for David Neeleman. He may have been successful before, but that was somewhere west of the Hudson River. This was New York City, where the press corps had seen its share of wunderkinder come and go.

"We want to be New York's new low-fare hometown airline," Neeleman assured them in a display of what could either be seen as naïve confidence or remarkable chutzpah, coming as it did from a third-generation Mormon from Utah. Striking on all the points he knew travelers would respond to, Neeleman promised New Yorkers—and the world—a new kind of economy travel aboard planes with wider, all-leather seats, extra legroom, preassigned seats, and more overhead storage space than other carriers delivered. Moreover, all of this would be provided at a price that was up to 65 percent less than the competition. Furthermore, there would be no requirement for staying at destinations over a Saturday night to qualify for the lowest fare, as the major carriers mandated. Even the price of walk-up tickets would be below the standard fares many airlines charged for flights of a similar distance. On the ground, JetBlue would offer quick, computerized, touch-screen check-in. Perhaps most notable of all, in the air, passengers would be able to watch 24 channels of live TV displayed on individual monitors mounted in every seatback. JetBlue would be the first airline in the world to make this entertainment amenity available to all passengers.

As always, Neeleman had his doubters. Hometown newspaper the *New York Times*, in reporting on the press conference, labeled his promise to bring humanity back to air travel "one of several pledges that may one day return to haunt him."

Regulatory authorities took a less jaundiced view of Neeleman's aspirations. After examining JetBlue's request and business plan, on August 31, 1999, the Department of Transportation found that the company was "fit, willing, and able" to provide scheduled air service, and awarded Neeleman and his team air carrier certification. Two weeks later, on September 16, a press conference hosted by Senator Charles Schumer was arranged at the DOT's offices in New York. It was here that U.S. Transportation Secretary Rodney Slater granted JetBlue an exemption to the high density rule, approving the 75 takeoff and landing slots for Kennedy Airport that the carrier had requested. It was the largest number of slots ever awarded to an airline, start-up or otherwise. Both Schumer and Neeleman took the opportunity to sound their populist themes.

Schumer declared that "JetBlue is the perfect airline to break the monopoly power which other airlines used as ransom to hold Upstate's economy hostage," while Neeleman proclaimed "an end to the regimen of high fares."

Would New Air have ever gotten those slots without the senator's help? Would it have ever taken off if it couldn't have used Kennedy as its home base? "It would have been harder, it would have been a different risk profile," Lazarus admits. "But would we have done it? Probably we would have done it anyway. But it really made the difference."

INAUGURAL FLIGHTS

The first of JetBlue's new A320 aircraft, one of eight leased from Airbus to bridge the gap before the planes the airline purchased were completed, arrived in New York in December 1999. Its first flight was a brief jaunt around the skies over Manhattan soon after. A Learjet with a camera crew acted as a chase plane, getting footage of the Airbus for JetBlue commercials and promotional material. Onboard the A320, Neeleman acted as host to a select group of investors, top executives, and friends. Few aboard were accustomed to cruising in an airliner at a mere 2,000 feet, an altitude selected to allow for inspiring panoramas of the plane soaring over the spires of midtown.

The silver-haired Neeleman was in high spirits as he patrolled the aisle. "I was trying to get the pilot to buzz underneath the Verrazano bridge," he quipped, breaking into quotations from a favorite movie, *Airplane*. "What's your vector, Victor?" he asked no one in particular, before taking out his cell phone and pretending to make a call. "I just want to see if this thing really does throw off the navigation system," he announced, straight-faced.

With the plane canting into a 40-degree bank for the cameras— a much steeper turn than commercial airliners typically make— Neeleman crouched down in the aisle and struck a surfer's pose, arms outstretched, like he was riding a towering wave. Indeed, he was. Service was scheduled to begin on February 11, with flights to Fort Lauderdale, followed by service to Buffalo. In the week since JetBlue began taking reservations, it had already sold more than $1 million in advance tickets to the two destinations. While skeptics remained, most observers were climbing aboard the JetBlue juggernaut. *New York Magazine*, ever the arbiter of what is in and out in the city, called the airline "as urbane as a Stoli cosmopolitan," before its first scheduled flight left the ground.

As one analyst remarked, Neeleman was performing the kind of tricks and getting the type of buzz that was normally only afforded to pre-IPO dot-com companies.

At 8:55 A.M. on Friday, February 11, 2000, JetBlue's first scheduled flight pushed back from its gate at JFK's Terminal 6 bound for Fort Lauderdale. A new era in low-fare aviation—and in David Neeleman's life—had arrived. Whatever sense of accomplishment this landmark event provoked for Neeleman would likely be brief and be soon overtaken by his relentless push to refine, improve, and strive toward perfection.

At a press conference before the flight, in addition to thanking the dignitaries for their help, Neeleman introduced the innovation that would become one of the airline's most distinctive features: the 24-channel LiveTV in-flight entertainment system. While the system wasn't installed in the planes yet, it soon would be, and JetBlue wanted to show future passengers what they could expect.

That same morning, Neeleman went aloft in another of his new airplanes again, this time on a ceremonial trip to Buffalo, New York. The upstate city would be a JetBlue destination beginning a week later. Aboard with Neeleman were Senator Charles Schumer and other politicians who had helped the airline get slots at Kennedy Airport.

A month after its first flight, Tampa was added as another JetBlue destination. Meanwhile, now that he didn't have Southwest's bureaucracy to thwart him, Neeleman pushed to combine the efficiencies of scale he'd observed at that airline with the nimbleness in responding to market conditions he'd practiced at Morris. In April, for example, JetBlue introduced a "Get-It-Together" fare for the Tampa market. Customers booking as little as 24 hours in advance of their flight still got the lowest possible fare—as long as they found at least one other person to travel with them.

Orlando was added to the company's route schedule in June. By the end of the year, service was also available to Rochester,

New York; Burlington, Vermont; West Palm Beach and Fort Myers in Florida; Ontario, and Oakland in California, as well as to a destination that had a particular sentimental attraction to Neeleman: Salt Lake City, Utah.

"I was just 25 when we launched Morris Air here in 1984," Neeleman said when the JFK-SLC run was inaugurated in November. "I guess time flies when you're having fun. Sixteen years later, it's great to be flying home with JetBlue."

As for those who doubted the airline's projections of load factors, JetBlue answered them less than three months after the carrier's launch by exercising its option to buy seven additional A320s from Airbus Industries.

In those early months, the challenge for the airline wasn't finding customers to fill its planes. Instead, JetBlue faced competition for talented employees in what was a tight market for airline professionals. The economy was booming, driven by an explosive technology and Internet revolution. The major airlines were expanding routes and hiring many new pilots. Flight attendants and even ground crews were also in heavy demand. JetBlue was the risky start-up that offered lower pay (at least for those with seniority at another airline) and seemingly less job security than the more established carriers. What's more, it was picky. JetBlue only wanted workers of the highest quality who could provide the kind of top-notch customer service it was determined to be known for.

"No question about it, our largest job is finding great people," David Barger, JetBlue's president, said at the time.

Despite the tight labor market in which it launched service, it turned out that JetBlue had little problem attracting promising applicants. How did the airline do it? By creating incentives and a work environment that made taking a chance on JetBlue both profitable and fun. It all began with an underlying philosophy: You must first do well by your employees (or crewmembers, as JetBlue calls them) before you can expect them to be good to your customers.

"Taking care of our crewmembers is the first rule," Neeleman says. "That means doing everything you can to select the right people, train them properly, and compensate them fairly. Give them a piece of the rock. These are bedrock principles that help people succeed at any business. And although they are not radical ideas, a lot of people don't stick to them. It's easier said than done when you're faced with real situations, but I try very hard not to waver."

The airline's hiring and human resources policies were—and are—overseen by a department that is simply called "People." The policies of the department were established by Ann Rhoades, one of Neeleman's earliest recruits at JetBlue and the woman famous for the innovative personnel policies she had previously instituted in the People Department at Southwest Airlines.

Those interested in working for the airline discovered right away that the only way to learn about and apply for a job—from executives and pilots on down—was through the company's web site. Instituting this requirement helped to reduce the costs associated with processing applications. More important, it immediately eliminated anyone who wasn't computer literate—a necessary skill for a company so reliant on technology to retain its competitive advantage.

A PEOPLE-FRIENDLY EMPLOYER

The airline has continued to tweak and refine its recruiting process over the years, but many key elements remain unchanged. For instance, JetBlue tries to initially contact everyone who meets the minimum requirements for an open position by phone. This telephone screening is an important component of the selection process, as crewmembers are expected to be articulate, and friendly. A follow-up phone interview awaits those who make the first cut, and the best of these are asked to come in for an in-person interview.

The number one job qualification to work for JetBlue is that prospective crewmembers must like people. During the initial interview, applicants may be asked to give an example of a difficult customer situation they were involved in and what they did to keep the customer happy, or they might be quizzed about a problem encountered in a project they were working on and what they did to solve it.

"You would be surprised how many people can't even give you one example of that," Neeleman says. "Those people are probably not working for us today because we want people who will chip in and help out and will make a company successful."

Prospective crewmembers who make it to the in-person interview phase of the process meet with top executives of the department in which they'd work if hired, so they can be filled in on what a typical day on the job is like—if there is such a thing.

"If you are used to structure, this is not the airline for you," says one senior JetBlue human resources executive. As for the job description, "It changes every day. It's really fast-paced."

Throughout these meetings, company recruiters look for signs of the fun-loving, team-oriented spirit its crewmembers are known for, as well as behaviors that mirror the values JetBlue is built on. Applicants are also interviewed about the company's five core values of caring, fun, passion, integrity, and safety. An eight-member hiring committee, composed primarily of front line crewmembers themselves, makes the final decision on whether someone gets the job.

When it comes to pilots, technical qualifications and flight experience are important. More critical, however, is whether the applicant fits the JetBlue mold. "There is no sim [simulator] evaluation, no tests, no grilling, no pain," Barger says. "We're not screening logbooks. We're hiring a personality and a set of values. Our objective is: 'Do you fit with us and do we fit with you?'"

Says one pilot, "Working there [at JetBlue] is like being a part of a big family. It is not uncommon to give and get lots of hugs from the gals, and the guys are kind of like brothers. You have a very warm and personal feeling about the company," he says. "This is the best of the best."

All pilot applicants who meet minimum qualifications are also first screened via telephone. Those who make it in for an interview may talk with Neeleman, Dave Barger, and the vice president of flight operations (Al Spain, who first held this title, was succeeded by Mike Barger), as well as a representative of the People Department. Having top executives and pilot applicants meet is one way JetBlue hopes to retain its small-company feel as it continues to grow. "They [the applicants] all have the ability to meet senior leadership on day one. It shows there are real people tied to these titles," Dave Barger says.

As with other prospective hires, pilots are asked to cite past examples of how they've dealt with problems. Rhoades recalls one pilot who told of solving a difficult situation by calling a flight attendant to the cockpit and giving her detailed orders on how to handle it. When asked why he chose that course of action, he answered, "I'm the captain and so I told her what to do." Says Rhoades, "That's not the kind of thinking we want."

Conversely, Rhoades recounts one flight attendant applicant, a retired fireman, who answered, "I was in a burning building, and some of my guys were inside, and the building was coming down, and I had to go in and get them out of there." The hiring committee's response? "We said, 'You're hired!'" The ex-firefighter is now considered one of the airline's best flight attendants.

Indeed, current qualifications for flight attendants are more stringent than they were when the company put its first recruitment ads in the *Village Voice*. Today applicants generally need two years of customer service experience, preferably "face-to-face." That's to help prepare them for unique situations such as an inebriated passenger at 37,000 feet, to paraphrase one People department executive.

"I am looking for an artist who can get on the PA and make announcements and have fun with it," Barger says. "I'm looking for people who can come out and talk to the customers. I want people who have the ability to empathize with the customers. That's what I'm looking for.

"I don't like to interview in the office," Barger adds. Instead, he's apt to take a management position applicant along on a Jet-Blue flight for a job interview. "This is the best way for somebody to evaluate what JetBlue is all about. This is a great way for somebody to experience the airline."

While the initial screening may sound touchy-feely, it's all business when it comes to background checks. JetBlue conducts some of the most thorough and extensive in the industry. For instance, private investigators have been hired to collect training records for the airline's pilots. Letters of recommendation and references are carefully checked. And the airline goes far beyond that.

"We talk to people who worked at the same airline [as the applicant]," Rhoades says. "We want to know about their ability to fly, but also whether they get along with other team members. By the time we're done, we know as much about you as your mother."

"It was the most extensive background check I've ever been through," admits Kevin Kelly, an A320 captain with the airline.

"They even called my next-door neighbor. Their attention to detail is phenomenal."

Hearing management talk about searching for people who "are willing to think outside the box" and who "find a way to say yes" sounds rote, but the results speak for themselves. The airline has had much less turnover than projected, a testament to both the hiring practices and the working environment. About 1 in 30 interviewed applicants is accepted. And the People Department itself thinks outside the box in developing novel programs that expand the airline's pool of potential hires.

JetBlue hires college students looking to take a year off from school with its in-flight crewmember recruiting program. The student signs a one-year contract agreeing to fly at least 70 hours a month. A sum equal to what traditional employees of the same level get for benefits and profit sharing is given to the students to help with living expenses. At the end of the contract period, the flight attendant has an option to renew with the approval of the in-flight department, becoming part of a traditional flight crew.

In addition, a job-sharing program dubbed "Inflight Friends Crew" allows two flight attendants to share one job. Interviewed and hired as a team, the two job-sharers cover one full-time scheduled position, comprising a minimum of 70 hours per month. For scheduling, the airline stays out of the way and lets the employee pairs manage themselves. The company doesn't care which member of the team shows up on a given day, "as long as one does," Rhoades explains.

Using friends eliminates one major headache of job-sharing arrangements: interpersonal problems. "In other job-sharing situations I've been in, one person will blame the other for not doing something or not informing the other one of what's going on,"

Rhoades observes. Underscoring the close bonds uniting some of these job-sharing partnerships, JetBlue currently has several mother-daughter teams and, as of this writing, at least one mother and son duo; the son is a college student, and his mother covers his shift when classes intervene.

More than 10 percent of the airline's flight attendants are involved in the job-sharing program, and the airline would like that figure to rise to one-third.

The airline also uses part-time employees. Despite the quality of its hires and the good working conditions, being a flight attendant is a stressful, demanding job, more so given JetBlue's accent on customer service. Both job-sharing and part-time work help prevent job burnout, while at the same time opening up opportunities for qualified people whose schedules might not otherwise allow them to take the position. "It's a win-win situation," says Wendy Stafford, president and senior recruiter of Airline Inflight Resources, an Altamonte Springs, Florida, recruiting company that hires for the airline industry.

"They work fewer hours and are able to enjoy other aspects of their lives, such as their family," Stafford says. "This flexibility allows them the freedom to thoroughly enjoy their relationship with the airline. Some airlines offer part-time employment to senior flight attendants, but if they would only extend the offer to new hires, they would have a vast market of untapped talent who have never considered a flight attendant career simply because they would have to be away from home so frequently."

All of JetBlue's more than 800 telephone reservations agents work from their homes in the Salt Lake City area, another example of the airline's innovative People policies. As Neeleman likes to quip, when you call the airline's reservations department, chances are the person on the other end of line is working the keyboard wearing comfortable clothes and fuzzy slippers.

"Those employees [have demonstrated] superior performance being at home as opposed to being right here where we could stare at them," Neeleman insists. "But no [company] does it. I find it almost comical that there's this Big Brother kind of control thing with the employee."

Neeleman points out that with today's technology, employers can get the exact same information about their workers whether they're sitting at home or in a cubicle 50 rows down in some monstrous call center. Plus, because the prospect of working from home is so attractive to many, it allows the airline to hire better people. The concept has worked so well, other airlines are now exploring this telecommuting option themselves. JetBlue is happy to share what it has learned about the innovation because Neeleman thinks it makes for good business.

"Once a month we host companies to come to Utah [and] sit down with our vice president of reservations," he says. "Delta Airlines went out there—our mortal enemy—and sat down and said, 'How do you do it?' We showed them, because I think it's just right for humanity that people have the option to work from home. So if you don't have people working at home, and you think you need control over people, shame on you. Change your ways, and go out to Utah, and we'll show you how to do it."

To foster camaraderie and keep the at-home workforce focused on common goals, JetBlue has regular meetings and social gatherings. Groups of about 30 reservationists gather monthly for a four-hour meeting with their supervisors to discuss issues and to socialize. A small party caps the get-together. There are quarterly socials at which all the reservationists gather, and an annual picnic, which Neeleman often attends. One measure of the program's success: Call centers typically have employee turnover rates in the vicinity of 30 percent per year. At JetBlue, the figure is 6 percent. Meanwhile, the virtual call center, which Neeleman can claim to have developed first, saves the company on all the costs associated with building and maintaining a centralized call center.

Many JetBlue executives and managers also work out of their homes, especially those located outside of the company's New York headquarters. The airline covers all costs associated with setting up and maintaining these home offices.

A FOCUS ON TRAINING

Following the rigorous up-front screening process, and after ensuring the right people have been hired, JetBlue next sets its sights on making sure crewmembers are well prepared for their jobs. Neeleman and his executives gave the design and implementation of training considerable thought during the airline's earliest days of planning. "We decided that we were going to train real well, that we were going to spend a lot of money on training," Neeleman says, "which is kind of counterintuitive because a lot of people that are starting their businesses for the first time . . . want to cut corners. They want to make sure that people are trained as little as possible because it costs money to train people."

The company established JetBlue University to ensure its people are properly trained. "We don't have a mascot or a football team," says Neeleman, "but we have the College of Flight and the College of In-flight, and the College of Customer Service."

Once hired, pilots and flight attendants alike are sent to Florida for their initial training. The company is currently building a new training and maintenance facility complex at Orlando International Airport for this purpose, which is scheduled for completion in 2005. A major difference between JetBlue's training program compared to that of other airlines: JetBlue pays its trainees while they're learning the ropes.

"Certain other big airlines, when they hire pilots, they say, 'You're privileged to work for us, so we're not going to pay you while you're in training. [Moreover] we're going to make you pay for your own hotel [during the time you're training].' And then little wonder people come out of the class mad because they had to borrow money or they had to sacrifice, and they didn't really respect the company because they took advantage of them."

JetBlue decided to follow a different approach. "We not only pay our pilots [and flight attendants] for training, we pay for all of their accommodations," Neeleman says. "We also sign a five-year contract guaranteeing them employment with us that [does-n't allow us] to lay them off. In essence it [is] a guaranteed contract." The net result, according to Neeleman, is that employees are convinced the airline cares about them. It's the kind of culture he wants to make pervasive throughout the entire organization.

Indeed, Neeleman also makes an effort to meet all new hires across the ranks. Among other topics, he explains JetBlue's culture and their part in preserving it. "Dave Barger and I try to hit every single new orientation when people come to work, and I talk about all of these things," Neeleman says. "And somebody raises their hand and says, 'What are you going to do when your maintenance costs start going up?' We say, 'Wait a second! You work for us now. What are *we* going to do? We're in this thing together!'"

Neeleman's own personal values, forged in part during his time living and ministering in the *favelas* of Rio de Janeiro, are reflected in the company's relationship with its people. Yet he seems intent on ascribing his rationale largely to sound business thinking.

"If you hide the ball, hold back information, speak down to people, and treat them like they are just employees, you will not be successful, particularly in a service-sector business like ours," Neeleman insists. "You have to be totally honest with people, and if they trust you and know you've never lied to them, they will go anywhere with you."

"Taking care of your own people [ensures] that they will take care of customers," Neeleman says. And, he adds, "It's a heck of a lot better to service your existing customers well than [having to] constantly find new ones."

NON-UNION BUT WELL-COMPENSATED WORKERS

Traditionally, airlines have never been known for their high wages—with the possible exception of senior pilots at the major airlines, who can bring in sizeable six-figure salaries. Beyond that, flight attendants rarely make more than $40,000 a year, and that's if they have years of experience. Ticket counter and reservations agents earn even less. Neeleman knew that to attract good talent, he'd have to do more than just create a welcoming environment in which for them to work.

"I tell our people all the time that 'This is a great place to work and we want you to feel valued and feel like people respect you,'" he says, "'but it's not just holding hands and singing *Kumbaya*. You'll actually make money working here at JetBlue.' So we pay people really well."

JetBlue's workforce is entirely nonunionized. One thing that most infuriates Neeleman is when people talk about how the airline won't be successful once workers decide to change that by forming a union. He takes issue with the assertion because he feels the allegation insinuates that JetBlue is being built on the backs of its people.

"It's not true," Neeleman insists. "We pay our people very well. They're very well compensated, and they've got lots of upside in the company. And they're doing very, very well as a workforce."

While Neeleman often speaks of his opposition to union representation at JetBlue, it's not the talk of an angry, paternalistic oligarch. It's the same voice that explains how his other seemingly altruistic stances are driven by pragmatic business principles.

"We know there's a reason for unions," Neeleman says. "I think they did a great thing for our country at a certain time. But unions are an offshoot of management that didn't take care of their people properly. And I would prefer to deal directly with the people that we are paying, and be ethical enough to anticipate their needs well enough. [I'd like to] take care of our people on traditional issues like pay and benefits. and contemporary issues like working conditions, so they never need to go to a third party that needs to tell us how to take care of our people. Our people are the most valuable asset we have."

Although Neeleman often boasts about how well compensated JetBlue employees are, the airline's salaries are far from the highest in the industry. But a profit sharing plan Neeleman put in place helps to bring the pay of JetBlue employees on parity with—if not higher than—that of its unionized competitors.

"We came up with an incentive program because we want to be fair and we want to share. Fifty percent of all our pretax profits from the company go back to our crewmembers," Neeleman says. "Not in money that they could spend immediately, but in a tax-deferred profit sharing account that they could take with them that would be 100 percent vested when they left. And because we wanted to avoid some of the pitfalls that some of the other airlines had with defined benefit programs and pension programs, which they all suffer from today, we would also come up with a very generous 401(k) program, where we would match

100 percent of what the contributions were from the very first day into the 401(k) program."

Neeleman tells of one flight attendant he met who had amassed more than $40,000 in her retirement plan after only three years of service. Considering that her annual salary is little more than two-thirds of that amount, it was quite an accomplishment that could only come through such an incentive program.

"I thought it was very important that every single person at Jet-Blue had the opportunity to own a piece of the rock, that they felt vested in the company, that they really felt like it's not my company or Dave's company, but it's *our* company," Neeleman adds.

By hiring the best, paying them well, and making sure they were committed to customers, JetBlue's dedication to excellent service helped to propel its steep ascent in the first months following the carrier's inaugural flight. Customers may have been drawn to the airline by its low fares, but they came back for the hospitality. As one passenger raved, "JetBlue offers some of the best customer service both in the air and on the ground. At the check-in counter, I have been greeted by a friendly and patient person every time." Says another, "The employees at JetBlue strike the right balance. They smile, they ask if they can help, they perform their jobs quickly, and they *always* maintain an appropriate level of professionalism."

Of course, there was another amenity that proved instantly captivating to JetBlue flyers: the individual 24-channel live TV service available at every seat. Never before had live television been provided to all passengers aboard a commercial aircraft. It was as if TV had waited half a century to find its ultimate killer app. Yet the revolutionary system that enabled this technology to take place was never part of JetBlue's original plan. In fact, the service came very close to missing the plane altogether.

CHAPTER 9

Making Air Travel Entertaining

Soon after mankind realized its long-held dream of achieving flight, it awakened to the reality of airborne boredom and ennui. The takeoff and landing were exciting, but the view of earth from above soon grew tiresome—particularly when flying over a cloud deck. Thus, the history of in-flight entertainment is almost as old as that of powered aviation. You can trace it all the way back to the founding of the Mile High Club almost nine decades ago by pioneering aviator and bon vivant Lawrence Sperry, whose inventions included the turn and bank indicator, the autopilot, and retractable landing gear. In November 1916, the Curtiss flying boat in which Sperry was giving lessons to a New York socialite crashed over Long Island. The duck hunters who came to their rescue found the pair naked. Sperry is considered to have given birth to the Mile High Club that day. (All too typically, the woman's vital contribution to this historic aviation first often goes uncredited. For the record, she was Mrs. Waldo Polk.)

By 1925 the search for airborne amusement led to the first inflight movie, a screening of *The Lost World* aboard a converted World War I Handley-Page bomber during a 30-minute flight near London. A scant seven years later, in-flight television de-buted aboard a Western Air Express F-10. But these screenings were little more than publicity stunts. Mass in-flight entertain-ment didn't come of age until the early 1960s, as commercial companies unveiled onboard projection systems and airlines be-gan installing movie screens and TV monitors aboard their air-craft. The first feature film shown on a regularly scheduled commercial flight, *By Love Possessed*, starring Lana Turner and Efrem Zimbalist Jr., was seen on a TWA Boeing 707 in 1961.

In-flight entertainment progressed almost in tandem with home entertainment in succeeding years. Yet by the turn of the new cen-tury, engineers were still struggling to bring one of the most basic and ubiquitous entertainment devices to the sky: live television. JetBlue became the first to provide this service on individual mon-itors to all passengers. But the hardware might never have been developed were it not for inquiries about providing in-flight TV for none less than the President of the United States.

In the early 1990s, Harris Military Technology—a division of the Harris Corporation, the world's largest supplier of electronic equipment to the military—was asked to explore the viability of installing live television aboard Air Force One. At the time it was completely unfeasible. No method of receiving a continuous signal aboard a platform traveling hundreds of miles an hour existed, nor was any ground station or satellite capable of transmitting such a signal. Engineers began examining what it would require to make this technology, taken for granted on the ground, a reality in the sky. Glenn Latta was among those working on the project. In the midst of his research, he began to think: If the leader of the free world wants to watch TV while flying on Air Force One, reg-ular airline passengers would no doubt like to do the same thing.

Could such technology be incorporated into commercial aircraft as well? Harris, intrigued by the possibility, gave Latta the go ahead to pursue this concept further.

But putting live TV aboard a commercial airliner was a far greater challenge than installing it aboard Air Force One. For one thing, "there's really no cost constraint" on the president's plane, Latta notes. "You could buy many aircraft for what it would cost to put TV on Air Force One" at the time. Fortunately, right as engineers began tackling this challenge, direct broadcast satellite television systems were evolving, with DirecTV and EchoStar leading the way. Latta and his team were able to use some of the technologies and breakthroughs discovered by these companies to create a design of their own. (As to whether they were able to get live TV aboard Air Force One before this, all Latta will say is "I can't talk about that.")

By 1998 Harris had a partially completed commercial aircraft live TV system developed and was looking for a launch customer. The company couldn't go much further until an airline was willing to try out the system. You see, in order to win approval for installation from the Federal Aviation Administration, the last phase of development requires demonstrating the system's operation aloft. (This would also show off the system's reliability to potential customers.) Once a piece of equipment and installation method are demonstrated to be safe, the FAA grants what's known as a Supplemental Type Certificate, or STC, allowing the device or equipment to be installed on any aircraft of the same type—all Boeing 737s or Airbus A320s, for example.

Unfortunately, while Harris could boast its superior technical expertise, the company had no experience dealing with the commercial aviation market. So Harris set out to find a joint venture partner to take its technology into the commercial aviation arena. In February 1998, B/E Aerospace, the world's largest supplier of cabin interior equipment to the commercial aviation market, bought a 51 percent stake in the company through its in-flight entertainment business unit. The newly formed joint venture company was christened as LiveTV. B/E Aerospace then began trying to sell the system. Latta, as the one person with the most knowledge about it, became the point man in the company's sales effort.

"In trying to attack the marketplace, we did not want to compete against the incumbent, entrenched in-flight entertainment providers," Latta recounts. "So we did an analysis on what areas of the market we wanted to attack. Ninety percent of all flights in the continental United States had no in-flight entertainment at all. That's because they were narrow-body [single-aisle] aircraft that typically don't have in-flight entertainment systems because most flights on these planes are shorter than the duration of a typical movie. . . . So even if the equipment was onboard, it flew dark, so to speak, because unless you had a five-hour flight they didn't show you the movie," or anything else, for that matter. And even those flights that had onboard entertainment offered something that was less than ideal. Passengers couldn't choose among various options. The airline selected a movie, and maybe a short feature or two, but these programs clearly weren't of interest to everyone on board. "We saw that as a great opportunity to bring what we thought—and still believe—was the perfect amenity for that type of flight: the at-home experience," Latta says. "Why create a unique entertainment experience, when you can take a familiar, enjoyed experience and just move it into a new environment, called a commercial aircraft?"

But none of the airlines that B/E Aerospace pitched with LiveTV shared Latta's enthusiasm.

"I had been told 'no' by at least nine major airlines," Latta recalls. B/E Aerospace finally made inroads with Dallas-based Legend Airlines, a new carrier that promised to offer first class service at coach fares. The airline was gearing up to fly 56-seat DC-9s and boasted such amenities as wide leather seats, more legroom, and gourmet meals. Before JetBlue, Legend was the best-capitalized start-up in aviation history, with $60 million in up-front investments.

While sitting in Legend's office negotiating that airline's contract, Latta spotted another—and, in many ways, more exciting— prospect for his product in the *Wall Street Journal*. "I read an article about New Air and David Neeleman and [him raising] $130 million," Latta recalls. "And I said, 'You know, that's somebody that I really need to talk to.'"

Latta was convinced it was a great fit. He figured a new airline trying to make a name for itself by providing great customer service would be able to set itself apart even further from rivals by offering such a discriminating feature as live television. B/E Aerospace helped Latta arrange a meeting with the JetBlue executives in charge of aircraft configuration. He was told that among the issues the executives wanted to be briefed on was in-flight entertainment.

Tom Anderson, JetBlue's executive vice president of technical operations, ran the meeting at the airline's unassuming Kew Gardens office in Queens, New York. Their discussion was one of several focused on seats and galley equipment (the latter obviously quite minimal, as the airline didn't plan to offer any food service beyond its signature blue potato chips and a few other snacks). When Latta stood up to make his presentation, Anderson suddenly realized who he was.

"Oh, you're the in-flight entertainment guy," Anderson said. "Before you get started, I've got to tell you, I have another meeting in ten minutes, but we've made a corporate decision not to put any in-flight entertainment on any of our aircraft."

Latta made the most of Anderson's limited time and interest. He told the executives at the gathering their decision confirmed two things: "One is that they were probably the smartest airline out there [by deciding] not to put a product onboard that didn't make any economic sense and didn't really create value for the customer. Second, they would make a decision to put our product onboard if it would pay for itself, and if it would provide value for what they wanted—short-haul entertainment."

Latta gave the executives a business proposal for a revenue sharing arrangement, with LiveTV covering the cost of installation hardware, and JetBlue paying a service fee and splitting any revenue derived from passenger rental of the equipment. Even though the JetBlue team didn't know much about in-flight entertainment, they realized no one had ever developed a system for installing screens in every seat in a narrow-body aircraft. It was also the first time a satellite would be used to broadcast a live television signal to a commercial aircraft.

"You know," Anderson said when Latta finished his brief pitch, "that's the only proposal of in-flight entertainment I've ever heard that's halfway interesting. I'll run it by my guys, and we'll call you back if we're interested."

Latta did hear back from Anderson. JetBlue was interested and wanted to know more. Several weeks later a second meeting was held at JetBlue's offices on Park Avenue in Manhattan. This time David Neeleman was in attendance, as was Dave Barger, Amy Curtis-McIntyre, and other key members of the JetBlue team. Latta and his associates brought along airline seats, mounted a demonstration of the system, and went over the details of their proposal.

The JetBlue executives were impressed, but they were concerned because the technology was unproven. They knew a malfunctioning system could seriously damage their brand.

"It's like when you use your telephone at home. You can't imagine it ever not working. You'd flip out, right?" observes Michael Lazarus who was JetBlue's chairman at the time. "And if you're on the plane and you say to yourself, 'I'm stuck for four and a half hours,' and your TV doesn't work, yet everyone else's does, there's nothing that's going to fix that experience."

TELEVISION IN THE SKIES

Many companies had imploded in the process of bringing in-flight entertainment systems to market. For instance, Boeing originally hired an outside firm to design a specialized seat-back entertainment system for its 777 aircraft. When the product failed to work as advertised, the company behind the system went out of business, and Boeing had to go back to the drawing board. Though Latta was confident about the technology he'd developed, given past history, he couldn't be certain it would operate exactly as planned.

"What we didn't know was whether we could meet the cost constraints of a low-cost airline, and reliability was absolutely our number one priority," Latta says. "There are probably ten [similar failed companies in the industry] where people tried to do something that was state of the art, and it ended up being too costly, unreliable, a bad experience, and so on. We thought we had done a good job, but we [couldn't be certain about how reliable this low-cost platform would be] until we actually got it up and flying on an aircraft."

Nevertheless, Neeleman was very enthusiastic about the concept. He immediately felt that if it worked, it would have a huge positive impact on the overall customer experience. Not everyone on his staff agreed. John Owen, the airline's money man, was adamantly opposed to the installation of LiveTV. Intent on following the Southwest Airlines model, where expenditures on frills of any sort are shunned, he gave the proposal a thumbs-down.

Ultimately, Owen was overruled. JetBlue wanted to be the first airline to offer this new, cutting-edge technology, despite the well-founded objections coming from Owen.

JetBlue board member David Checketts, a fellow Utahan who was at the time president of Madison Square Garden, helped negotiate a contract with DirecTV for the content that would be shown on LiveTV's technology. The initial 24 channels would include Bloomberg Television, CNN Headline News, CNNfn, the Weather Channel, ESPN, A&E, the History Channel, Discovery Channel, and Animal Planet, among others.

The contract between JetBlue and LiveTV called for a $5 fee for customers to use the TV, regardless of flight length, but the agreement contained a provision for converting the service to a free amenity, in which case JetBlue would pay LiveTV a higher service fee, to make up for the revenue-sharing shortfall. JetBlue's initial three aircraft were all targeted to be outfitted, but one would have to undergo the installation and testing first, in order for it to receive an STC allowing for installation on the rest of the fleet. LiveTV agreed it wouldn't institute the revenue sharing arrangement until all three aircraft were equipped, and JetBlue wouldn't charge customers a usage fee during this trial period.

Contrary to popular belief, JetBlue didn't start out from the gate with LiveTV service. It came about two months after the launch, debuting on its first plane in April 2000. John Owen's conspicuous absence from the promotional pictures taken at the system's launch event was interpreted by some as a sign of the depth of his antipathy for the project. But as LiveTV was brought into the fleet, the impact it had on the customer experience quickly became apparent. The overall reactions of customers with and without TV on the same routes could be observed firsthand. It was as if the airline was a media laboratory conducting experiments with a statistically valid population and control groups. Station managers soon nicknamed the TV-equipped A320 "the happy aircraft." By watching customers disembark, they could tell right away whether the plane had television service by the expressions on their faces.

Some JetBlue executives also observed with their own eyes the power of having LiveTV onboard. President Dave Barger, for instance, was on a full flight, including 40 to 50 children, that got delayed on the runway for an hour and a half due to poor weather conditions.

"Nobody said a word," Barger marveled. "No complaints; everybody's in their seats [watching television]; everybody's happy."

During the first 500 flights aboard the equipped aircraft, the LiveTV system boasted a 99.9 percent reliability rate. To ensure high quality, LiveTV has a built-in test system embedded in the product that continuously monitors every element of the system during flights. The data is wirelessly linked to the LiveTV network operating center in Melbourne, Florida, where it's all analyzed by a software program developed by the company. The onboard system also supports a number of communication technologies, many so far untapped, that will enable new features and capabilities to be offered in the future.

Installation on the last of the three A320s in the fledging JetBlue fleet was scheduled for completion on July 1, 2000, at which time the contract called for the system to be offered on a fee basis. But as that date approached, qualms were building about charging customers for the service. JetBlue was especially reluctant to implement the charges over the July 4 weekend. The imposition of fees and celebrations of freedom hardly went hand in hand. Neeleman and the JetBlue executive team sought some way to delay the enactment of customer charges while they pondered the situation. LiveTV agreed to proceed without customer fees on a month-by-month basis, and negotiated for JetBlue to pay a larger service fee than it would have under the revenue sharing arrangement.

"The problem with aviation is you never know what's fair or what's real," says Lazarus, summing up the thinking at JetBlue regarding customer perceptions about having to pay to watch television. "You can call every day to United and get a different price (for a ticket). The reality is you get nickel-and-dimed. And more importantly, the customer thinks 'You're screwing me.' So it's better to just ask one price. You want to keep the service offerings very simple. The whole key is keeping trust in the system. It's just common sense, and my gosh, has it paid off."

Later that July, Dave Barger met with the LiveTV team and informed them JetBlue had decided it wanted to provide the service for free on a permanent basis. "It's too important a part of the customer experience," Barger told them. "We just think it has more value, providing it as part of the integrated JetBlue experience, than getting the product paid for through customer revenue." The biggest supporter of the concept of giving it away for free: John Owen, who had opposed its installation in the first place because of cost considerations.

"David was right," Lazarus says about taking the gamble to install the untried system. "Americans love screens, they love TV, they want data, and they want it live."

In retrospect, one factor that made the project work was the ability of the two sides—JetBlue and LiveTV—to adapt together to changing conditions and realities, which is an important lesson for the success of any business relationship.

"They [JetBlue executives] were always a great business partner," Latta says. "Anytime we needed help with something, or they needed help with something, it wasn't a situation where we'd both go to the contract and we'd read the provisions and figure out what the contract says. I don't know that either one of us ever did that, because we always wanted to do the right thing. And it was really a very, very positive relationship. There were issues and problems we had to solve on both sides, but it was a very positive relationship."

JETBLUE MAKES ITS FIRST ACQUISITION

The relationship between the two companies was about to get even closer. B/E Aerospace's ownership share of LiveTV was held in its in-flight entertainment business unit, which catered primarily to wide-body aircraft. B/E Aerospace decided to get out of that business, and reached an agreement to sell its interest in LiveTV to Sextant Avionique, S.A., a transaction conducted in two phases several months apart. When the deal was concluded, Sextant owned 51 percent of LiveTV. But Sextant's strategy of where it wanted to take LiveTV differed from that of Harris Corporation, still minority owner of the technology, creating an inherent conflict in what was supposed to be a joint venture. The two companies finally concluded that either one of them would have to sell LiveTV to the other, or the entire venture would have to be sold to a third party.

One of the provisions in the JetBlue contract called for the airline to be notified in the event LiveTV was ever put up for sale. Once JetBlue heard about the opportunity, it conducted due diligence and concluded that even if the system was never sold to another airline, it made sense to buy it purely in terms of the costs and fees associated with installing LiveTV throughout the carrier's expanding fleet. Moreover, it was clear other airlines would indeed want the service.

JetBlue struck a deal to buy LiveTV for $82 million in September 2002. The price included the hardware aboard all JetBlue aircraft (which was considered to be LiveTV's property) and the assumption of $40 million in debt.

"When I first walked into that meeting and they said, 'We made the decision not to put any in-flight entertainment on the aircraft,' I never expected that one day JetBlue would own the company," Latta, now a company vice president, admits. "They [JetBlue] continue to invest in the product and the technology and they understand the value of what we do, and they're interested in advancing the technology, so it's just been wonderful."

Virtually the same week the deal closed, LiveTV signed a contract with Frontier Airlines to install the system on several of that airline's own Airbus aircraft. Frontier wound up installing LiveTV under the same revenue sharing arrangement JetBlue originally agreed to, whereby passengers were charged for the service. As a result, the deal has produced profits for Frontier, just as LiveTV projected it would in its proposal. More recently WestJet, the Canadian low-cost carrier co-founded by Neeleman, signed a contract to wire its fleet with LiveTV in January 2004.

As for concerns that JetBlue would give up its competitive advantage by letting other airlines have the same service, Neeleman believes JetBlue's leadership in this arena is established, and is convinced that profiting from wiring other fleets with the technology makes sense from a shareholder value perspective.

Says Latta, "We've had a great lead in the industry for many years in being the first to do this, and JetBlue was able to leverage that as part of its launch as well. Eventually other people will be able to do what we do, so why not leverage our competitive advantage and provide a return to shareholders for the investment that JetBlue made in buying the company?"

CHAPTER 10

Keeping Customers Happy

Within six months of initiating service with just three planes, JetBlue was already profitable, as its financial projections had forecast. The airline boasted a fleetwide load factor of 71.6 percent, meaning on all the miles flown by the carrier, an average of more than 70 percent of the available seats were sold.

"I love to prove people wrong," Neeleman said of the skeptics who had claimed JetBlue wouldn't be successful so fast. "It gets you motivated. It gets you up in the morning."

By August 2000, the airline was operating 48 flights a day and had logged 4,328 departures and arrivals with only ten cancellations. On-time performance (judged by whether a flight arrives at the gate within 15 minutes of its scheduled time) was 80.25 percent, compared with 73.6 percent for the nation's ten largest carriers. This was especially impressive in light of the severe weather conditions that affected the East Coast that summer. As for consumer metrics, the Department of Transportation had received a total of three complaints about the airline from passengers during its first six months of operation, translating to 0.6 complaints per 100,000 passengers. The ten biggest airlines averaged five times that number of passenger unrest. In the misplaced luggage department, another bane of the air traveler, JetBlue recorded 2.7 mishandled bags per 1,000 enplanements, compared to 5.04 mishandled bags averaged by the 10 biggest carriers. Everything was working as Neeleman and his team had planned.

During the Labor Day weekend, JetBlue flew its 500,000th customer. By October 2000, its on-time performance ranked as number one in every market it served. It was so good, JetBlue took to calling its home base at JFK "New York's most on-time airport." By the end of the year, more than 1 million customers had flown on JetBlue. Neeleman's recipe for the achievement: "The right mix of a strong business plan, an experienced management team, dedicated employees, a great product, and service, service, service."

The high level of service, as we have seen, was the result of hiring the right people and treating them well. As Neeleman says, "Taking care of your own people makes sure that they will take care of customers." The connection is made more explicitly on the company's web site: "Experience indicates that our Customers return not only because we offer low fares, but also because we provide them with a more enjoyable air travel experience. Hiring the best people and treating them as we expect our Customers to be treated are essential to achieving this goal."

Neeleman was determined to create a customer-friendly environment that immediately set JetBlue apart from competitors, something he believed was essential to the success of every business. "It's critically important that when that first customer comes to the door he has a 'Wow!' experience," Neeleman says. "One of your goals should be having a customer say, 'Wow, I love doing business with that company.'" But to serve customers well, you also must listen to what they have to say.

Neeleman demonstrates his focus on customers and the importance of their opinions in a very direct way. At least once a week he boards a JetBlue flight to find out firsthand what people think of the JetBlue experience. Neeleman starts off by walking to the front of the airplane, grabbing the microphone, and making an announcement over the public address system.

"I'm David Neeleman and I'm the CEO of JetBlue Airways," he begins. He then thanks customers for flying on the airline and reminds them of the company's goal: "We're trying a little harder to be the best airline in America," he says. "And I hope you notice the difference."

Neeleman actually starts his work on the flight even before the first passenger is buckled into a seat. Occasionally he helps luggage handlers load bags into the cargo hold. Other times he assists customers in stuffing their carry-on bags into overhead bins. This practice is something JetBlue flight attendants are taught early on, because the airline believes it's the little things that often matter most. Flight attendants are trained to approach passengers with carry-on luggage as they board, to help them to quickly get it secured in the increasingly crowded overhead bins.

"I have never seen a normal, unionized flight attendant do that," observes an admiring Kristin Zern, who is executive director of the Association of Travel Marketing Executives. "They won't even help somebody with a bag. They simply won't do it. They're so union-oriented, and they think it's a little beneath them. And they also don't want to hurt themselves." But Zern admits there's an underlying reason JetBlue's flight attendants, who tend to be younger than those found on the legacy carriers, are so helpful in this area: "In order to get the plane out of the gate fast, finding room for somebody's bag as they're getting on is paramount."

Neeleman himself acknowledges that while customers gush about how helpful the flight attendants are, their assistance is, in fact, driven by a desire to get the plane boarded and moving as quickly as possible. Attendants know the bins and how best to load them, so pitching in helps everyone out, including the company.

Neeleman's practice of personally conducting airborne customer satisfaction surveys goes back to his days at Morris Air, when Carla Meine used to urge him to talk to customers as a way of getting a true feel for the state of the business.

"David," she would tell him, "when you fly your own airline, everybody knows who you are, so you're never going to get a true experience. That's the great thing about getting feedback from the people who travel with you. Listen to your customers, because they tell you what's going on, what you will never see. When you travel your own airline, you don't get treated the same way everybody else does [by your employees]."

Neeleman eagerly put her advice into practice. "David got really good at listening to customers' experiences on our airline and saying, 'We've got to make this better. We can't have these things happen where people have no clue about why they're being delayed and why they're not being told anything, and why they're told it's going to be ten minutes and two hours later they're still there,'" Meine says.

Once airborne and at a safe cruising altitude, Neeleman announces that he'll be passing through the cabin and that he wants to talk to each person onboard. He proceeds to the rear of the aircraft and dons the apron flight attendants gave him in recognition of his service. "Snack Boy," it reads, alluding to his primary job for the flight. Neeleman is charged with making his way up the aisle, handing out such goodies as blue bagel chips, cookies, blue Terra chips (the official snack of JetBlue), and biscotti. The fact that Neeleman and the flight attendants hand-carry refreshments is, in itself, another nod to keeping customers satisfied. The idea came to Neeleman as he sat on a flight one day before Jet-Blue took to the skies. He began to observe what an inconvenience food carts posed to customers. The carts bumped against passengers as flight attendants maneuvered them down the aisle, and trapped them in their seats until the service was complete. Early on, Neeleman made the decision at JetBlue not to have carts. That choice was made easier given the airline's lack of a meal service, but plenty of airlines still use bulky carts to ferry snacks and beverages every bit as simple as JetBlue's up and down the aisles.

As Neeleman hands out refreshments, he converses with customers one on one. "I go through and speak to every passenger, find out what their concerns and comments are, and collect a lot of business cards," he says. In characteristic style, rather than jotting these suggestions in an organized fashion, he often scribbles them on napkins or on the backs of those cards. But rest assured, every comment gets attention—if not from Neeleman, then from one of his associates. It usually takes Neeleman about two and a half hours to make his way through the A320. By the time he's through, it's often time to return to his seat and fasten his belt snugly across his lap for landing. On longer trips, once he's talked with every customer, he makes his way into the cockpit for a chat with the flight deck crew. "I'll land up front with the pilots because they tend to lead kind of an isolated existence," he says.

Listening to customers is vital for the organization to continue to succeed, Neeleman contends. But that's only part of what these missions accomplish in terms of assuring continued superior customer service. "More importantly, I need our crewmembers that are on that flight to know that their CEO cares about the customers," Neeleman says. "Even though I'll never fly with every single flight attendant, every one of them knows that I go on flights and I spend time with the customers. And I spend time with [flight crews] and I do their job. I crawl around under the seats and pick up the trash that's been left there, because I want them to know that their jobs are vital and important to the success of JetBlue. I've heard it said that a fish stinks from the head, but I guess it also smells good from the head. I'm just trying to be as good an example as I possibly can."

Neeleman admits these forays also serve another important function: They get him out of the office and provide a socially acceptable outlet for his hyperactivity.

Neeleman's ideas about customer service, like all of his business philosophies, are culled from a wide range of sources. Even his experiences trying to get his shirts cleaned became a lesson in keeping customers satisfied. Back in Salt Lake City, his dry cleaner opened early and stayed open late. They kept his credit card number on file, which made doing business with them rather simple. But when Neeleman moved to Connecticut, he suddenly found himself in dry cleaning hell. The local cleaner was supposed to open at seven, but never did. As a result, the early riser Neeleman could never drop off dirty shirts when he wanted to. Worse still, the store closed at six, before Neelman returned home. Consequently, if he managed to get any clothes to the laundry at all, he could never get them out. "I kept buying more and more shirts," he says. But Neeleman claims his life was altered by the appearance of a new laundry service in town.

"I got a card from somebody in the mail that said, 'I want to be your dry cleaner. I'll drop a bag by your house. You put it in the garage. I'll come in once a week, give you your dry cleaning, and keep your credit card on file.' That was a dry cleaner who would really make a difference in my life!" Neeleman gushes. "I was really excited about it." He was so excited he mentioned it to a reporter from *Fortune* magazine doing a story on JetBlue. The magazine ran a sidebar about the dry cleaning service, and the re-sulting publicity helped make the new business a rousing success. As Neeleman points out, it all started with customer service.

"It wasn't the cheapest dry cleaner on the planet," Neeleman says, "but it was something that fit with me and fit with the area and the needs of the people, and now he's very successful because he created a new way of doing business."

PAYING ATTENTION TO THE SMALL STUFF

Likened to a sponge, Neeleman absorbs an astonishing amount of raw data. In his speaking engagements he's fond of bringing up the concept of "insuring" a customer to one's brand—an idea he says came from an article called "The Constant Customer" that was based on research done by the Gallup organization.

"If people want a cup of coffee, they'll go an extra block to go to Starbucks," Neeleman says about what happens once a customer is insured to a brand. "They'll walk past three or four coffee houses to go to Starbucks because they just like the way they feel about it."

As paraphrased by Neeleman, the research identified three ele-ments that insured customers to a brand: First, flawless execu-tion. Second, make things right with customers when things go wrong, because no matter how flawless you try to be, sometimes things will go wrong. And third, a company needs employees that are ambassadors for their brand, who are proud to belong to the organization. "We try to follow these at JetBlue," Neeleman says.

Flawless execution is, of course, a constant goal of the airline. That's particularly hard in an industry like aviation where weather and other external factors can affect operations. Still the company strives for perfection—tracking, for example, the time it takes to get luggage off all its flights and to the baggage claim area. And when any performance parameters are exceeded, the president of the airline knows about it.

JetBlue also goes much further than most in making things right with customers when things don't go as planned. First, flight crews are forthright in communicating with customers when delays or other problems occur. No one is left in the dark, wondering what's going on and what is being done to correct a problem. And JetBlue is very quick to compensate customers with free tickets or coupons for substantial discounts on future flights if they are inconvenienced by delays or other deficiencies of service—even if it's not the airline's fault.

During JetBlue's first year of operation, a delay caused one customer to miss his son's wedding. In response, Neeleman instituted weekly three-hour training programs for managers on how to handle delays. He also directed customer service personnel to call every person aboard the delayed flight to ask each of them what they felt JetBlue could have done to "improve the situation." The customer who missed the wedding was given three free round-trip tickets.

After a Christmas snowstorm played havoc with JetBlue departures from Kennedy, the airline gave back $2.5 million in credits toward future flights to its customers. That meant an immediate hit to the young airline's bottom line, but Neeleman felt it was worth it. "You know, I've met some of the people we gave the credit back to, and they like JetBlue more than had they not had that experience in the first place," Neeleman says.

In its monthly expenses, JetBlue budgets a sum to compensate passengers for inconvenience, and Neeleman is adamant that all of it be spent. As for having employee-ambassadors, "They're not afraid to wear a shirt that says 'JetBlue,'" Neeleman says of crewmembers. "People say, 'Oh, you work for JetBlue. That's exciting. What's it like to work for such a great company?' I'm not sure everyone who works in this country would be happy to let people know where they work, or be proud of it."

"I want to have a company where people are insured to our brand," Neeleman says, "where JetBlue becomes a verb. They want to JetBlue down to Florida. It's just something that you do. You want to JetBlue down to California. People don't even think about flying anyone else, they want to fly on JetBlue."

It all makes perfect sense, except for one detail: The article Neeleman alludes to contains almost none of the points he so meticulously limns. Nothing about three rules, about "insuring" a brand, about brand ambassadors. Somehow he's combined elements from the article with ingredients he found elsewhere to create a new, original recipe for customer satisfaction, without even realizing it.

The low prices that go along with its friendly service are another product attribute JetBlue customers clearly enjoy. But pricing of goods and services is one of the most difficult decisions for any business. In JetBlue's case, the company starts by trying to cap its most expensive fares at a level it considers to be "very reasonable," so customers don't feel like they're ever being taken advantage of. In 2004, JetBlue was holding the line on its most expensive walk-up fare—that is, a ticket bought on the day of departure without advance booking—at $299 one way. These walk-up fares are real moneymakers for traditional airlines. They are usually purchased by business travelers on expense accounts who have no choice but to hold their nose and pay these high prices. Not on JetBlue.

"We don't discriminate against business travelers," Neeleman maintains. "We don't charge $2,000 fares, because we don't need that business to be successful. Besides, I don't think that many businesses are going to come back and be willing to pay those fares. During the go-go times of the 1990s, people would pay anything. But I think we're past that cycle and that the high-priced business traveler may not come back for a long, long time. So for a low-cost operator like us, it's a good position to be in."

The other way of soaking business fliers—requiring a Saturday night stay to get a low fare—has also been dispensed with at Jet-Blue. The company typically sets its lowest, nonsale fare somewhere near $119. Everything in between the lowest and highest is based on supply and demand.

"If the flight is selling well, if it's almost sold out, we get $299," Neeleman says. "If it's a dog and we don't have that many people on board, you can buy it for $119."

Promotions and sales often bring the fare well below $100, and many short-haul routes are priced for under this figure. The airline's average ticket price at the beginning of 2004, by JetBlue's calculations, was $140 to $150.

OPERATING FOR SATISFACTION AND PROFITABILITY

Another practice that sets JetBlue apart and adds to customer satisfaction is its policy of not overbooking. Other airlines routinely overbook flights, because they don't want to lose revenue associated with no-show passengers. Some air travelers might look at overbooking as something between a crap shoot and the lottery, because airlines dangle increasingly attractive offers of free tickets and other inducements to pry enough willing bumpees off a flight. But it also leads to passenger anxiety if a traveler can't afford to be bumped, or isn't able to get to the airport early enough to secure an assigned seat before the airline starts playing musical chairs with its remaining open spaces.

Nevertheless, JetBlue isn't afraid to institute policies that appear on the surface to reduce convenience, as long as the rules allow for the greater good of all customers. For example, JetBlue tickets are nonrefundable. This minimizes accounting time and further helps to control costs, thus keeping fares low. However, an unused ticket is good (and transferable to anyone else) toward any other JetBlue flight for one year, minus a $25 fee for changing the booking. Neeleman says this $25 fee alone more than covers the cost of the time a telephone reservation agent spends on a rebooking, yet it is about 75 percent less than what most other airlines charge for such changes or cancellations.

Passenger comfort is another major concern at JetBlue, epitomized by the constant allusion to its "all leather seats." Leather is obviously more comfortable than scratchy cloth, but it isn't the fabric usually associated with low-fare airlines. On the major carriers, leather is reserved for the first class cabin. But, once more, Neeleman's counterintuitive decision to use leather has an economic benefit as well. It's true that leather costs twice as much as cloth, but it also lasts twice as long. Moreover, leather is easier to clean. At the same time, the comfort is more likely to induce a customer to return to the airline. Therefore, the overall effect is to improve the bottom line even while it enhances the overall customer experience.

On JetBlue's first anniversary, February 11, 2001, Neeleman announced that in the final quarter of 2000, the airline had achieved its first quarterly profit, proclaiming "the sky is the limit" for the company's prospects. Meanwhile, Congress's interest in the airline industry, spurred by customer complaints and news accounts of deteriorating service, heated up. Senators John McCain and Ernest Hollins introduced the Aviation Competition Restoration Act, S-414. A key provision of the proposed legislation called for the Secretary of Transportation to investigate the use of gates and facilities at the 35 largest airports in the United States, to determine whether they were being fully utilized or, as some contended, were monopolized by major airlines to keep competitors out. In mid-March 2001, Neeleman traveled to Washington to testify before the Senate Commerce, Science, and Transportation Committee in support of the bill.

Noting that the airline industry was developing a reputation for being "uncaring, uncomfortable, and expensive," Neeleman told senators, "The answer to many of the problems plaguing the industry is not a re-regulation of the industry, or laws governing how big an employee's smile ought to be, but rather the capitalist cure known as competition."

A week later, JetBlue's way of doing business was validated in the form of the annual Zagat Airline Survey, which covers more than 70 airlines. The 30,000-plus fliers surveyed rated JetBlue the number two domestic economy carrier, earning scores above those for many of the major airlines. (Midwest Express, now known as Midwest Airlines, was voted number one, largely because it had no middle seats and served high-quality in-flight meals at the time.) The ratings were based on "comfort, service, and food," with the last category earning JetBlue a rating of "fair to good," even though it only offered snacks aboard its aircraft.

Said Neeleman of JetBlue's rapid acceleration to the forefront of the industry, "Somewhere, somebody forgot that passengers are customers. They're not people to tell to sit down and shut up, and buckle your seat belt. There's a different way to do it so people feel like they're appreciated, like, 'I am a customer.'"

Neeleman's focus on customer service was proving its value. But little of this human touch would be possible without JetBlue's mastery of a cold and heartless competitive advantage: technology.

CHAPTER 11

The Technology Advantage

Memorial Day weekend traditionally kicks off the start of the summer season. It's one of the year's busiest travel periods. Clogged highways, standing-room-only beaches, and long lines at airports have become as much a part of the holiday's imagery as ceremonies for the fallen soldiers the occasion was created to honor. As Memorial Day 2001 approached, JetBlue crewmembers at Kennedy Airport's Terminal 6 were armed for the onslaught, ready to battle the expected crowds with a new weapon: a hand-held, wireless, curbside check-in system. Should lines begin growing too long, roving JetBlue staffers equipped with the devices could check in customers and luggage and print boarding passes almost anywhere inside the terminal or its vicinity. Based on a wireless radio frequency network, the line-busting device also provided a real-time connection to the airline's Open Skies reservation system, enabling staffers to quickly check flight and passenger information in the master database. The device, the first of its kind in the United States, was the latest result of president Dave Barger's edict to JetBlue's information technology crew: "Let's keep pushing the envelope."

From the start, no airline has put modern-day technology to work more effectively than JetBlue. If the question among customers and observers was how JetBlue would be able to offer new airplanes, leather seats, individual live TV *and* cheap fares, technology was—and is—the answer. Automation helps to slash operating costs, while increasing efficiency.

"Some people say airlines are powered by fuel," says Barger, "but this airline is powered by its IT infrastructure. We're always looking at our technology and saying, 'Is there a way we can improve this?'"

Not a surprising stance in a company founded by a man who was the co-inventor of e-ticketing.

The airline industry was one of the first to embrace technology and explore its potential. Electronic reservations systems gained acceptance in the late 1950s. American Airlines led the pack, developing a system that would give each of its offices real-time flight information, while integrating and automating its booking and ticketing processes. The result was the Semi-Automated Business Research Environment, a system more commonly known by its acronym, Sabre. Launched in 1964, Sabre's main innovation was its ability to track seat inventory on all flights in real-time. This information was instantly available to reservations agents around the world. The ability to electronically monitor inventory led airlines to set various pricing levels, based on how fast or slow seats were selling.

In the 1970s, computerized reservations systems (CRS) were linked to monitors on the desks of travel agents, allowing them to view the inventory of seats on almost all airlines instantly, and make reservations without calling the carrier. This innovation saved the airlines millions of dollars, as computers cut down the work required by the in-house reservations staff. United's Apollo CRS system was the first to be installed in travel agencies in 1976, closely followed by American's Sabre. This put people in the travel industry at the forefront of professionals who understood the power of technology—long before computers became a staple of the business world.

The CRSs were not only convenient, they were extremely profitable. Airlines that owned the systems charged other carriers a fee for each booking, while travel agents generally paid to lease the terminals. By the late 1980s, almost every major airline had developed a central reservation system of its own, including Delta, Eastern, and TWA. Before long, these systems expanded beyond airline bookings to include automated hotel, car rental, and even cruise reservation capabilities. Travel agencies without a computer terminal were suddenly in the Dark Ages, making the devices a necessary part of doing business.

While the industry began to consolidate in the 1990s, especially as some of the sponsoring airlines went out of business, the demand for computerized travel arrangements only increased. With the advent of the Internet, a growing number of airline reservations are now made electronically. This is becoming increasingly true for hotel and car reservations as well. Neeleman and his old boss June Morris were among the first to realize that technology was essential to maximizing the efficiencies of the travel industry. It's a realization Neeleman has carried forward in numerous ways at JetBlue.

POWERED BY TECHNOLOGY

As the projected launch date for the hip new carrier neared in late 1999, JetBlue's leadership team worked as aggressively at bringing the company's technology online as it did at getting its brick-and-mortar infrastructure in place. Among the innovations planned: a paperless cockpit—the first in the airline world to boast this—with all charts generated electronically on the instrument panel's screens, and aircraft flight manuals loaded onto laptop computers carried at all times by pilots. A hard copy of these manuals for a commercial airliner—the operator's bible that explains all of an aircraft's systems along with standard and emergency procedures—is about the size of a set of the *Encyclopaedia Britannica*. The charts and books of landing and takeoff procedures, which go out of date every 90 days, can easily fill a large briefcase. The airline and the FAA worked together as partners in completing the certification process that would eliminate the need for any hard copy of this material—even for backup—to be carried aboard. For JetBlue, certifying the paperless cockpit meant significant savings in operational costs. For the FAA, it was a chance to learn more about the technology envelope, which its managers would increasingly deal with as more airlines sought to take advantage of similar new technologies.

"It's a great testament to Dave and David's commitment to getting everyone in as a partner," said Ann Rhoades of the close cooperation. "You've seen start-up companies complain about the federal government. We didn't complain at all. We knew they were a partner, and we used them that way, and they used us that way. They learned from us and we learned from them."

JetBlue would also be the first 100 percent e-ticket airline. While other airlines used electronic tickets, none at the time relied on them exclusively. Indeed, the majority of travelers still preferred to have a paper ticket in hand, as physical proof of their reservation on a flight. Neeleman wanted nothing less than to change the public's attitude and behavior.

In early January 2000, a month before its inaugural scheduled flight, JetBlue hired Jeff Cohen, the chief technology architect at US Web/March First, as an information technology consultant. Stocky, with something of an impish air conveyed in his ready smile, Cohen was tasked with helping to handle FAA certification issues involving technology, and with assuring that JetBlue's IT network was stable enough to handle the expected volume of online reservations. He also worked to set up the voice over Internet protocol (VoIP) lines that served as the telephone reservations system's backbone, connecting the airline's 600 reservation agents working in their homes to the outside world.

The first week of the web site's operation, JetBlue sold 20 percent of its tickets online, more than twice the figure of most airlines at the time. And customers calling to make reservations had no idea the agent they spoke with was sitting in her house and even possibly wearing those "furry slippers."

Cohen's passion for the mission matched his bosses', and three months after arriving as an outside consultant, Neeleman and Barger hired him as JetBlue's first full-time chief information officer.

"One of the things I promised my bosses when I came on board was that we would always be the most technologically advanced airline in the sky," Cohen says. "But one of the caveats was that we would never buy technology just for the sake of technology, but rather to improve our efficiency and customer service."

Cohen's job was to figure out how to use technology to keep JetBlue a low-cost airline "without bringing in huge ideas that will cost a huge amount of money and aren't aligned with our business model." And the *low cost* mantra was definitely reflected in the IT department's budget and ethos. Like a movie director who wants every dollar to show up on the screen, Neeleman kept the IT department, as others, lean. After all, Neeleman had experience in this area. He and David Evans had developed the Morris Air Reservation System pretty much on their own, as they had

Open Skies. The two of them had flown circles around the big IT departments of the major airlines in developing their software. Why copy the dinosaurs now?

With a staff of some three dozen people at the airline's launch, a quarter of them programmers, the IT department was encouraged to try out new ideas and develop its own skunk-work projects. JetBlue uses off-the-shelf Microsoft Windows–based software that it customizes to its own specific needs. The IT department also maintains beta-testing arrangements with Microsoft. Developing its own software this way helps keep licensing fees low, as well. (JetBlue's IT budget is typically about 3 percent of gross revenues.) But both the company and the department never forget that technology works only if it can improve the bottom line.

Ultimately, projects must answer the question Barger posed of all new IT developments: "Does it drive efficiency?" The answer isn't always yes. The handheld check-in devices unveiled days before the Memorial Day weekend are an example. JetBlue determined that agents manning the 40 check-in positions at the terminal did the job more quickly, so the devices actually caused degradation in performance. By the end of the following year, the wireless check-in system was scrapped. Says Cohen, "It if doesn't make you efficient, it's not cool."

But most of the technology innovations developed by the JetBlue team clearly enhanced efficiency and trimmed costs. The paperless, computerized cockpit was one of them. All pilots are issued Hewlett-Packard laptop computers early in their training. Cockpit crews use their laptops to perform the weight and balance calculations necessary to assure a plane is within its operating limitations, determine fuel needs, and all other essential flight planning functions. At other airlines, this work is done by the dispatch office, which can create long delays, especially when data must be reworked in the event of a wind change, for example, that causes the airport to change the runway in use.

"Now whenever the airport changes runway configuration before takeoff, JetBlue is always first from the gate," Cohen says. "That's because everyone else has to send their figures back to their dispatchers to recalculate. Our pilots can turn on their HP computers, do the calculations, and they are ready to go straightaway."

By having pilots handle the paperwork—or, more properly, *screenwork*—on their computers, the planning takes less time, and JetBlue avoids the need and cost of a large dispatch department. In 2002, the airline estimated that having cockpit crews take over flight planning saved it 4,800 hours of operational time across the fleet, enough to make more than 1,500 flights between New York and Florida, or add about 16 extra flights to each day's schedule.

"This helps maintain passenger satisfaction and keeps our costs down in a highly competitive environment," Cohen adds. "In the future we hope that we'll even be able to use wireless technology to enable pilots to receive flight releases without leaving the cockpit."

Says John Kasarda, an industry expert at the University of North Carolina's Kenan-Flagler Business School, "They [JetBlue] took what was cutting-edge in terms of digital business and translated it to aviation. It was surprising somebody hadn't done it sooner."

There's a bit of kismet in all this. JetBlue came along at a time when technology had reached the point that made this soft revolution possible. What's more, Neeleman understood the technology and was gifted in adapting it to the wants of the traveling public, as well as to the needs of the airline. JetBlue's clean-sheet concept gave it a huge advantage over the previous century's carriers, which were saddled with legacy systems and expensive labor contracts.

USING HIGH-TECH PLANES

The company's focus on technology extends to its aircraft. It's not surprising that Neeleman preferred the Airbus A320 over the rival 737 from Boeing. Like JetBlue itself, the A320 is more technologically advanced than its competitors, offering similar advantages: more efficiency, lower operating costs, and better service.

The digital fly-by-wire system that controls the aircraft—in contrast to the physically linked systems in the B737, for example, where the pilot's actions on the yoke and pedals are transmitted mechanically to the control surfaces (ailerons, rudder, and elevator)—is less prone to malfunction. This also eliminates the maintenance associated with checking the rigging of mechanically linked control systems. As a matter of fact, the A320 doesn't even have a yoke on the control column that the pilot grasps, as in a traditional airliner, but rather a side stick that resembles the controls of a video game more than those of a $50 million flying machine. There are no previous-century dials or gauges on the panel, either. Data is displayed on six cathode ray tube (CRT) screens—two side-by-side in front of the pilot and co-pilot, and an over-under pair in the middle of the panel—with electromechanical instruments discreetly arrayed above them, providing backup.

The A320 also has an electronic nervous system that does its own troubleshooting. In the event the airplane has a problem, it automatically informs crews of the situation, reducing the maintenance time associated with troubleshooting, and eliminating the need to track down intermittent squawks, or "gremlins," creeping into systems—the bane of maintenance departments and technicians around the world. Additionally, the use of composite materials instead of metal in portions of the airframe reduce weight, improve aerodynamic design, and allow various parts to be worked into more complex shapes. Airbus estimates the A320 saves its operators an average of $625,000 annually in operation costs compared to the 737.

The A320s are efficient in every way. Seating in the aircraft's all-coach configuration comes in two choices. In one option, seats are an inch wider, "adding noticeable comfort in the six-abreast layout," according to Airbus. The narrower seat configuration has a six-inch wider aisle, facilitating "easier passenger movement and meal service." Clearly meal service wasn't going to be an issue. But getting customers on and off in a hurry would be. That's why JetBlue went with the wide-aisle configuration.

Introduced in 1984 and first flying in 1988, the A320 has the lowest fuel burn, emissions, and noise footprint of any aircraft in the single-aisle airliner class. Further enhancing the aircraft's efficiency, JetBlue's jets are powered by V2500 engines from International Aero Engines AE. The A320's range of 3,450 statute miles gives it long enough legs to operate on any route in the continental United States. Even with the roomier aisle, thanks to a cabin that's seven inches wider, the seats are still bigger than on a 737. The A320 also has more headroom and the overhead bins hold 10 percent more.

The use of a single aircraft model throughout the fleet reduces costs associated with spare parts inventories, as well as maintenance and training costs. It further leads to enhanced knowledge of the aircraft in use, which in turn improves productivity and efficiency. Because JetBlue's aircraft are new, they need less maintenance and can be scheduled to fly more hours without cancellations due to equipment failure. JetBlue's aircraft operate an average of about 13 hours per day, thought to be the highest among the major airlines. The carrier's point-to-point route system minimizes ground time associated with hub-and-spoke models, in which aircraft wait to enplane passengers who arrive on feeder flights from smaller cities. Additionally, JetBlue emphasizes quick turnarounds at the gate, accomplished by a tightly choreo-graphed routine of on-loading and off-loading customers and baggage, and servicing of the aircraft.

Cleaning crews are another frill JetBlue dispenses with. Flight attendants and pilots take care of cleaning chores (while some-times asking customers to pitch in by taking their refuse with them), reducing the amount of time needed to prepare the plane for its next departure and, yes, saving on the cost of hiring sepa-rate personnel dedicated to this task. The relatively uncongested traffic of its home base at JFK during many of JetBlue's hours of operation also helps—long taxiing and hold times don't have to be factored in to flight times. It all means airplanes can spend more time in the air. The extra fuel costs associated with in-creased flying time are gladly incurred when an airline is operat-ing with load factors like JetBlue's.

The efficiencies of the airline's human assets are also made pos-sible by technology. Electronic systems enable an exact study of tasks and optimum deployment of personnel. "IT has made a huge impact on our number one cost, which is labor," Barger says. "It allows us to do more with fewer people and it also allows us to take better care of the people we do have." JetBlue's labor costs represent 26 percent of operating expenses compared to 38 per-cent at Southwest. At the major carriers, labor costs are well into the 40 to 50 percent range.

OPERATING AT MAXIMUM EFFICIENCY

JetBlue's distribution costs are also lower than the competition. It remains the only airline that offers nothing but electronic ticket-ing. E-ticketing eliminates paper costs, postage, security issues in-volved in guarding ticket stock, and back-office processing expenses. If anyone knows how to make the most of the customizable e-ticketing reservation system the company runs on, it should be Neeleman, the person who co-developed the technology behind it before selling it to Hewlett-Packard.

The airline's web site, www.jetblue.com, is designed to make online transactions quick and simple. As an incentive, the company clips $5 off the fare for online bookings. Today, more than 60 percent of JetBlue travelers book their tickets online. Each Internet transaction costs the airline only 50 cents. In addition to the savings, JetBlue encourages online bookings by making the process almost effortless. Even those with limited computer knowledge can easily navigate through the airline's web site. By clicking on the "Buy Tickets" icon, customers are taken to a page with a drop-down list of cities and dates of travel. After entering whether you are going one way or round-trip, and indicating the total number of passengers, customers simply click on "Search for Flights." This takes them to a page with schedule and fare information for each flight. They then need only select the flight wanted, click on "Continue," and fill in the blanks with contact and payment information.

JetBlue's virtual call center also helps to keep distribution costs down by eliminating the expense of building and running a centralized call center. The system that enables the company to use at-home reservations agents (who, research shows, are more efficient than those operating from conventional call centers) works exactly as if all the agents are doing their jobs from a centralized location. Each of these home offices has two phone lines—one connected to a computer, and another that opens a bridge to the call center. Calls are cued up just as they would be at a traditional command center. To take a break, the agent simply goes on "unavailable status," and the phone cue automatically bypasses that line until the agent returns. Phone transactions cost the airline an average of $4.50 each. Since no travel agents are involved, Jet-Blue doesn't have to pay the commissions and expenses associated with these bookings. (Travel agency–generated bookings cost airlines an average of $14 per ticket, after factoring in commissions and other charges.)

JetBlue's nonrefundable ticket policy eliminates complex back-office bookkeeping headaches and isn't as draconian as it sounds. Unused tickets can be transferred to anyone and are good toward any other JetBlue flight for one year, less a $25 rebooking fee. As previously mentioned, the $25 fee more than covers the cost of having live telephone reservations agents available to make the change. What's more, the airline's payroll processing, expense approvals, and other routing tasks are done digitally as well.

The bottom-line results of JetBlue's technological innovations are relatively easy to quantify. Instead of the sometimes amorphous ROI (return on investment) by which the cost of technology is typically gauged, the airline looks at the impact on CASM (cost per available seat mile), the industry's standard metric of efficiency. This is the expense of flying one passenger one mile. Available seat miles (ASM), a benchmark of an airline's total capacity, is calculated by multiplying the total of all seats available on every route by the length of the routes. If you divide an airline's total operating costs by the ASM, the result is the CASM. Airlines also pay close attention to RPM, or revenue per passenger mile. RPM is the number of seat miles for which the airline is actually filling a seat and making money. Divide the RPM by the ASM and the result is the airline's load factor. (Load factors can't be determined simply by averaging the occupancy of each flight, because the length of the flights figures into the result.)

By most measures, JetBlue operates more efficiently than its competitors. Its CASM is under 7 cents per mile, 25 percent below industry average for major carriers. Of course, RPM may not always measure up to other airlines because JetBlue's fares are lower (which helps to boost load factors), thanks to its efficient use of technology. (For example, RPM was 8.8 cents at JetBlue versus 12.0 cents at Southwest.) These metrics allow JetBlue to quickly determine the impact of new technology solutions on the company's balance sheet.

Technology also gives the airline an edge in real-time information. All operational anomalies are tracked electronically through JEM, the JetBlue Event Management system. Incidents involving safety issues, weather delays, baggage handling irregularities, and passenger injury are all reported and cataloged. Crewmembers use BlackBerry PDAs to report and respond to these events. They also uses Pocket PCs to ask customers about their level of satisfaction, and relay this information to headquarters using wireless technology. Neeleman carries his Black-Berry wherever he goes. It gives him instant information on all aspects of the airline's operations, down to how fast bags are being unloaded from planes, and he uses it to constantly send messages to people throughout the operation. Technology hound that he is, Neeleman further can often be seen using the calculator on his Casio wristwatch, punching in numbers in his endless search for more efficiency.

The ADD program that calculated operational and financial data at Morris Air, which Neeleman used to much advantage, has found its latter-day equivalent in JetBlue's Blue Performance program, developed by the airline's IT department. Blue Performance tracks data updated on a flight-by-flight basis. The program runs on the company's intranet, keeping data secure while allowing it to be shared with flight crewmembers.

"Having that kind of real-time information at your fingers is really more critical than anything," Neeleman says. "Other, older airlines spend billions and billions of dollars and use staffs of hundreds to try to pull this stuff, and we have it baked into the system."

The technological innovations at JetBlue are unprecedented in the industry. But you can be certain they are being closely monitored by the competition and will no doubt become commonplace in the industry, as have so many of the other advances Neeleman has pioneered during the course of his career.

CHAPTER 12

Getting the Word Out in Style

Two pilots are in the cockpit, performing their preflight checks, as restless passengers sit in a packed, cramped, and crowded cabin.

"Welcome aboard, folks, this is your captain speaking," one of the pilots announces over the PA system. "Just sit back and enjoy DirecTV, free at your comfy leather seats, on our brand-new planes."

The passengers look perplexed and extremely uncomfortable, especially one elderly woman sitting next to an overweight passenger stuffing his face with potato chips.

What in the world is the pilot talking about, she wonders? This plane is anything but comfortable, there's no television, and the aircraft is obviously old.

The pilots erupt in laughter, clearly enjoying their prank.

"Just kidding folks," one of them quips, following a short pause, "I mean, this *isn't* JetBlue."

"That's not funny," the elderly woman tells her neighbor back in the cabin.

"I love it when you do that, man," the co-pilot tells his colleague.

"I know," the other pilot replies, as the two continue snickering.

Humorous scenes like this, which are usually followed by a tagline like "JetBlue—it's not the only way to fly but it should be," or something similar, are indicative of the way the airline uses clever television advertising to distinguish its service while tweaking the noses of its competition. Another commercial shows a young JetBlue passenger trying to carry his own TV on the plane, only to be assured by a friendly ticket agent that, being JetBlue, there is already one on board. Then there's the ad portraying a sad-sack pilot whose admiring young son, after waxing enthusiastically about JetBlue, tells him, "Dad, when I grow up, I want to be a pilot just like you." When his dad explains he doesn't fly for JetBlue, the son woefully observes, "No wonder Mom left."

From the beginning, JetBlue has marketed itself by using off-the-wall and often comical campaigns. When the carrier launched service to Denver, it invited passengers to "Join the Mile High (City) Club." When JetBlue started red-eye flights from Seattle to New York, it encouraged residents to "Sleep Less in Seattle." And while the airline has made memorable waves with its paid advertising, it has also managed to gather incredible free media attention, dating all the way back to before Neeleman's July 1999 press conference where he announced the formation of the airline and the innovative experience he promised to deliver.

THE PR EFFORT TAKES SHAPE

By the summer of 2001, JetBlue was serving 15 destinations from New York with its 15 aircraft. Although it operated only 80 flights a day, compared to 2,500 flights for American Airlines and 4,800 for United, JetBlue enjoyed an outsized media profile that wasn't mere happenstance. It was carefully crafted by two veterans of marketing and public relations who had done it all before for yet another big brand famous for its clever campaigns.

Amy Curtis-McIntyre began her career in the travel and tourism division of Hill & Knowlton, the powerhouse New–York-based public relations firm. A native of New York City, she jumped over to the client side in time-honored fashion, becoming Celebrity Cruises' director of advertising and promotion. Richard Branson then brought her to Virgin Atlantic to help launch his transatlantic airline service. Virgin needed to establish a strong brand in order to survive its battle over the North Atlantic with British Airways.

Curtis-McIntyre was instrumental in positioning Virgin Atlantic as the cool, fun underdog that people in the know preferred. She created an image for Virgin that mirrored that of its founder: hip, brash, on the cutting edge, yet fond of the good life. But Virgin Atlantic, unlike JetBlue, wasn't making a low-cost appeal. Branson's bread and butter was the business and upper-class travelers the airline targeted with its door-to-door limousine service, airport "clubhouses" with putting greens, hair salons, gyms, masseuses, and individual VCRs aboard the aircraft. These travelers wanted pampering, just not the old-fashioned, stuffy kind. Ironically, Branson, who appealed to the hippie sensibilities among the traveling public with his counterculture and music connections, was actually more conservative than the soft-spoken Mormon-raised Neeleman, who was determined to liberate the public from the hegemony of the high-priced carriers.

When Neeleman and his investment backers met with Branson and his New York team to discuss a partnership, they were immediately taken by Curtis-McIntyre. "She has a great kind of New York humor—a little sarcastic and a little whimsical, a little off-center," former JetBlue chairman Michael Lazarus says. And she certainly "got it" as the discussions progressed about the low-fare U.S. airline that Neeleman would run. With her raven hair and sharp banter with Aussie colleague Gareth Edmondson-Jones, Curtis-McIntyre reminded more than a few of British actress Diana Rigg. Edmondson-Jones, who was responsible for generating the steady stream of glowing media coverage for Branson and Virgin Atlantic, also hit it off with the Yanks.

The two were based in New York, so the spiritually inclined could argue they were fated to join Neeleman's team. They made a great pair, with spirits and temperaments that seemed to complement each other. The equity positions the two would receive in the new airline also made the decision to come aboard that much easier. Several other Virgin staffers eventually followed them to JetBlue as well, adding their considerable talents to the mix.

Edmondson-Jones took charge of generating publicity for the enterprise, while Curtis-McIntyre developed JetBlue's corporate identity, brand platform, advertising, web site, and the overall in-flight and airport product.

From the beginning, price was to be the carrier's primary selling point. While it's not that difficult to get the public's attention when you're offering the same basic service for about one-third the cost of everyone else, price alone doesn't make a successful brand. The new airline, which had no name beyond its temporary "New Air" moniker when Curtis-McIntyre came aboard, needed an identity.

True to his roots and disposition, Neeleman wanted a happy,

friendly feeling to go along with the low-price advertising pitch. "Cheap and cheerful," is how he described it. Curtis-McIntyre aimed for something loftier: "I wanted cheap and chic," she says. Their battles over the direction of the advertising led to more than one job-threatening confrontation. But on the whole, Curtis-McIntyre found Neeleman's famously attention-span-challenged mind to be beneficial to the creative strategizing process. "It's great," she said of his characteristic transient lack of focus. "We can keep going back to him with idea after idea until we get it right."

The creative differences between Neeleman and Curtis-McIntyre culminated in a compromise that couldn't have more perfectly blended their thoughts, either conceptually or phonetically: "cheap and cheeky." Bold, sassy confidence was what JetBlue was all about, and it was what New York was all about, too.

The airline needed an advertising agency to help craft and execute its message and media plan. Neeleman, who had single-handedly changed the religion of 200 Brazilians on a budget of $850 per year—and who got Morris Air off the ground with little more than a couple of classified ads—wasn't predisposed toward the Madison Avenue way of doing things, nor the arrogance and condescension of some of the ad execs he called on. The airline went through more than one shop as it sought to establish itself.

"We had these big ad agencies in New York that would say, 'Hey, we're going to create your brand. We're going to make your company, and we're going to charge you $150,000 a month,'" he recounts. "And I was like, 'You know, actually, it's good to have the image and have the look and have the great advertising, but if people come and get on our flights and they don't have a great experience, then actually they'll never come back.'"

Curtis-McIntyre had a total marketing budget of $10 million to launch the airline—a relatively flinty amount, especially given reports in the trade press that the budget would be closer to $100 million. To compensate for the shortfall, she planned to utilize guerrilla marketing and word of mouth to spread news about JetBlue to the hometown crowd. Instead of paying $80,000 to hang a promotional banner in a sports arena, for example, as one marketing expert suggested, JetBlue spent the same amount on small gifts to give to the taxi drivers who brought customers to the airport every day. "Drivers can start a virus, spreading the word throughout the city about the great new airline," Neeleman said of the plan.

Other low-cost ideas for establishing the airline included offering discounts on tickets for public employees, and selling Lotto tickets and Metro fare cards aboard the aircraft. To throw competitors off the scent, a dollop of disinformation was put into the mix. Minneapolis, Detroit, and Dallas were mentioned as cities in need of JetBlue's services, yet five years later JetBlue had yet to touch down in any of them.

The marketing budget for introducing JetBlue in the five cities it would initially serve was "absolutely nothing," Curtis-McIntyre says. This was technically correct, since the marketing department's funds come under the operations budget, reflecting a company philosophy Curtis-McIntyre strongly endorses: "Product and marketing should be intimately involved—in each other's face and on the same side of the fence," she explains. Curtis-McIntyre raided her small sales and product development budget to buy a few TV ads. The rest of the money went into making the product distinctive: logo design, snack service, and the look of the gate area. "There's just not one thing with that brand that she doesn't have her fingers in the middle of," Lazarus says.

Like Neelman, she embraced Jan Carlzon's *Moments of Truth*

philosophy—that every point of customer contact is a marketing opportunity and a test of the brand. Curtis-McIntyre had Terminal 6 at New York's JFK Airport decorated to exude the aura of hip fun the airline sought to be known for. The walls were hung with framed covers of old LPs, complemented with retro-chic furnishings of tufted banquettes and brushed-steel lamps, suggesting the look, as one reporter called it, of "a Greene Street loft."

Edmondson-Jones, meanwhile, was generating literally millions of dollars worth of free press coverage for JetBlue. With his droll observations and Australian bonhomie, he was fast becoming a sought-after source the media could rely on for providing a regular stream of pithy quotes.

"So many entrants have come and gone based on, 'We're going to have low fares, and that's going to be it,'" Edmondson-Jones observed in one interview, contrasting JetBlue's marketing approach with that taken by previous low-fare carriers. "Low fares will get them [passengers] on, but you've got to enjoy it [the flying experience], especially in the New York market. Look at Starbucks. We're built on the same principle. Brands these days get emotional commitment, not just financial commitment. What you buy says something about you. You buy it because you like that badge. We're going to be the Starbucks of the sky."

One area where Curtis-McIntyre was determined not to scrimp was on crewmember uniforms. "Great-looking uniforms project a lot more than the obvious," she insists. "When a customer sees an employee that looks fabulous, they think, 'If they care about the uniforms, then they care about the aircraft, their on-time performance, and more.'"

The airline hired designer Stan Herman, president of the Council of Fashion Designers of America—who was responsible for designing TWA's uniforms in 1974 at the height of the jet set era—to create the look for JetBlue's crewmembers.

"JetBlue's home is New York City, the fashion capital of the country," notes Curtis-McIntyre, who worked closely with Herman on developing the utilitarian yet chic design. "So, while our uniforms had to be comfortable and functional, it was important that they be stylish and distinctive as well."

For the first JetBlue uniforms—Curtis-McIntyre served as the clothes dummy for the design—Herman created a "Prada-esque" look featuring a windowpane-check midnight blue shirt and matching tailored trousers or skirt. Male crewmembers wore ties patterned to echo the design of the tail fins of the airline's aircraft. Female crewmembers wore blue check or polka-dot scarves. And JetBlue's pilots, unlike those at other airlines, went hatless.

"Even if they brought a fedora in, we'd say, 'No, get that off your head!'" Edmondson-Jones joked. "We didn't want to go for the militarized look. We wanted our pilots to be as approachable as our flight attendants."

"There is a certain aesthetic they take very seriously," Curtis-McIntryre says of JetBlue's flight attendants, who are, after all, performers at heart, onstage before an audience when they're at work. "They want to look good—and they have to put this thing on every day, too."

In the minds of JetBlue executives, the lack of attention to uniforms at other airlines was an additional indication of the estrangement between management and labor, an additional impediment to delivering superior service to customers.

"That's just another symptom of how those airlines run their business," Curtis-McIntyre maintained. "They tend to be male-dominated businesses that don't bother to ask the front line what they want to wear."

A year after JetBlue took to the skies, the carrier's uniforms were featured in the Museum at the Fashion Institute of Technology in an exhibit called "Work in Uniform: Dressed for Detail," tracing the evolution of uniform design in the twentieth century. Commenting on the honor Curtis-McIntyre proclaimed, "Our uniforms set Jet-Blue apart from other airlines as much as all our other amenities."

A VISIBLE CEO

Then, as now, Neeleman was one of the airline's best and most vocal promotional tools. He routinely accepts invitations to address groups of all sizes, from college classes to corporate functions, where he eagerly spreads the gospel of air travel according to Jet-Blue. In February 2000, as the airline was first taking to the skies, Kristin Zern, executive director of the Association of Travel Marketing Executives (ATME), asked Neeleman to be the keynote speaker at the group's annual convention. "There was already a buzz about JetBlue," she recalls. Neeleman quickly accepted the invitation to the association's late-May gathering in Miami Beach. Because he was scheduled to speak on a Thursday morning, Zern expected to see Neeleman at the convention hotel the night before. But he still hadn't appeared by breakfast. As the ballroom began to fill for his presentation, Neeleman remained missing.

"I was totally freaked out," says Zern. Moments before his address was scheduled to begin, Neeleman, looking more than a little rumpled, strode into the room with a hanging suitcase slung over his shoulder. He'd come straight from the airport, he told the audience. An airline snafu—not his airline, of course—had forced him to buy a ticket for a red-eye from California on a "regular" airline that cost $663. His "can-you-believe-it?" tone was mixed with the steely determination of a man ready to take on the town bully.

The 300 travel marketing pros in attendance were used to seeing airline CEOs get up and deliver blustery, ego-stoked presentations. But Neeleman was "a distinctly different personality than anyone I've ever seen in that position," Zern recalls. "He stood absolutely still, didn't do that [walking] back and forth, didn't come into the audience, didn't ask for a lavaliere [microphone], he just started to talk." He also came without the entourage airline CEOs typically surround themselves with. Speaking sans notes, as he always does, Neeleman proceeded to explain what JetBlue was all about, and how and why it was going to be different from other airlines.

"Even though he spoke in soft tones, not your typical fervor, every word he spoke, everything he said, was a jewel," Zern remembers. "He said, 'It's going to be an experience. This is what the product is going to be like. It's not going to be like flying on any other airline, even though we're going to be cheaper than anybody else.' I thought positioning the airline as a product was really interesting, something an airline had never done before."

JetBlue was really positioning itself to be the anti-airline. The goal of "bringing humanity back to air travel" was antithetical to the way legacy carriers operated. JetBlue underscored the difference by highlighting those things that distinguished it from the competition: courtesy, comfort, and punctuality. Furthermore, the message was delivered with wit and panache. Billboards in New York promised "Free TV With Every Purchase," while a whimsical TV spot portrayed a subway ride recast as a JetBlue flight, with crewmembers dancing through the car, making passengers comfy with pillows and blankets, and even pouring coffee into the cup of a beggar collecting change.

"The messages we heard time and again were, 'JetBlue makes me feel welcome' and 'JetBlue is genuinely happy to have me onboard,'" Curtis-McIntyre said of the consumer research behind the campaign. This led to yet another catchy advertising tagline: "Somebody Up There Likes You."

By the summer of 2001, JetBlue had gone from start-up to upstart. It led the industry in load factors, on-time performance, and profitability. A new Airbus was being delivered every five weeks, about the same rate JetBlue was adding new destinations. Then, as now, rigorous research and analysis preceded the splashy debuts and witty announcements of new destinations and service offerings. Factors such as potential market share, elasticity (how demand in a market changes in response to changes in ticket price), opportunity cost, and profit and loss comparisons were calculated before adding any new destinations. Neeleman was quick to dispel any notions that JetBlue had a grand design behind its route expansion, as if engaged in some aerial chess game with the Darth Vader-like giants of the industry. "There are some strategic things that enter in, but for the most part we just go where we can make the most amount of money. We're not in this for market share. We're in it to make a profit," he insisted.

As the financial folks worked their calculations, the numbers showed the airline's greatest potential profit wasn't in route expansion, but rather in increasing service to current markets, which showed more elasticity than anticipated. In other words, the low fares uncovered crowds of untapped customers that even surprised Neeleman. "There is such demand for our product that it behooves us from a cost perspective to just add frequencies and tie the cities together," he said, explaining to the press why the company would scale back its plans for adding new destinations from Kennedy. "That's our number one preference, because that way you can add flights less expensively, keep costs down, and better utilize your existing crewmembers."

The airline's capitulation to reality was the equivalent of the famous Wall Street edict, "Don't fight the tape." But any suspicions that this represented a retrenchment in plans were preempted by the contract JetBlue signed in June 2001 to buy up to 48 additional A320s. The $2.5 billion deal brought the total number of planes JetBlue had on order to 131. Deliveries would continue through 2011. But JetBlue was already near to maxing out its space at Kennedy. Where would all those jets go? A partial answer came in July when the carrier and the Port Authority of New York and New Jersey announced that JetBlue would take over the rest of Terminal 6. The five-year, $60 million lease would allow JetBlue to expand from 6 to 10 gates and double its operations at the airport. The airline projected it would operate 100 flights a day from its 6 gates at Kennedy by the end of 2001. With the new lease, that number almost doubled by the end of 2003.

The expanded base at Kennedy would relieve immediate concerns about overcrowding. But Neeleman and his crew weren't waiting to face another real estate crunch. They had already analyzed, calculated, and selected the airline's next base of operations. Again the choice fit with Neeleman's counterintuitive business sense, the kind of decision that at first hearing elicits puzzled surprise, yielding to musings of "Why didn't I think of that?" But, despite being the best-capitalized start-up in the history of aviation, the budget to launch the new operations base would be lean and tight. Imagination and unconventional tactics would have to take the place of dollars. Curtis-McIntyre, Edmondson-Jones, and the airline's marketing and PR crew faced the same challenge when they introduced and promoted JetBlue to the media and the world two years before. They knew the methods a situation like this called for. It was time to get out the guerrilla suits.

MOVING OUT WEST

California has been the promised land for those seeking riches ever since gold was discovered there in 1849. From that time on, the state has drawn more than its share of dreamers and schemers. Many airlines had profited handsomely over the years by hauling people back and forth from the East Coast to the Golden State, spawning the concept of the bicoastal lifestyle and the 2,500-mile commute. To JetBlue, Los Angeles represented a mother lode of potential customers. There was a hitch, however: Los Angeles International Airport (LAX), the preferred portal for air travelers, was too clogged and congested to permit the kind of fast turnarounds JetBlue prospered with. But 21 miles south of LAX lay Long Beach Airport, with a terminal that was a throwback to the earlier days of air travel. Instead of walking down jetways to board aircraft, passengers strolled across the tarmac and up airstairs. Parking directly in front of the terminal was a few dollars a day, a fraction of what most other airports charge.

Several carriers had come and gone from Long Beach over the years, leaving the airport relatively underutilized, and minimizing departure and arrival delays. Nevertheless, city ordinances passed to preserve the scale of airport operations limited the number of available departure slots to 27. With its eye on the prize, JetBlue began quietly negotiating with the city fathers and the airport authority about getting those dormant slots. In May 2001 JetBlue announced that Long Beach would be its second base of operations, with plans to phase in 27 daily departures over the next two years. Service would commence on August 29, 2001, with two daily nonstop flights to JFK.

But just as Long Beach was off the radar screens of the major carriers (a situation that would dramatically reverse itself once JetBlue got interested in the facility), the same thing applied to potential customers, who were used to flying out of either LAX or even the increasingly popular Burbank airport.

"We have a big job to do here," Curtis-McIntyre said, summing up the marketing challenge the team faced in California.

Most people had never heard of JetBlue, which was primarily making a name for itself in the East, and many didn't know that Long Beach even had an airport. Going back to the guerrilla marketing playbook, the team developed a strategy that focused on reaching influential potential customers one-on-one. As usual, JetBlue wasn't trying to capture market share from other carriers as much as it was using low fares to find a pool of potential travelers who had ample reason and desire to fly coast to coast, but not the budget for it.

JetBlue hired college interns and dispatched them to beaches, bars, and hot spots to scout for prospects. The interns were armed with giveaways of JetBlue tote bags and bumper stickers, emblazoned with the line "Goodbye LAX." Nine Volkswagen Beetles painted blue and adorned with the JetBlue logo cruised local streets and performed beach patrol duty for a month, with drivers spreading the word about the new airline. Hotel concierges, bartenders, and other influencers and opinion shapers were courted with gifts. An introductory fare of $198 round-trip to New York was promoted. Neeleman himself helped out by speaking at the local Rotary Club and making himself accessible to the media. Painting itself and the airport it served as mavericks, JetBlue called Long Beach "an anti-airport to go with the anti-airline."

The strategy worked. Shortly after JetBlue's twice-daily service began at the end of August, customer demand was such that the carrier decided it would add a third daily flight, commencing barely a month later. The campaign's success also underscored a valuable lesson for Neeleman. "I used to think I knew all there was about branding and marketing," Neeleman said, "but now I know enough to get out of the way and let Amy and her team do it."

Industry experts often credit the airline's success to its image. Would the bedrock low-fare, on-time, leather-seated, TV-sated experience that JetBlue offers fail without the veneer of hip, edgy cool that the airline strives to project? Perhaps not. But smart branding and positioning have clearly been effective in giving the airline its distinctive personality, and a reason for customers to turn into devoted fans. As for big ad budgets, who needs them when your airline draws 60 percent of its new business from word of mouth, and only 15 percent from advertising, anyway?

With the latest marketing challenge met, another important milestone was already in the works: taking JetBlue public. While Neeleman made the airline's success look easy, the prospectus for the stock offering laid out the many potential pitfalls the company still faced: JetBlue had a limited operating history; its business plan and growth strategy had yet to be proven; and, like all airlines, it was subject to unpredictable increases in the costs of fuel, maintenance, labor, and insurance premiums, not to mention unforeseen regulatory and competitive changes. JetBlue couldn't even guarantee it would be able to renew its gate leases. Nonetheless, the public eagerly anticipated getting a piece of the company, and the airline set a filing date for its IPO: September 11, 2001.

CHAPTER 13

Dealing with Disaster

September 11, 2001, was to be a historic day for New York's hometown airline. JetBlue was set to file the papers for its initial public offering, a milestone on the way to becoming a publicly owned company. But in the purposeful, roll-up-the-shirtsleeves atmosphere of JetBlue, no one paid much attention to the outside world—even if it involved financial machinations they had a personal stake in. David Neeleman has always let it be known that he ignores stock prices and concentrates on operating his airline, which, unlike the fickle volatility of Wall Street, he can do something about. So it was business as usual at the company's headquarters that clear September morning.

Benny Stabile saw it first. He was sitting with Ann Rhoades, vice president of JetBlue's People Department and the woman he was about to succeed. The week before, Rhoades had been elevated to JetBlue's board of directors. No more commuting back and forth to Albuquerque every week. Rhoades was relinquishing her day-to-day responsibilities in favor of ramping up her human resources consulting business, which she had postponed to help get JetBlue airborne. The two were discussing transitional issues when Stabile glanced out the window of Rhoades' office, with its singular view of the World Trade Center.

Smoke was rising from the North Tower. Neither Rhoades nor Stabile had any idea a plane had caused the damage. Anyone following the news that morning knows the confusion and conflicting reports that first accompanied the images seen countless times since. And the very size of the stricken building initially minimized recognition of the scale of the calamity. Some eyewitness callers to morning news programs already in progress claimed they had seen a plane fly into the tower, but they were wildly divergent in their reports of the size of the aircraft. The possibility that it was a deliberate act was never even raised. Who would have imagined something so incomprehensible?

As Stabile and Rhoades watched, an orange burst erupted from the South Tower. In that instant, the true dimensions of the horror revealed themselves. Within moments a crowd was packed into Rhoades' office, transfixed by the growing plumes visible in the distance. Someone rounded up a radio.

Dave Barger and JetBlue's dispatch office were immediately notified. Barger called in the airline's emergency care team. Created to deal with disasters, this was the first time it had been activated. At 9:25 A.M., the FAA gave the order to shut down U.S. airspace, the first nationwide grounding in history. Planes began landing at the closest suitable airport. At JetBlue headquarters, like those of other airlines, time passed uneasily as employees waited to learn which companies' aircraft had been involved, and whether other planes were still unaccounted for.

JetBlue's employee assistance group was also activated to help crewmembers cope with the tragedy. Counselors were sent to the airport. With planes grounded and the roads in and out of Manhattan closed, many travelers were stuck at airports. JetBlue officers went to Kennedy to talk to customers and crewmembers.

Flight attendants were especially devastated. Rumors circulated that some attendants at other airlines were quitting, having lost all desire to fly. Others worried more attacks would follow. Jet-Blue wanted to assure its people and customers the company was there for them.

That afternoon, Jane Garvery, the FAA administrator, convened a conference call with the heads of all U.S. airlines to discuss security needs and measures. Neeleman and Barger participated. With information at a premium in the coming hours and days, Neeleman and Barger began sending out e-mails at least once a day, updating people on what the airline knew about the service suspension, what JetBlue was doing, and continually thanking those who were volunteering their time and efforts. JetBlue crewmembers took to making copies of the communiqués to give to employees of other airlines, who in many cases heard nothing from their leadership.

COPING WITH TRAGEDY

The attacks of September 11 devastated the entire airline industry. Every carrier was severely impacted. Not only were flights grounded completely for two days, but anxious passengers refused to fly for long after that, leaving airports and airplanes virtually empty for weeks.

The blow these attacks struck to the already teetering U.S. economy further slashed demand for air travel, as companies and consumers cut back on spending. By the beginning of October, massive layoffs and cancellations of aircraft deliveries had been announced by a number of carriers. The recovery process would not be fast, nor would it be easy. And the effects would ripple throughout the entire travel industry, impacting hotels, restaurants, amusement parks, and tourist attractions as well.

As the airlines struggled to cope with the new post–9/11 economic and security environment, passengers returning to the air found long airport lines and burdensome random inspections aimed at preventing further acts of terrorism. The inconvenience made many travelers decide it was easier to just stay home. Even Neeleman was troubled by the price society was being asked to pay—sometimes needlessly, in his opinion.

"The most discouraging thing about September 11 was when people said, 'Our lives have changed forever, we will never be the same.' Well, why do good people have to be hassled every time they go to do anything?" Neeleman asked.

Finding himself on the front lines of the debate over security tactics and civil liberties, Neeleman began advocating a passenger screening policy based on profiling that was as pragmatic as it was impolitic. Neeleman called for focusing screening efforts on foreign-born passengers based on such characteristics as nationality, age, and gender. In his mind, it just made good sense. "I would like to eliminate the 80-year-old ladies from the equation," Neeleman said. "Like retired school teachers living in Queens that we know are not capable, [nor do they] have any desire to do terrorist acts. They shouldn't be hassled every time they go to the airport. We're sitting there, you know, patting down 80-year-old ladies. We shouldn't be messing with that. Security is so important, and we need to really focus on those people that have a potential [to be a threat]."

Before 9/11, the question of how to make airlines safer from terrorism had long been fodder for debate. Airports in Europe had installed bomb detection equipment and programs to positively match luggage with passengers, ensuring that no one packed a bomb in their bags, checked them in, and skipped the flight. U.S. carriers had resisted such measures as being unnecessary. Instead, they began experimenting with the Computer Assisted Passenger Prescreening System (CAPPS), a computer program designed to assign a risk assessment "score" to each passenger. Scores were based on a variety of information gathered from the passenger, including form of payment and nationality. In theory, those deemed at a high risk would be subjected to greater scrutiny. The first generation of these systems was introduced in 1996. Privacy advocates, civil libertarians, and other critics immediately raised concerns that the system was flawed and incapable of consistently spotting threats.

The industry's attitude changed following the explosion of TWA Flight 800 shortly after takeoff from JFK on its way to Paris in July of 1996. The crash was initially thought to be caused by a bomb or missile. An aviation safety commission, chaired by Vice President Al Gore, was established to study U.S. aviation policies following the disaster. In 1998 the commission concluded that a CAPPS I should be deployed as a temporary measure, until a baggage screening program could be implemented. Additionally, the CAPPS I system scores could be used to determine which passengers should be screened more rigorously. But few took the need for such measures seriously before 9/11.

TAKING THE RIGHT STEPS

While others talked about various ways security could be improved in the aftermath of the terrorist attacks, Neeleman took action. By the end of October 2001 the entire JetBlue fleet was equipped with bulletproof, Kevlar-fortified cockpit doors, at a cost of about $10,000 per aircraft. This was before the government mandated such action.

"We just said, 'Hey, if the cockpit doors were the problem,' which they [were], I didn't want to get on a plane with a flimsy cockpit door, [so we decided] 'Let's bulletproof the cockpit doors in all of our planes,'" Neeleman explains. "We were smaller [than other airlines]. It was easier for us to do it." Soon after, JetBlue also became the first airline to make positive bag matches of passengers against all checked luggage.

In addition, the innovative onboard LiveTV system was used to provide greater security in the cabin. Untapped communication capabilities built into the operating unit allowed JetBlue to install cabin cameras throughout the fleet following 9/11. This gave pilots a view of the cabin at all times, allowing them to monitor any situations involving passengers without having to leave the safe environment of the cockpit.

"It was one of those things where David found out about it, and said, 'We're going to do it, period,'" says Glenn Latta, a LiveTV vice president and one of the architects of the system. "And it was a very quick decision."

Neeleman further proposed creating a national travel card that would be given to all U.S.-born citizens. Holders of this card would be subject to less rigorous screening than those without one. Using himself as an example, and citing his Brazilian birth, Neeleman said, "Maybe the first go-round, don't give me a card. Make me fill out a 30-page questionnaire, then give me the card." He also proposed cooperation between the airline industry and the government, specifically as it relates to data mining, to help identify individuals who presented the greatest security risks. "We'd like to see the federal government get involved," he said. Neeleman noted that the government had many databases with everything from tax returns to Social Security information already at its fingertips, which would make the process easier.

Throughout the fall and into the winter following the attacks, JetBlue remained profitable, despite an overall downturn in air travel that saw major carriers plunge into bankruptcy. While capacity had doubled over the previous year, the number of customers and profitability at JetBlue more than kept pace. "We were built for recession," Gareth Edmondson-Jones proclaimed, "and from an operating perspective this is just like a tough recession."

The industry giants battled to remain solvent. American Airlines shed 20,000 of its 112,000 employees. United cut a similar number from its 95,000-person payroll. US Airways laid off 11,000 of its 42,000 workers, while Northwest, Continental, and Delta shed another 11,000, 12,000, and 13,000 jobs respectively, representing 28 percent, 18 percent, and 20 percent of their workforces. Losses for the domestic carriers were estimated to be $6 billion in 2001. Internationally, Air Canada furloughed over one-third of its 25,000 employees, while Swiss Air, Alitalia, British Airways, and even Virgin Atlantic collectively cut jobs in the thousands. Among established domestic carriers, only Southwest and Alaska Airlines avoided layoffs. Among start-ups, only JetBlue didn't cut its payroll.

Legislators in Washington began discussing a bailout plan for the industry, and they were interested in what Neeleman had to say.

"I [would] go to Washington a lot and sit in the room with other airline CEOs," Neeleman said at the time, "and they would be talking about, 'Give us money or we're all going to fall apart and go home.' I was just astounded at the defeatist attitude that was amongst a lot of these other airlines."

Congress moved swiftly, if not always advisedly, to legislate relief for the beleaguered airline industry. The Air Transportation Safety and System Stabilization Act, passed on September 22, 2001, created the Stabilization Board, which was charged with disbursing $5 billion to the airlines for losses associated with the terrorist attacks. The Board was also given the power to guarantee up to another $10 billion in loans from private lenders. In return for granting the loans, the government got stock warrants and other equity positions in the airlines as compensation for its demonstration of faith. JetBlue announced it had no plans to seek any of the loan guarantees offered by the government to buoy the struggling carriers, though it eventually took some $20 million in federal aid. (US Airways received the largest loan, at $900 million. Applications by National, Spirit, and Vanguard were all turned down.)

Some airlines were forced to file for bankruptcy protection despite this government assistance, and others went out of business altogether after being turned down for loans. UAL, the parent of United Airlines and the nation's second largest carrier behind American, declared Chapter 11 bankruptcy in December 2002. Before that, US Airways did the same. Both carriers sought—and got—labor concessions in order to lower operating costs and enable them to more effectively compete with more efficient low-cost airlines like Southwest and JetBlue. Nevertheless, even with these cuts, the legacy carriers were straddled with high embedded costs on everything from pensions to aging aircraft, making it almost impossible to ever catch up with the efficiencies enjoyed by JetBlue.

GOING PUBLIC

As the spring of 2002 approached, JetBlue's IPO was back on the calendar. The airline filed its notice of intent to go public with the

SEC on February 12. "Amid . . . changes in industry dynamics, we intend to maintain a disciplined growth strategy by increasing frequency on our existing routes and entering attractive new markets," the filing stated. Neeleman's vow to never be undercapitalized—a lesson learned following the collapse of his first business—had paid off again. Because it had plenty of cash reserves in its coffers, JetBlue had no need to rush to the capital markets and was comfortably able to wait for Wall Street to rebound from its post–9/11 depths. Morgan Stanley was hired to be the lead manager of JetBlue's IPO. The firm had also been slated to handle Morris Air's IPO in 1993. Back then, Neeleman had struck up a friendship with Kevin Murphy, who was Morgan Stanley's airline analyst. But since Southwest Airlines wound up buying Morris, that deal ultimately evaporated.

During the late 1990s, when Neeleman began making trips to New York—trying to sell the concept of JetBlue to investors, government officials, and civic leaders—Murphy offered to let Neeleman sleep at his East Side apartment. The ever-frugal Neeleman gladly took him up on the offer. Now Neeleman was about to pay his friend back. In addition to choosing his firm to manage the IPO, Neeleman let Murphy invest almost $125,000 of his own money in the airline.

The company originally planned to sell 5.5 million shares of stock. Several days before the planned April IPO, shares were priced at $22 to $24 each. At the time, the airline industry was in the dumps. So was the overall stock market. There hadn't been an IPO involving an airline since Air France had offered some shares three years before. Still, JetBlue was unfazed and Wall Street seemed eager to buy in. "There's definitely a lot of interest in it," said one fund manager, who also hit on a reason for the offering's popularity: Investors knew the product. "There are so many buy-side people in New York and so many of us have flown JetBlue."

The day before the offering, demand continued to grow. In response, more shares were put on the market and the share price was upped to $27.

JetBlue made its debut on the NASDAQ stock exchange on April 12, 2002, under the symbol JBLU. By the end of the first day of trading, shares had been bid up almost 70 percent above their opening price of $27, the best first-day performance of a newly listed stock in a year. The offering of 5.9 million new shares of common stock, representing 16 percent of the company, raised $147.3 million. That still left 71 percent of the company in the hands of the original investors, with an additional 13 percent owned by Neeleman and other top managers. JetBlue's auspicious debut brightened what had been a dreary environment on Wall Street. "JetBlue is an absolute gift for IPO buyers," said Morningstar.com analyst Ben Holmes. "It's the hottest deal this year."

Within a month, JetBlue's share price had doubled. And it would go on to even loftier heights, becoming one of the most talked about stocks on any exchange. At one point, the total market value of JetBlue was greater than that of American, United, and Delta Airlines combined. Only Southwest Airlines, Neeleman's model company and former employer, was worth more.

At the end of its initial month as a publicly traded company, the airline's first quarter results revealed that JetBlue's load factor had climbed to 80.8 percent, again the highest in the industry. Flight completion had reached 99.9 percent. Operating revenues had more than doubled over the previous year's figures. Operating expenses per available seat mile had decreased more than 8 percent. And net income, at $13 million, had almost doubled the previous year's figure of $6.7 million. It was the young company's fifth consecutive profitable quarter.

Fearful that some business travelers were avoiding the airline rather than lose out on the frequent flyer benefits offered by competitors, that June JetBlue unveiled its own customer loyalty program called TrueBlue—the name Neeleman once considered calling the airline. Even prior to the program's introduction, JetBlue had taken steps to acknowledge its best customers, realizing such regulars are the backbone of any business. Using data from its e-ticketing software, the airline was able to identify several hundred of its most active flyers. Each had been sent a voucher for a free ticket as a show of gratitude.

In creating its own frequent flyer program, JetBlue sought to avoid some of the pitfalls experienced by other carriers, most notably the accretion of owed flights that end up on a company's ledger as liabilities. Under TrueBlue, customers simply get a free ticket for every 10 flights they take, which must be used within a year. Additionally, there are no mailings of statements or other administrative costs normally associated with such programs. A customer's mileage balance is only available for viewing online, which means it costs the airline little to keep TrueBlue members informed of their status.

FACING CHALLENGES

Meanwhile, back on the West Coast, JetBlue's hegemony at Long Beach airport was challenged once word of its deal to lock up the airport's remaining available slots became public. Alaska Air and American Airlines—which previously had little interest in the airport—threatened to sue the city of Long Beach if they weren't given some of the slots as well. JetBlue responded by accelerating its expansion plans to make use of the gates, although it wound up relinquishing a small number to head off the threatened legal action.

But this distraction did little to slow the carrier down. JetBlue's performance numbers only got better as the summer travel season commenced. By August 2002 the carrier's flights were more than 90 percent full, even as the number of seats grew with each new airplane coming on line. Flight completion—the percentage of scheduled flights that operated without being cancelled—reached 100 percent. What's more, the airline's following was increasing, as it developed an army of fanatical, devoted customers—the best marketing force any company could ask for. This was further underscored when *Condé Nast Traveler* readers voted JetBlue the "Best U.S. Airline" in November.

As JetBlue grew, the airline's brain trust became increasingly engaged in success control. Despite the huge base of loyal customers the airline had amassed, Neeleman knew he couldn't become complacent. He also realized that no matter how good you are today, there's always room for improvement.

"We're not perfect," Neeleman is fond of saying. "We know we'll never be perfect. But we're working really hard to try to be better and better every day, to be the best service company. I tell our people all the time, 'We may be the best airline in the country and still not be all that great. So let's just make our goal to be the best service company because that's what we do. We're in the service business.'"

The company has long observed several practices that help keep it on track. For instance, numerous regularly scheduled weekly meetings monitor specific areas of operational performance, including baggage handling, the length of check-in lines, and on-time performance. Every Tuesday the airline holds a three-hour management conference, the first half of which is devoted to operations planning and the second half of which deals with strategic marketing. Tuesday afternoons the company's four top executives (Neeleman, Barger, CFO John Owen, and general counsel Thomas Kelly) convene a four-hour meeting. Anyone out of town attends via phone. These executive sessions always cover three main topics: people, performance, and prosperity.

Barger develops the agenda for these meetings. "People" can cover training or recruitment issues. "Performance" looks at how both the airline and its competitors are doing compared to various DOT metrics. "Prosperity" examines any variety of economic issues that are bound to impact the bottom line.

Neeleman, as he did back at Morris, is still apt to abruptly leave a meeting in progress, go down the hall to deal with some other issue, and later return to pick up where he left off.

Barger tracks data about JetBlue's performance relentlessly, receiving detailed daily reports broken down by flight and city. Operational goals include a 95.5 percent flight completion rate; 13 hours a day of use per aircraft; and having the first bag from a flight off the plane and on the luggage carousel within 10 minutes of arrival, with the last one showing up within 20 minutes. That final measure is especially meaningful to Neeleman. "Why would you be so stupid to measure something so insignificant as how long it takes to get a bag to the carousel?" he asks. "[Because] it's the last thing you remember about JetBlue. You could have a flawless experience. Everything could go wonderfully perfect. And you could go to the carousel and wait 45 minutes and . . . screw up the whole thing. So that is one metric that we think is very, very important."

Passenger boarding and aircraft taxi times are also tracked, as are mishandled baggage, complaints, and the length of check-in lines. As JetBlue executives like to say, it's not sexy, but people will manage that metric if they're held accountable for it. And they are. Under JetBlue's TLC, or The Leadership Connection program, each officer of the company "owns" a city the airline serves. They make a minimum of four full-day visits each year to their operations base at their adopted city, keeping crewmembers up-to-date on what the company is doing, and meeting with airport management, control tower personnel, emergency services teams, and others. Actionable reports are created and each city owner is responsible for addressing any and all issues raised during these visits.

The single-aircraft structure JetBlue adopted has, among other things, helped it to control costs, as the same strategy did for Southwest and Morris Air. That made it all the more surprising when, in June 2003, Neeleman once more went against expectations and announced the company had placed an order for 100 Embraer 190 aircraft—a medium-range, 100-seat jet—with an option to buy 100 more. The $3 billion deal for 100 of the Brazilian-made aircraft represented another homecoming of sorts for Neeleman. After all, Embraer's headquarters is located in the state of São Paulo, Neeleman's birthplace.

Industry analysts questioned whether the addition of the second aircraft type, which will begin delivery in 2005, would undermine the successful formula and simple operating model that made JetBlue a success. Neeleman's rationale: He was convinced there was a market for jet service in scores of smaller cities if it could be offered at a price point that the Embraer made possible. Previously these markets were served either by turboprop aircraft, or more recently by the 50-seat Canadair RJs, or regional jets. Neeleman calculates that the capacity of the Embraer, which he calls a "category-killer plane," makes it much more feasible to drop the price to a point where the elasticity of the marketplace will show a dramatic stretch. Moreover, there are no competing aircraft. Since Fokker Aircraft went bankrupt, no other manufacturer is building a plane in the 100-seat capacity range. And Neeleman has locked up most of Embraer's production capacity for the new jet with the purchase contract.

DOING WHATEVER IT TAKES

In August 2003, JetBlue's load factor reached 91.6 percent, thought to be the highest monthly figure ever posted by a national airline. But an event that same month showed the company's character more than any statistic could. Just after 4 P.M. on Thursday, August 14, a blackout swept across the northeastern United States and into Canada. Across the region, much of life came to a standstill. Virtually every airport from the Midwest to the Northeast was affected. Neeleman was determined the event wouldn't stop JetBlue. "We hate canceling flights," he said in damn-the-torpedoes fashion.

JetBlue had flown more than 20,000 consecutive flights without a single cancellation in the months leading up to this day. When the blackout occurred, other airlines promptly began canceling flights practically across the board, especially since many passengers couldn't even get to the airport. Air traffic controllers also faced technical problems, and other terminals faded to black as the power went out. But while some airlines decided to suspend operations, ride out the blackout in limbo, and strand hundreds of angry passengers, that wasn't JetBlue's approach.

Lights were rigged in Terminal 6 thanks to a backup generator, but without air conditioning, it became uncomfortably hot. Using auxiliary power, JetBlue crewmembers were still able to check in and board passengers. But doing so required the resources of everyone, from the top of the airline on down. Neeleman and other executives drove from JetBlue headquarters to

JFK to help out. Though takeoffs were delayed by air traffic control, the planes were air-conditioned and passengers could watch TV while they waited on the tarmac. Still, other complications arose. At one point the airline needed fuel for its aircraft, but couldn't get it from its usual supplier because the blackout disrupted operations. Unless they were able to find an alternate supply, several flights would have to be grounded. Neeleman went out patrolling the tarmac at JFK to see if he could find some spare jet fuel. Spying an airport supervisor's truck racing along the apron, he flagged it down.

"I need fuel for five airplanes," he told the supervisor.

"I'm not sure we have any," the driver answered.

"Let's go looking for it," Neeleman said, as he hopped into the cab.

The supervisor stared at him, as if his disapproving expression could drive Neeleman out of the truck.

"I can't really get out," Neeleman told him. "I've got planes. I've got people in the planes waiting to go."

Together they found enough fuel to feed JetBlue's waiting aircraft, which were subsequently able to depart. The last flight out left at four o'clock the next morning. JetBlue had cancelled just two flights that night. By contrast, most other carriers closed down operations altogether, stranding passengers for at least one day. JetBlue didn't come out completely unscathed, though. On the day after the blackout, 20 of JetBlue's 200 daily flights had to be cancelled. But because of the unusually high number of no-shows, no one wanting to get out was left stranded.

"I think the measure of a good company is how you handle adversity," Neeleman said, recalling that night. JetBlue had handled this major disaster almost without incident and kept its passengers happy in the process.

A BLOW TO JETBLUE'S IMAGE

JetBlue was indeed flying high. It had proved it could weather the challenge of hard economic times, and it dealt with unforeseen emergencies that crippled other carriers. But the golden image the airline had earned and cultivated was about to be tarnished. A travel writer interested in privacy issues, Edward Hasbrouck, discovered a presentation posted on the web by Torch Concepts, a company working under an Army contract to help improve security at military bases. The presentation contained information about JetBlue customers. The breach of customer privacy "was immediately apparent," Hasbrouck says. Alabama-based Torch Concepts matched this data against information from other databases in an effort to develop software that could identify high-risk individuals who posed a potential security threat. This was the kind of data mining Neeleman had proposed in the wake of 9/11. But sharing this data violated JetBlue's own privacy policy. Hasbrouck posted the information on his web site, reporting that JetBlue had shared the records of some 5 million passenger transactions—representing a vast majority of the airline's total ticket sales. *Wired* magazine picked up the story from Hasbrouck and on September 18, 2003, posted the story on its web site.

The Department of Homeland Security (DHS) and the Federal Trade Commission (FTC) both launched investigations. The DHS sought to determine whether government officials had violated privacy laws in helping to coordinate the project. The FTC was moved to action by a complaint from the Electronic Privacy Information Center, a Washington, D.C.-based advocacy group that urged federal action for violation of the company's own privacy rules. Two passenger groups, one in Utah and one in California, filed class action suits against the airline for invasion of privacy.

Some 1,500 customers complained to the company over the next week. The Army even began its own inquiry.

JetBlue took immediate action to head off what was building into a significant scandal. The story received prominent attention from the media and created a firestorm of condemnation, yet the image of honesty and integrity the airline cultivated made its fall from grace more inexcusable to many observers. "They peeled the banana, they threw the peel down, and then they slipped on it," says noted public relations expert Howard Rubenstein, of New York–based Rubenstein Associates, Inc.

Neeleman personally apologized to customers in two different e-mails, and also posted an apology on the company's web site. He said he had "no knowledge" of the affair, admitted it was a mistake, and said no further passenger information would be given out. He declared that, as far as the company was concerned, the matter was closed. No one at JetBlue was made to be the scapegoat and no one was fired. Said Neeleman, "All of us at JetBlue are very anxious to support our government's efforts to improve security." The airline also announced steps to examine its privacy policy and prevent future abuses, including the hiring of the accounting firm Deloitte & Touche to review internal practices.

Most commentators were of the opinion the company exercised extremely poor judgment for sharing the information, yet had done well in quickly dealing with the issue once it became known. Larry Smith, president of the Institute for Crisis Management, a public relations consultancy in Louisville, Kentucky, said, "It's our experience that a company can screw up once in a while. As long as they take responsibility for what they've done, the American people are pretty forgiving."

After the initial finger-pointing and recriminations from outside the company, the controversy cooled and JetBlue's business continued as usual. Neeleman insisted that the crisis had no impact on business, and any customer frustrations were short-lived. It was later discovered that JetBlue wasn't alone in sharing information. American, United, and Northwest Airlines also reportedly provided passenger records to either the FBI, government contractors, or both. For its part, JetBlue quickly accepted blame and tried to put the matter behind it. Nevertheless, questions about the privacy breach remained unanswered. Among them was why Neeleman seemed to feel that an attempt to help the government was enough justification for sharing passenger data in the first place. One cannot help but reflect on Neeleman's Mormon heritage and wonder if the patriotism, loyalty, tight-lipped conservatism, and respect for patriarchal authority its adherents are known for could have created an environment in which this action was viewed as acceptable. One is reminded of another airline CEO who, perhaps of less benign intent, hired many Mormons for these same qualities: Howard Hughes, the noted owner of TWA.

Despite this controversy, JetBlue was again voted Best Domestic Airline by *Condé Nast Traveler* readers in 2003. It was also named the best low-cost airline in the United States by *Business Traveler*, *Entrepreneur*, and *Skytrax* magazines. Other accolades it won in 2003 included Airline of the Year from *Airfinance Journal*, Editors' Choice award from *Travel Holiday*, Outstanding Inflight Entertainment from *Onboard Services*, and Best Budget Airline from the annual World Travel Awards.

Reflecting on the underpinnings of JetBlue's success, Neeleman recounts lessons that are applicable to any company. "We didn't know about 9/11 when we started. We didn't know about Gulf War Two when we started. We didn't know the kind of difficulties we would encounter," he explains. "But we knew we had a bunch of airlines that had predatory pasts that would essentially try and put us out of business. So it was very important for us to have three things: have the best product, have the lowest cost, and have the most money. I believed at that time, and I believe it even more today, that if you're going go through difficult times, you want to do it with the best product and the lowest cost.

"I don't care what business you're in. If you're in the dry cleaning business or if you're in the gas station business, if you have the best product and you're the lowest cost, you're going to do well, even in bad times."

CHAPTER 14

Preserving the Culture

Although he's CEO of the company and recognized by all, he's rarely seen without it in public. Whether in the office, at the airport, or in some far-off city preaching the gospel according to JetBlue, David Neeleman wears his employee ID badge in a plastic pouch around his neck, close to his heart. Perhaps that's because it contains so much of his identity. And it's not just because his picture and employee number are on the badge. The pouch also contains a printed list of the company's principles of leadership and five core values: safety, caring, integrity, fun, and passion. All JetBlue crewmembers carry these principles and values with them, in the pouch with their IDs, a reminder of the rules they should live by.

The principles of leadership and core values were developed, in part, to help assure that all crewmembers stay focused on the company's goals and remain true to its mission of bringing humanity back to air travel. Neeleman and his executive team developed these five core values before the first frontline crewmember was hired, as a means of developing a corporate culture that would provide a foundation for long-term success.

They were also designed to enable the organization to weather any storm or turbulence it encounters along the way.

At the top of the list is *safety*. Without safety, Neeleman says, there is no airline. This emphasis on safety can be seen in Jet-Blue's fleet of new planes, which incorporate the most sophisticated and proven technology, and which are exceedingly reliable because of their low time of operation. Furthermore, the hiring of the best possible pilots, along with the emphasis the company places on training for all crewmembers, further underscores Jet-Blue's commitment to this core value.

Caring is seen throughout the organization. It starts with the way the company watches over and supports its people. It is further emphasized in the spirit of cooperation the airline fosters among its employees, all of whom pitch in to help each other. It all translates into the way the company and its people care for their customers.

"I believe that our company has a heart and has a soul, and it wasn't because I put it there," Neeleman says. "It's countless acts of kindness that happen on a day-to-day basis that create this heart and soul. And I'm trying to set an example through principles of leadership and getting all the leaders properly trained and setting the bar, letting everybody know where the bar is for leadership . . . so that when I'm gone from JetBlue, that example will live on."

In the fall of 2003, and again in the winter of 2004, unusually severe weather brought heavy snows to the Northeast, interfering with both ground and air travel. JetBlue waived its policy on charging for changes in reservations, to help travelers who had difficulty getting to the airport for their scheduled flights. The airline would have been within its rights, and within common industry practices, in sticking to its policy. But that would have violated its values of caring.

Integrity isn't a quality one associates with an airline. Most carriers seem to operate from behind a curtain like the Wizard of Oz. But JetBlue demonstrates integrity in its policies, its openness, and in its commitment to doing the right thing for its people and its customers. That's one reason revelations about the sharing of private passenger data hit the airline so hard. Although he had good intentions, Neeleman realized the company's integrity was at stake, which is something he works very hard to protect.

Fun seems an odd quality, and it's one that's certainly alien to many airlines—especially the old-line carriers. Many face fractious strife between labor and management, and some are engulfed by economic calamity. A hostile work environment like that doesn't leave much room for fun. By contrast, JetBlue creates an atmosphere where people can look forward to coming to work, while enjoying both their jobs and being around their fellow crewmembers. This emphasis on fun and camaraderie even carries through to the names of the airline's planes, all of which contain the word "Blue." The planes are named by crewmembers. Those who come up with the winning names get a pair of free round-trip tickets to any destination of their choice—and not just those JetBlue serves. Sometimes they even get to fly on the new planes during their inaugural flights over from Europe.

The names of the airplanes themselves and the promotional rollouts that sometimes accompany them further underscore the spirit of fun that pervades the airline. For example, in conjunction with the release of an Elvis Presley compilation album, the company christened a new aircraft "Blue Suede Shoes."

Passion captures the almost evangelical fervor JetBlue's crewmembers bring to their roles, which they see more as a mission than a job. They're out to change air travel as we know it. Tackling a huge job like that requires lots of passion. This is underscored in the letters JetBlue gets all the time from customers expressing gratitude and astonishment for the extra lengths crewmembers go to in order to insure that customers have a pleasant flying experience.

If you want to work for JetBlue, you must demonstrate that you share these values. "At JetBlue, what happens to you counts 10 percent and how you react counts 90 percent," Neeleman says, noting that this applies beyond one's duties at the airport. "I truly believe that those people who can rise to the occasion—and can have the best attitudes—will always succeed in any environment."

By developing careful hiring policies designed to identify candidates who believe in and support these core values, JetBlue has been able to create a workforce that dazzles its customers. In return it has achieved results, in terms of performance and profitability, far beyond what the established airlines—or other start-ups— could accomplish. But as the company grows, it knows that merely having employees committed to the company's core values isn't enough to ensure success.

PRESERVING THE CULTURE

Maintaining the small-company corporate culture at JetBlue was relatively easy at first. Early hires were members of a vanguard, and the company was tiny enough that everyone knew their co-workers. But Neeleman and his team recognized the challenge they faced in trying to keep this family-like feeling as the enterprise grew. Having Neeleman and other top executives meet with pilots called in for interviews whenever possible, and trying to get them to orientation programs to personally meet new crewmembers, is one way of combating the creeping impersonalization necessitated by growth. Having accepted the company's core values, Neeleman tells new recruits that the recipe for success at the company is simple: "Show up to work on time sober, with a good attitude, go take care of each other first, and then go take care of the customers."

All along, he was convinced those simple rules—when applied aboard an aircraft, in the terminal, or out on the apron taking care of airplanes—would insure that JetBlue stayed on the right track. For a while they did. But unforeseen problems began to emerge as the workforce increased. The growing number of crewmembers made it impossible for officers who initially oversaw operations to have as much contact with their personnel. In response, they delegated more authority to newly minted supervisors pulled from among the ranks of crewmembers who appeared capable of overseeing the operation. Naturally, the company selected as supervisors senior crewmembers in the various departments who had shown the most diligence in applying the values and rules the company espoused. But they were put in charge of their peers without receiving any formal management training. No one in upper management noticed that anything was wrong with this structure until they looked over the results of the 2002 crewmember survey.

To be certain the company is observing its own teachings, JetBlue hires an outside firm, Market Matrix, to conduct an annual confidential survey of all crewmembers (administered online, of course). The 68-item questionnaire examines nine job-related categories, including pay, benefits, attitudes about the company, and working conditions. Employees are encouraged to write comments and suggestions, as well. Indicative of the level of crewmember involvement in the process, the company has received over 1,000 pages worth of single-spaced messages along with the survey results. Management uses the survey scores as a report card on its own effectiveness, assuring that executives, too, are accountable for their actions. The results of the 2002 survey surprised them.

"We found a lot of negative comments about the people who were in leadership in the company," Neeleman admits. Putting people in charge without preparing them for the special demands of supervision was having unintended consequences, Neeleman came to realize. "If you do that absent any kind of training or experience for what it takes to be a great leader, you tend to become dictatorial and you tend to be rule oriented and inflexible," Neeleman says of those who are thrust into the position of "boss" with little or no preparation.

Neeleman and his team recognized they needed to develop an internal management training program, one that would instruct crewmembers in the art of being a "servant leader"—one who supports rather than criticizes, and one whose goal is to help people grow. At the same time, supervisors needed to know how to coach and counsel those who didn't respond to mentoring, while being able to identify the 10 percent of new hires who didn't fit in with the organization and should be let go. JetBlue expeditiously developed a management training program within JetBlue University. The University is overseen by Mike Barger, the former Top Gun instructor who is also a pilot for the airline and brother of company president and chief operating officer Dave Barger.

"Probably the most important thing that we're going to do to become bigger and better is that we have put about 800 of our leaders through a program called Principles of Leadership," Neeleman says. "It's very important that we bake into the DNA of every single one of our leaders the JetBlue way of doing business, and that we all are singing from the same hymn, singing from the same page, that we're all doing things exactly the same. They either lead the way we ask them to lead, and the way we think is the right way, or we ask them to find another job."

There are two-day, three-day, and five-day management courses for teaching crewmembers how to best make the transition to more senior roles. Like the company's core values, the principles of leadership themselves are simple, yet all encompassing. They are also five in number: Do the right thing. Communicate with your team. Inspire initiative. Inspire innovation. Inspire greatness. There are subsets to these principles as well, such as "Live the golden rule," "Be visible," "Be sociable with your crewmembers," and "Be humble."

The company teaches these leadership principles to all crewmembers, explaining that they define how leaders are supposed to act. Each manager is asked to review the principles before every workday begins. If subordinate workers feel a leader is not living up to these principles, they are encouraged to ask supervisors how the conduct in question complies with the principles, thereby providing for accountability. And there are defined procedures for moving the conversation up the chain of command until all involved feel the issue has been resolved.

"They know that they are being held accountable to those principles that they have around their necks," Neeleman says. In theory, this translates into a cohesive crew dedicated to putting humanity back into air travel. "I really believe that if somebody wakes up in the morning and they say, 'Yeah, I like to go to work, I like my job, I respect the people I work with, I like my leader, I respect my CEO,' then that has an effect on the customers."

But no matter how nurturing, how positive a work environment, not all will respond well to it. Neeleman is adamant about the need to recognize this and do something about it. "Work really hard to hire the right people, train them really, really well, pay them really, really well, give them the best tools to work with. And then if it's not working out, make sure that you get rid of them, because the foundation of JetBlue is our people," Neeleman advises.

"Even world-class companies, when they make decisions on

hiring, do a great job 90 percent of the time. That means you've got 10 percent that you either have to try to rehabilitate, or try and change their behavior, or you've got to get rid of them," Neeleman says. "It's very, very important that when you determine that somebody isn't tuned in to the JetBlue way of doing business, that they don't really like people, that they just kind of faked it in the interview, you just have to have them go find another job."

"You have to be accountable every single time," Neeleman adds of the demands of leadership. "And it's a lot of hard work. It's so much work, listening to people, fixing problems, and making it right with people. It's very, very difficult. But it's essential to the success of the business. And I don't care what business you're in. It's essential."

W here do these values and leadership traits come from? Neeleman often maintains that a fish stinks from the head. His efforts to set an example are meant to create an organization that has the scent of a winner from the top down. Anyone looking for the source of JetBlue's character, therefore, must start with Neeleman.

Neeleman says the strong Mormon faith he was born into forms the bedrock of his values. He refers to his two years as a missionary in the *favelas* of Rio de Janiero, performed in the service of his faith, as "essential" to building and forming his character. The experience directly influenced his leadership philosophy, which is seen today in his willingness to pitch in and help with any job that needs doing.

"This class distinction thing drives me crazy, and it has ever since I was a missionary in Brazil," Neeleman says. "I was put in the most humble of circumstances for two years in my life. I was with people that were in abject poverty but were totally happy. And they would give you anything that they had. I learned to love those people more than anything in this world. Now as a CEO, as I'm running JetBlue, and I see someone who's out on the ramp loading heavy bags and sweating and working their tail off, I'm incapable of treating that person any less important than our president of the company."

HELPING YOUR FELLOW EMPLOYEES

The values that emanate from the top are evident in the pay package Neeleman negotiated for himself when the company was being established. He kept about 8 percent of the company's stock to distribute to company officers, so they'd have the piece of the rock he's long believed all employees are entitled to. Once this was set, the airline's board asked Neeleman what he wanted in terms of his own personal stock options.

"I said, 'Are you kidding me? Why would I need stock options? I already own like 12 percent of the company. Why would I need stock options?' And they said, 'Well it's kind of traditional.' I said, 'Well I don't need stock options because if this thing goes public, I'll have all the money I'll ever need. In fact I already have all the money I'll need. I don't need any more.' I knew that if I was offered 200,000 stock options, and if I took them, there would be less for other people," Neeleman insists.

Then the subject of salary came up.

"I said, 'I'll just take an officer's salary, whatever the officers get.'"

That salary was $200,000, far below typical CEO pay, but it was fine with Neeleman. Then, he said something surprising. "I really don't need the money," he told the compensation specialists, "so why don't we create a crisis fund for our crewmembers that they can donate [to] and I'll match it dollar for dollar? I'll match $200,000 a year into the crisis fund so we can raise $400,000 a year to help our crewmembers with their needs."

The JetBlue Crewmember Catastrophic Plan now helps employees in need of special assistance. The tax-free corporation is run by employees, who serve on its board and decide how to spend the money. Both Neeleman and company president Dave Barger donate their entire $200,000 salaries to the plan. Other workers contribute what they can afford.

"There are so many things that come up in our lives of a catastrophic nature that maybe isn't covered by our health insurance or by any kind of insurance," Neeleman points out, in describing the plan's purpose.

For example, one crewmember's wife had cancer. That employee had to keep working to support his family. The plan provided the employee with money to have someone come take care of his children and make life a bit easier at home. Another crewmember lost her house to a fire. She had no insurance to cover all the personal effects she lost. The JetBlue Crewmember Catastrophic Plan stepped in and paid for everything to be replaced in her house.

"We've been blessed," Neeleman says in deflecting praise for his contributions. "We [company executives] have done well with the growth of the company and don't need the money, but it sends a great example to our people—that we're here to help them help themselves by matching funds so they can help their fellow crewmembers."

One unwritten value that also comes through at JetBlue is *believe in yourself*—don't be immobilized by what others think or by the doubting of experts. That can be seen in the lesson of a businessman Neeleman is fond of invoking: Sam Walton.

In 1962, Walton opened his first store in Rogers, Arkansas. It was big and he was highly leveraged. "He borrowed a bunch of money to open this one big store," Neeleman observes. "The folks in Troy, Michigan, at Kmart had been around for 45 years and they laughed. 'That was the stupidest thing in the world, to put a big store in a little, teeny town' [they thought]. 'Why would anyone do that?' All the Kmart guys, the ones that were invincible and unstoppable, had to do was to go open a store in that little town in Arkansas and they would have put him out of business just like that." That's not the way things happened. In 2003, after filing for bankruptcy, the value of Kmart's original stock was completely erased and it was delisted from the New York Stock Exchange. Wal-Mart, by contrast, had become the largest retail organization on the planet. It all started from a single idea: Merchandise your product bigger, better, and cheaper than the competition. "Sam Walton was a brilliant merchandiser," Neeleman says. "He put little blue vests on everybody with the big sign across the back that says, 'How can I help you?' People who went to Wal-Mart got what they wanted to get, they got it for a fair price, and they had friendly people that would care about you. It was a very simple formula . . . but it's hard to do it every day. It's hard to make it happen." Like Wal-Mart, JetBlue keeps trying all the time.

In speaking about the importance of having strong values, Neeleman offered the following advice while delivering a commencement address for graduate school students: "My first lesson is that there is no correlation between wealth and happiness. My second lesson is that the only way of achieving joy and happiness in life is serving other people."

These are values Neeleman has demonstrated in his own life, first during his time as a missionary, and more recently when he decided to found JetBlue. In 1998 Neeleman needed support for his idea, not just from investors and managers, but from his family. "We were very comfortable, and we had everything that we needed in life, and we had nine children that we were raising, and [I said to my wife], 'Honey, I would really like to move to the East Coast and start an airline.' She said, 'Are you insane?' And I said, 'No. We could really make a difference in a lot of people's lives. We can really make a huge difference.'" Put that way, Neeleman's wife, Vicki, couldn't refuse. But the rest of the brood weren't so easily convinced. His oldest daughter, a senior in high school, was dead set against the move. "She didn't want anything to do with New York City," he says. Now she's enrolled at New York's Fashion Institute and thinks the Big Apple is "the greatest city in the world," Neeleman says.

Neeleman believes the ultimate litmus test of whether one's business—and life—is serving others is by asking the following question: "Do you matter?" To Neeleman, this is the ultimate measure of the value of a business, or a person. "If people were to wake up tomorrow morning and your business was sucked from the face of the earth, would your customers care or would they just say, 'Oh, there's a place I can buy stuff just down the street. There was nothing special about that particular business.' When your employees came to work, would they say, 'Oh, it's just a job, nothing special about that job, I'll go find another job.' Because if you don't matter, if your company doesn't matter, then you're not going to be a success over the long term," Neeleman maintains.

This serial entrepreneur feels it's useful for one to continually reassess whether they matter to themselves, to the people around them, and to co-workers. "Do you matter? Are you a great leader? Are you inspiring greatness in other people? Are you making a difference in people's lives?" he asks. "I think that's the secret to happiness. That's my own personal opinion—that joy and happiness comes from helping others and from mattering and making a difference. I think that's what I'm trying to do and that's what we're trying to do at JetBlue."

CHAPTER 15

Looking to the Future

On April 15, 2003, passengers boarded a sold-out flight to West Palm Beach, Florida, from a stunningly refurbished terminal at New York's John F. Kennedy Airport. Many checked in using self-service electronic kiosks and were greeted by personnel telling jokes and trying to make the travel experience fun. On board, passengers sat in leather seats throughout the all-coach cabin. While it hadn't been installed on this particular aircraft yet, they were told that before long, the plane would have a state-of-the-art in-flight entertainment system, including live television at every seat.

By all accounts, this sounds like just another JetBlue flight, right? In reality, it was the inaugural journey for Song, the low-fare carrier spawned by Delta Airlines in direct response to competition from JetBlue.

In creating Song, Delta copied just about everything JetBlue was doing right, and then tried to go one step further. It first chose to use all one aircraft type, in this case Boeing 757s. While it didn't buy brand-new planes, it completely gutted existing aircraft and redid everything from the inside out to make them look factory fresh. The 199-seat all-coach planes were fitted with leather seats from the cockpit to the tail. Outside, the clean white jets were painted with flourishes of lime green and the stylish but simple-looking Song logo. The pricing structure was simple, with no one-way fare selling for more than $299. Reservations could be made through a clean-looking and easy-to-navigate web site. Meal service was sparse, consisting of free beverages with other snacks available for purchase. And, unlike parent company Delta, Song's planes would be run with a leaner staff, both at the airport and in the skies, with everyone pitching in to help control costs.

When Song president John Selvaggio unveiled plans for the new airline, it was reminiscent of the speech Neeleman gave when talking about JetBlue for the first time. "Song is introducing fun, entertainment, and choice to the air travel experience," Selvaggio said. "Our goal is to make the Song experience enjoyable on every level, from making reservations to checking in and waiting at the gate area, and especially while on board."

Song even opted to go head-to-head with JetBlue's route structure, starting off with service from JFK to West Palm Beach, and eventually adding flights to Fort Lauderdale, Las Vegas, Boston, Washington, D.C., Fort Myers, Tampa, and Orlando—all of which JetBlue either served or hinted it planned to serve in the near future.

"Here's someone who wants to take our lunch box," Neeleman said of Delta and its proxy competitor. "But we know the secret isn't in the technology, it's in the people we have. We're going to go and kick their butts."

In a display of competitive defiance, Neeleman announced that JetBlue planned to start flying to Hartsfield International Airport in Delta's hometown of Atlanta. In honor of this event, he christened JetBlue's 39th A320 aircraft with a bottle of Coca-Cola, Atlanta's homegrown beverage, at Hartsfield, naming the aircraft

"Song Sung Blue." Further thumbing its nose at Delta, JetBlue hired a local pop group to perform at the rollout, thus, in the airline's words, launching service to Atlanta "with a song."

Despite the competition from Song, and word from United that it planned to start a low-fare subsidiary of its own called Ted, JetBlue began its fourth year of operations in good form. Economic performance for all of 2003 was once again stellar. The company just missed, by $1.6 million, becoming a billion-dollar business in its third full year of operation, a distinction no other airline or private business has come close to achieving. Had it not been for a series of early winter storms that lashed the Northeast and affected operations, JetBlue would have undoubtedly hit that magic number, qualifying it in the DOT's taxonomy as a "major" carrier. As it was, the $998.4 million in reported operating revenues represented a better than 57 percent increase over the previous year's figures.

As the calendar turned to 2004, JetBlue had 55 aircraft and was operating 220 flights each day. Fourteen more planes were scheduled to join the fleet by the end of the year. The company now hires about 2,000 new crewmembers annually, and new destinations continue to be added to its route system. Boston was added in early January, concluding a long battle the airline had waged to gain access to Logan Airport.

By any measure, JetBlue has been a resounding success, and Neeleman's vision and patience over the years have been amply rewarded. Up to this point, the story of Neeleman's career and the building of JetBlue has been of one great accomplishment after another. He has done many things right and managed to prosper in what famed investor Warren Buffett has called "about the toughest business" there ever was. "If you go back to the time of Kitty Hawk, net, the airline transport business in the United States has made no money," Buffett observes. "Despite putting billions and billions and billions of dollars, the net return to owners from being in the entire airline industry, if you owned it all, and if you put up all this money, is less than zero." Buffett has even quipped that the first flight by the Wright brothers was "one small step for mankind, and one huge step backwards for capitalism."

Neeleman has been able to defy the odds with not one but three different airlines: Morris Air, WestJet, and now JetBlue. But as JetBlue heads for its fifth anniversary, Neeleman and his team will continue to face a number of challenges as they try to sustain their winning formula. One thing's for sure: The battle for the hearts and wallets of air travelers will be a fierce one, with JetBlue no doubt taking the brunt of the bullets being fired by the major carriers.

Perhaps the first visible smudge on the company's good fortune, which proved it wasn't infallible and would have to face some real tests as it grew into new frontiers, came in October 2003. That's when JetBlue decided to pull out of Atlanta, six months after commencing service there. JetBlue entered the market with great fanfare. Its flights to Long Beach were the first nonstops to the West Coast from Atlanta offered by a low-cost carrier. But both hometown giant Delta and discounter AirTran Airways already had a strong presence in Atlanta. They pulled out all the stops to defend their prized territory. In a display of the power a major airline can unleash, Delta matched JetBlue's low fares on competing routes, awarded triple miles to members of its frequent flyer program, and added more flights on bigger planes, doubling its capacity at the three Los Angeles-area airports it serves.

The much smaller but just as competitive AirTran also offered low-fare flights of its own, and enjoyed the added advantage of being able to feed in passengers from its other flights going into Hartsfield International.

The gritty competition ultimately saw JetBlue cut its three original flights a day from Atlanta to the West Coast down to one by September. At the same time, AirTran added flights from Atlanta to Las Vegas and Denver, and announced it was ordering longer-range jets to beef up its service to the West. In Atlanta, at least, JetBlue wasn't the 300-pound gorilla it was in most of the other markets it entered.

Neeleman positioned the airline's decision to leave Atlanta as "a kind of a war between AirTran and Delta." Did the withdrawal from Atlanta represent a retreat or defeat? "We certainly, with our cost structure, could have stayed in there for a long time just to . . . prove a point, but we're not into proving points," Neeleman insisted. "We're just into making money." The previous quarter JetBlue made $29 million, compared to a loss of $164 million for Delta, the parent of Song. But in this market, that didn't matter.

There was one huge winner in JetBlue's fierce battle in Atlanta: local passengers. The low fares that came along with the competition have persisted beyond JetBlue's departure, at least so far.

CONFRONTING THE CHALLENGES

In JetBlue, Neeleman created a real rarity—a company of both style and substance. Here again some of the major airlines are copying his lead, starting with Delta's Song. Delta hired the hip fashion designer Kate Spade to develop the airline's look. Her husband, Andy, was charged with creating the subsidiary's human vibe, including scripting the patter its flight attendants deliver to passengers in-flight. In addition to United's new Ted airline, there are plenty of other upstarts that are now also trying to fly in the JetBlue pattern, including one in the works by Neeleman's former potential partner, Richard Branson.

In public, Neeleman puts a happy spin on the impact JetBlue has had on the marketplace when talking about how competitors are trying to emulate all that he's accomplished. "I applaud Delta for doing something," he says. He further contends he's not worried about the competition, largely because he believes they're coming out of the starting gate with a significant disadvantage. "The big guys are 0-for-5 with the low-cost airline concept," he offers. Moreover, Neeleman sees the act of creating a low-fare spin-off as detrimental to employee morale. "Launching a discount service also sends a mixed message to your people: 'Fly for this airline because it's better than the one you're working for.' How does that motivate people?"

Without question, the major carriers have failed at such endeavors in the past. Continental Airlines tried Cal Lite, United ran Shuttle By United, US Airways operated MetroJet, and Delta even had the now discarded Delta Express. American Airlines, despite its enormous muscle, has yet to launch a low-fare subsidiary, though it has been a fierce competitor nonetheless. American initially tried to defend its dominance at California's Oakland airport by launching low-priced nonstop service to JFK once JetBlue announced it was coming to town. But JetBlue proved a fiercer-than-expected rival. American ultimately ceded defeat and dropped the flights. Instead, American began capping transcontinental one-way fares to markets JetBlue serves at $299, while offering bonus miles on certain routes. In early 2004, to combat competition on prized routes it shares with JetBlue from Boston and New York to California and Florida, American responded with a "fly two, get one free" promotion. Passengers who took two flights on those routes over a three-and-a-half-month period got one free ticket to anywhere American flies around the world. United and Delta eventually matched the promotion. Song, which tried to look a lot like JetBlue, had something its smaller rival didn't: the global route structure and frequent flyer program of its parent, Delta Airlines. A free trip anywhere Song/Delta flies is much more valuable than one offered by JetBlue.

While Neeleman insists that, "From day one, we've had fare competition," he admits that 2004 is "a very competitive year," as will be the years to come. During the airline's first quarter of the year, Neeleman conceded that the promotions and cheap fares offered by rivals sliced three percentage points off JetBlue's profit margins. "It could have a bigger impact" in the future, Neeleman admits. At the same time, in a reverse of roles from JetBlue's attempt at breaking into Atlanta, Delta announced a major expansion at JFK in early 2004, saying it would add flights to San Diego, Denver, San Juan, Puerto Rico, and other cities from JetBlue's base.

The domestic airline industry as a whole remains battered. In the wake of 9/11, the federal government has provided $10 billion in grants and loan guarantees in the name of relief from the attacks of that day. But the problems some carriers face predate and run deeper than the damage caused by the terrorist acts alone. Questions continue to linger: Should the government step in to aid the troubled carriers? Should the free market dictate their fate? Will the JetBlue model replace the one established long ago by the legacy carriers? The commercial aviation industry is a major part of the national economy. It accounts for 8 percent of the U.S. gross domestic product. Therefore, the government doesn't want any of the large carriers to fail and is likely to do what's necessary to keep them in business. As a result, any low-fare airline—including JetBlue—that thinks it can topple the majors like a beaver brings down a tree must face the reality that it's simply not that easy.

One area JetBlue has managed to conquer that other low-fare carriers have not is the corporate travel market. Corporate travel managers, long hostile to the big airlines that held them hostage to high prices, are increasingly looking to JetBlue as a way of reducing travel costs. Because JetBlue uses its own reservations system, which is not networked into corporate travel departments the way other airlines are through the CRS networks, travel managers previously ignored JetBlue. The airline was essentially invisible to them. But with recognition of the savings JetBlue represents, corporate travel department practices have been changing. IBM, for example, instituted a policy whereby employees are to use standard booking channels to make airline reservations, unless they are traveling on JetBlue, in which case they can charge tickets on their American Express cards and simply seek reimbursement from the company.

Again, however, on routes where the majors have matched Jet-Blue's fares—and even offer additional travel incentives—corporate travelers will likely think twice before turning to JetBlue. Those who travel a lot often enjoy elite status in the frequent flyer programs maintained by the larger carriers. Many of those programs now offer such perks as free first class upgrades and bonus miles to elite members, giving travelers yet another incentive to avoid JetBlue, which has an all-coach cabin and a much more simplified and limited frequent flyer program.

The addition of Embraer 190 regional jets introduces new opportunities and risks to JetBlue's successful single-aircraft-type business model. After listening to Neeleman and John Owen explain the decision to go in this direction during a conference call to industry analysts, Robert Mann of New York–based R.W. Mann & Co., a respected member of the investment community, described the move, which he said he found surprising, as "brilliant, but not riskless."

The risks come in part from the unpredictability of this largely untried segment of the market. Commercial carriers have, at most, only dipped their toes into these waters, and have no idea how deep or shallow they are. In projecting potential traffic and determining whether establishing service to a particular destination is worthwhile, "airlines use historical data," Mann notes, "and if it's dismal data, because [previous] pricing has been so unattractive, they tend to go on to the next thing."

JetBlue will be the first airline to deploy the 100-seat jet, although it is a stretch version of the Embraer 170, which US Airways put into service in 2004. JetBlue hopes any bugs in the aircraft will be worked out through the US Airways experience before its first Embraer is delivered. Like JetBlue's Airbus fleet, the Embraer 190 features integrated avionics and fly-by-wire flight controls. In the cabin, all seats will have LiveTV.

How JetBlue will fare in the smaller markets it plans to serve with the Embraer aircraft is unknown. With smaller passenger loads, the relative costs of serving these markets are higher. Currently, passengers in many of these cities are forced to fly on either turboprop planes or regional jets and usually pay premium prices, reflecting the higher costs of offering the service. They rarely have access to competing carriers. JetBlue's entry could end the tyranny of these high fares. But if the strategy is successful, other airlines will no doubt try to replicate JetBlue's formula. Given the number of markets that could conceivably support such service, if it proves economical, a whole new era of airline service and opportunities could develop.

JetBlue has effectively blocked others from following its lead with the Embraer aircraft for at least the next few years. There is no manufacturer currently building a comparable plane, and

JetBlue will absorb most of Embraer's production capacity during the length of its delivery contract, which runs into 2011. At that time, it has the option to buy another 100 of the 190s. But who is to say whether other carriers will decide to put either larger planes or smaller regional jets to work to avoid ceding these markets to JetBlue?

The live seat-back satellite television service introduced on JetBlue raised the bar for onboard entertainment. But the industry wasn't about to let JetBlue have this field to itself. Discount carrier Frontier airlines has installed LiveTV and WestJet is putting the service in its 737s. (Fortunately, since JetBlue owns LiveTV, it will make money from these moves.) Song, meanwhile, is also offering onboard live television, though the service is being provided by a competitor to JetBlue's LiveTV division. Established carriers trying to compete on the entertainment front with their existing planes will face huge challenges, which works to JetBlue's advantage. Retrofitting aircraft with TV and other entertainment systems is costly and difficult. New entrants offering competing systems face the daunting challenge of developing and getting a system approved for installation, along with the technical challenges of having it operate consistently and reliably. JetBlue itself has further upped the ante for in-flight entertainment by introducing up to 100 channels of digital satellite radio through an agreement with XM Satellite Radio, and movie channels featuring 20th Century Fox movies and Fox TV programming. The service will be featured on the Embraer aircraft as well as JetBlue's A320 fleet.

The major carriers also have JetBlue to thank for changing the face of in-flight meal service. JetBlue made it hip to serve nothing but beverages and small snacks. Most every other airline has followed suit, stripping down meal service to little more than pretzels, peanuts, or stale sandwiches. If passengers want more, they pay for it. Or they can bring their own meals aboard, which many seem happy to do.

Then there's the issue of expansion. Neeleman says he'd like to increase JetBlue's routes into such places as Canada, Mexico, and the Caribbean. He has no interest in flying to Europe, the Far East, or other far-flung destinations. International travel is complex, the competition is stiffer, and some foreign carriers get government subsidies that give them an unfair advantage, he notes. It also requires larger aircraft than JetBlue operates to go overseas. As part of its strategy, JetBlue hopes to continue gaining market share in existing markets rather than by adding a lot more destinations. But that may become more difficult as competitors continue to bring out the heavy artillery.

Another strategy the company will not pursue, though it has the financial clout, is growth by acquisition. Besides the clash of cultures that would result, Neeleman remembers the lessons learned from People Express, which went on a buying binge and wound up going broke. Neeleman is happy growing the company plane by plane. While the airline's cost per available seat mile is around 6.4 cents, about a penny less than Southwest, Neeleman admits that maintenance expenses are at an all-time low now, thanks to the aircraft being new. He estimates costs will rise 0.3 to 0.4 cents per available seat mile as the fleet gets older, due to higher maintenance requirements. Still, the company's financial projections show that savings on others' costs, as the fleet gets larger, will offset at least some of these expenses. Administrative costs, airport operations, even advertising will offer economies of scale as the airline grows.

A jump in fuel prices could also hurt the airline, though that would affect its competitors as well. To minimize this risk,

JetBlue hedges about 50 percent of its fuel purchases. In other words, it has contracts it can exercise to buy fuel at preset prices in the future. The fuel efficiency of JetBlue's fleet also gives it an advantage in the fuel cost factor category.

JetBlue's competition going forward will come not from its past operating history, but rather from other low-cost carriers that have learned from its example and can exploit opportunities in markets JetBlue hasn't been able to reach because of its limited size and focus. Additionally, network carriers are expected to regain their financial footing by 2005–2006, at which time they will be in a more competitive position as far as the balance sheet is concerned. Once the majors are back on track, JetBlue will have a more difficult time competing head-to-head with them, as its experience in Atlanta demonstrates. Therefore, it must continue to identify and exploit areas of opportunity that have not yet been spotted by the competition (such as those created by its acquisition of the 100-seat Embraers).

Despite the cautious concern expressed by some experts, others remain bullish about JetBlue's future.

"For a long time there was a belief in the industry that 'Oh, it's all smoke and mirrors, it's all bullshit, just good PR spin,'" says airline analyst Stuart Klaskin of KKC Aviation Consulting in Miami. "Because nobody really took them [JetBlue] seriously at the outset, it gave them all this room to develop consumer traction. Now, they have trained the consumer [to know] you get a good deal on JetBlue . . . and always an extraordinary consumer experience. In today's environment, [consumers want] a fairly high level of customer service and consumer value in addition to the fare. One of the problems [is] the other carriers can't deliver that. Their systems are not optimized to deliver that." And if they can't compete with JetBlue on service, that leaves only price. Here, too, Klaskin believes, competitors are boxed into a corner due to JetBlue's lower operating costs. "It is a terrible, terrible mistake to think that you can get down in the mud in terms of low fare pricing against JetBlue and stay there very long," he says.

Still, the privacy issue is one JetBlue and the rest of the industry have not heard the last of. The Transportation Security Administration (TSA) and the FTC have yet to publish the findings of their investigation into JetBlue's passenger file sharing matter. A request from Congress to the Army to explain how the data was collected and exactly how it was to be used had not even received a response several months after it was sent. The fact that at least one other airline, Northwest, also provided passenger data to the government may help mitigate the harsh glare of attention focused on JetBlue for violating its own policy and possibly breaking the law. But other pressures will keep this issue before the public, most notably the lack of agreement between European and U.S. officials over the use of this data. European Union laws are much more protective of passenger data than are U.S. regulations. The United States demands passenger information from foreign carriers in order to screen for individuals thought to be a security risk. But it is against the law in Europe to provide all the data U.S. security officials seek. As international privacy policies are aligned, it will bring more attention to the issue in the United States.

BUILDING FOR THE FUTURE

JetBlue is in the midst of expanding its facilities at JFK. It is constructing a brand-new terminal with about 26 gates, capable of handling 250 departures a day. The company foresees more service to the mid-Atlantic states, as well as the Midwest and possibly the Caribbean. But, Neeleman cautions, it's not going to happen anytime soon. In a surprising move, the airline recently asked for slots at LaGuardia, the airport it once criticized as being too congested to operate effectively in.

Whatever success the airline enjoys in the future, Neeleman knows it will be hard-earned. While things have gone well thus far, he's learned that resting on one's laurels can lead to disaster.

"Don't think for a second that we're euphoric, that we think that we have figured this all out," Neeleman says. "We're just trying our hardest every day. I remember I read one time that someone had come up with eight steps of a development of a business, and I can't remember one through six—all I remember was number seven was euphoria and number eight was devastation. So we're not euphoric. We're humbled by the fact that we're in a very difficult business."

Also difficult is maintaining the welcoming culture that especially the legacy carriers will have a hard time duplicating. Then there's the matter of whether customers will continue to be impressed as other airlines begin to emulate the unique JetBlue experience. "People ask me all the time, 'What keeps you up at night? What is it that makes you worry?'" Neeleman shares. "And I only have one concern for JetBlue: How can we continue to inspire and motivate our people, and let them know what a tremendous impact they're having on our customers? I worry a lot about that. How do we do that? How can you keep the culture going? How can you continue to dazzle and excite your customers?"

Beyond the customers and crewmembers, the company has another constituency it must continue to serve well: its shareholders. JetBlue stock, once one of the darlings of Wall Street, has taken some lumps, losing half its value from October 2003 to January 2004. While JetBlue shares still trade much higher than their IPO offering price as this book goes to press, investors have reason to worry. JetBlue's retreat from Atlanta proved that with enough pressure, JetBlue could be forced to give in. New competition has also put a dent in the airline's operating margins and is starting to cut into revenues. The impact is slight, but investors were getting used to one glowing report after another. "This is still a company delivering a great product at a low price," says Lehman Brothers analyst Gary Chase. "They're facing more competition than they have in the past, but that doesn't materially alter their prospects as a company. It might alter the prospects for the stock."

That last point is critical. While JetBlue's stock price might be considerably more volatile going forward, that doesn't mean the company itself has lost its magic touch. Wall Street is pretty fickle by nature, falling in and out of love with stocks. That's one reason Neeleman insists he doesn't pay much attention to how much shares are trading for in the open market.

"Herb Kelleher at Southwest Airlines said something very insightful," Neeleman relates. "At the time it sounded shocking. He said, 'I don't care about my shareholders.' 'What do you mean you don't care about shareholders?' 'Because I just take care of my employees. I know if I take care of my employees, they'll take care of my customers, and my customers will take care of my shareholders.' So don't get it backwards. Don't focus so much on the bottom line that you spoil the broth, that you spoil the business. You have to build the business first, intrinsically make it important to your customers and to your crewmembers." That, Neeleman reasons, will lead to a higher stock price over the long haul.

Of course, Neeleman's legacy extends beyond JetBlue. WestJet, which he co-founded, continues to thrive. It arguably forced Air Canada into bankruptcy. In light of competition from WestJet, Air Canada altered its strategy by moving away from domestic routes and redeploying its assets to transborder and international flights.

Open Skies, the electronic reservations system Neeleman pioneered with David Evans, now powers the stand-alone computerized reservations systems of a growing number of airlines. In addition to JetBlue, Open Skies is used by AirTran, Frontier, WestJet, and RyanAir (the famed discount carrier in Europe), to name a few.

Neeleman has been involved in one successful venture after another. Each time, he's been faced with challenges similar to those being leveled at him now. He's managed to get through the tough times before, and few doubt he will be able to do so again.

It's important to remember that Neeleman is all of 44 years old. Quite possibly his restless spirit will take him—and JetBlue—in many new directions in the years to come. In fact, when first approached about this book project, Neeleman insisted that it was too early to tell the JetBlue story. Whether or not that's true, Neeleman's own story is quite rich indeed.

What areas might he try to conquer next? Neeleman has commented that one of the most exciting innovations he's seen in aviation is the development of small jets aimed at the personal owner market. Companies like Eclipse and Adam Aircraft are designing such jets with prices projected to be under $1 million. If Neeleman pursues his interest in this area further, perhaps one day he will have an airline called Taxi after all, with a fleet of hundreds or thousands of these aircraft taking people all over the country.

To be sure, many folks, including Uncle Sam, are interested in what Neeleman has to say. He was recently appointed to the FAA's Management Advisory Council by Secretary of Transportation Norman Mineta. It's certain the man who Southwest Airlines couldn't get to shut up will increasingly be asked to speak up.

What, Neeleman has been asked, will JetBlue look like 5 or 10 years down the road? "I would hope that doing business with us will be easier, that we would be better than we are today but a whole lot bigger," he says. "In 2011 we'll have 290 airplanes and I would assume that by the time we have 290 airplanes, we'll probably be in 50 or 60 different cities. Where we have 6,000 crewmembers today, going forward we're going to have 30,000 crewmembers. How is it that [you] can grow from 6,000 to 30,000 and be able to have the same culture? How do you become bigger and how do you become better as you become bigger? That is the question that we're wrestling with at JetBlue, and I think it's something that we focus on a lot. I believe we're going to be able to do it.

"My hope is that we can continue to have a thriving, prosperous company, that we're setting the standard in what we're doing in customer service, and that we'll continue to grow in the future."

CHAPTER 16

David Neeleman's Rules for Succeeding in Any Business

As you've no doubt gathered by now, David Neeleman has spent his life learning and practicing a set of rules by which he's built his many successes. Some he's developed on his own. Others have come through trial and error. Many have been learned from the smart people he has surrounded himself with over the years. Whatever the source, all have been evident in his many business ventures—including three successful airlines and a technology company. He applies them to his personal life as well.

Neeleman is now putting these rules to work at JetBlue. As he often points out, these principles don't just apply to the airline business. They are applicable to all industries and can benefit every businessperson. And while most may sound like common sense, it's amazing how few businesses actually live by them in their daily operations.

While Neeleman has clearly articulated several of these rules—and actively teaches them to his crewmembers and other eager students looking for his advice—others can be inferred through observing the deeds and strategies he has employed over the years. And though you've probably already culled many of these lessons while reading Neeleman's story, here, in a handy list form, are what I call "David Neeleman's Rules for Succeeding in Any Business."

RULE 1. FOLLOW YOUR PASSION

Growing up, Neeleman was haunted by the specter of future failure. A poor student who always fell behind his peers, he wondered how he'd ever find work, let alone be a success. That changed when he began to focus on something he loved: the travel business. Without that passion, he would have been lost. Indeed, his much-noted ADD prevents him from focusing on anything that he's not passionately interested in, and this goes all the way back to boyhood. Neeleman followed his passion when he left home to become a Mormon missionary in Brazil. And, while the odds were against him when he came up with the idea for JetBlue, he was passionate about his idea and followed it with all of his heart.

RULE 2. THINK OUTSIDE THE BOX

Much of Neeleman's success can be traced back to his creativity—his ability to think outside the box and his refusal to accept conventional wisdom. Those who have worked with him over the years still marvel when recalling how he is able to generate ideas nonstop—while admitting they aren't always good. This ability to see problems in new ways is critical to standing out and adapting in all walks of life. Far too many let their inner talents lie fallow, often because they don't have confidence in their ability to be creative. Neeleman believes in taking chances. He isn't afraid to fail, knowing that if an idea doesn't work out this time, it might the next time around.

RULE 3. WORK WITH AND LEARN FROM THE BEST

Leading by example has its corollary in "learning by following." Neeleman may have blazed many trails on his own, but he's discovered the value of emulating and gathering wisdom from the leaders in his chosen field. At Morris Air, he learned from June Morris, one of the country's most innovative travel agents at the time. Morris frequently had to temper Neeleman's wilder inclinations, though he was encouraged to be creative and take risks.

Early on, Neeleman made Southwest Airlines his model, and its chairman Herb Kelleher his hero. Neeleman sent Morris Air employees to Southwest to learn that carrier's operational methods. He then made those methods his own. Neeleman applied those lessons so well to his operation, Southwest wound up buying his company, largely because it was nearly identical to its own.

Neeleman further emphasized this principle when putting together JetBlue's executive management team. He recruited the best people he could find for each position. He also made hiring the highest-quality workforce—down to the lowest level—a top priority. When it came time to find investors, he went to the cream of the crop, including the legendary George Soros, who became the carrier's biggest underwriter. Neeleman has even stocked JetBlue's board of directors with savvy, independent-minded people who aren't afraid to contradict him.

Neeleman knows that great organizations require brilliant teams. After all, even a genius can come up with a lot of bad ideas.

Neeleman has always surrounded himself with teams he respects, can listen to, can bounce thoughts off of, and can learn from.

RULE 4. BE READY TO MOVE ON

Neeleman really didn't want to leave Southwest Airlines, but in retrospect he concedes the firing was a good thing—for him and for the airline. Since then he's exhibited a flexibility and willingness to get on with his life to great effect. For example, after helping to found WestJet in Canada, he left before the company went public. He was anxious to start the next chapter of his life, JetBlue. After turning Open Skies into a success, rather than holding on, he sold the company to Hewlett-Packard, pocketing a nice profit in the process. Even now at JetBlue, the company's willingness to reverse course, as demonstrated by its exit from Atlanta, shows that Neeleman is still able to gracefully accept failure, while not being tied down to imperfect assumptions, old ways of doing things, or complacency.

RULE 5. BUILD A BETTER MOUSETRAP

Neeleman has prospered over the years not just by doing things differently, but by doing them *better*. He calls it "building a better mousetrap." It might be a cliché, but to Neeleman it's a golden rule. JetBlue's better mousetrap consists of low fares combined with comfortable new airplanes, live in-flight entertainment, and great customer service. As Neeleman contends, anyone who can combine the best product with the lowest price, as JetBlue has, will be successful in any industry (just as Wal-Mart built a better mousetrap in the retailing business and triumphed over Kmart).

Don't be cowed by the size or strength of competitors, he urges. There's plenty of room for David versus Goliath triumphs. The major airlines are known for brutal combat. Traditionally they have eaten new start-ups for breakfast. Before taking them on, Neeleman carefully studied the big players. He knew their strengths and weaknesses, and decided to avoid the former while exploiting the latter. JetBlue's operations can be seen as almost a point-by-point answer to the deficiencies of his competitors. They showed a lack of caring for passengers, so he provided extremely good customer service. They flew beat-up old aircraft, so he acquired brand-new planes. They often weren't on time, so he operated from airports where delays were minimal. Throughout his career, Neeleman has never backed down. In building JetBlue, he did his homework, assembled all the necessary pieces, and didn't let fear of the competition deter him from pushing ahead.

RULE 6. BE WELL CAPITALIZED

Neeleman was on his way to making his first fortune while still in college. The travel agency he started grew to $6 million in annual revenues. But it all evaporated almost overnight for one reason: The airline he was dealing with went out of business, taking all of his money with it, and he wasn't sufficiently capitalized to continue on. He didn't have the cash cushion necessary to ride out this temporary storm. Since then, being well capitalized has been one of Neeleman's most important rules.

When Morris Air went from being a charter airline to a scheduled carrier, he had the Morris family put up more money than was needed. When he went to raise money for JetBlue, he followed the same rule. The $130 million he amassed made JetBlue the best-capitalized start-up airline in aviation history. Having this strong financial position has enabled the airline to comfortably do battle against the competition, while surviving—and thriving—in one of the toughest periods ever for aviation.

RULE 7. TAKE GOOD CARE OF YOUR PEOPLE

Neeleman repeatedly talks about how JetBlue's employees—crewmembers, as he calls them—are the primary reason for the company's incredible achievements. While downplaying his own role, he often cites the proper care of his people as JetBlue's number one priority. Whether a service business fails or succeeds is in the hands of its frontline people, Neeleman believes. These "moments of truth," which he ascribed to during his Morris Air days, occur when customers interact on a personal level with a company. These experiences have a profound effect on customers. Therefore, whether a plane is on time isn't as important as how a passenger feels he or she was treated during the flight. But if you don't have workers who believe they are being taken care of by you, they won't make an effort to take good care of your customers. If they're unhappy on the job, it's bound to show up in the service they provide—or the lack thereof.

By Neeleman's example, it's important to both tell and demonstrate your company's commitment to its employees. Communicate frequently and by whatever means available how much you value their contributions and how important they are to your company. For Neeleman, this communication extends to getting out and working alongside his crewmembers—loading luggage on the apron, serving snacks aboard aircraft, and even cleaning up trash in between flights. If these jobs weren't important, would the CEO waste his time doing them?

The airline also demonstrates its commitment in good old

"show me the money" fashion. Neeleman believes in sharing the wealth. Generous stock purchase plans and other benefits ensure that everyone does well, financially and otherwise. The fact that Neeleman donates his entire (though by CEO standards paltry) $200,000 salary to the employee catastrophe fund makes it personal, not just a corporate concern.

Working conditions add to this spirit of caring the company promotes. Innovative programs, from the virtual call center staffed by home workers, to flexible job-sharing arrangements, make for a happier and more productive workforce. Management policies create a positive and supportive environment, leading to satisfied employees and well-served customers.

RULE 8. RESPECT YOUR CUSTOMERS

Neeleman's pledge "to bring humanity back to air travel," which he announced during the initial launch of JetBlue, may sound grandiose. But it speaks to both his love of travel and the depths to which he saw the airline industry had fallen. The once glamorous and hospitable carriers had grown arrogant and lazy. The occupants of its seats were treated as mere fares, whom the airlines were ready to abandon without explanation for multitudinous reasons, from weather events to mechanical problems.

Neeleman's initial obsession with customer service was learned as a youngster working at his grandfather's convenience store. Treating people right was reinforced during his missionary service, when he saw how society treated a whole class of people wrong. At Morris Air, his customer-centric focus was fueled by the example of his hero, Herb Kelleher at Southwest. But Neeleman added his own touches, his imagination fired by ideas like those former SAS president Jan Carlzon outlined in his book *Moments of Truth*.

Today, everything a JetBlue customer encounters reinforces the company's interest in them, along with the airline's desire to make their encounter with the carrier a pleasurable experience. This respect for customers pays huge dividends. It creates loyalty that results in the best kind of advertising: word of mouth. Sixty percent of JetBlue's new customers come this way. Only 20 percent hear about the airline through advertising. JetBlue would therefore have to spend at least three times as much on advertising (which currently runs about $30 million per year) to get the same amount of business that simply being good to customers naturally brings in.

RULE 9. ADMIT YOUR MISTAKES EARLY, BUT DON'T LET THEM SLOW YOU DOWN

Strive to be perfect, but realize you never will be. Neeleman has often acknowledged that JetBlue is not exactly where he'd like to it to be. He always reminds crewmembers that while the goal of perfection may never be achieved, it is always within close reach. The reality is that there will always be stumbles and moments of abject humility along the path to this lofty objective.

Perhaps JetBlue's greatest tribulation began with a betrayal of its own policies on the protection of customer privacy, specifically the personal information customers entrusted to the airline. This information was shared with a government contractor for use in a passenger screening project following the events of 9/11. Neeleman, who has said he had no knowledge of the release of this information, promptly apologized to JetBlue customers, admitted the airline was wrong in releasing the data, and faced the maelstrom of ensuing queries and condemnations head-on. If it's possible to make lemonade out of lemons in a situation like this,

Neeleman and his company earned high marks for their openness in communicating with customers about the airline's conduct.

In doing so, JetBlue was able to quell what could have easily been a worsening storm. In fact, Neeleman insists that because JetBlue quickly confronted the issue head-on, it lost little, if any, business as a result.

RULE 10. PAY ATTENTION TO DETAILS

Neeleman isn't interested in details. People who have worked with him through the years will tell you he's only concerned with the big picture. But he's smart enough to know it's the little things that are important. That's why he hires people to attend to the details—the best he can find, in fact. JetBlue president Dave Barger is Neeleman's ultimate enabler. Barger is obsessed with operational details. Nothing at JetBlue goes unnoticed. If the first bag isn't at the carousel within 10 minutes of arrival, and the last within 20, management knows about it.

JetBlue orchestrates every detail of the customer experience. Marketing director Amy Curtis-McIntyre is equally vigilant in designing all elements of the airline's points of contact with passengers. From the thought that goes into crewmember uniforms and building the brand, to the food offered by the vendors in the terminal and even its clever television commercials, every detail of the customer experience is considered and optimized.

RULE 11. CONTROL COSTS—
JUST DON'T LET IT SHOW

Neeleman is obsessive about cost control. His frugality was evident in his earliest days as a missionary in Brazil, when he managed to live on about $1,700 over the course of two years. At Morris Air, operating as a charter airline with leased equipment and crews, the company couldn't get its costs under control. It was Neeleman who led the charge to bring expenses down. This was one of the factors that led him and his partners to turn Morris into a full-fledged airline.

As he was preparing to unveil the best-funded start-up in aviation history, this multimillionaire crashed at a friend's apartment on his visits to Manhattan, rather than pay for an expensive hotel room. Instead of providing meals, JetBlue serves its passengers inexpensive snacks. New planes increase fuel efficiency and keep operating costs down. And rather than hiring large janitorial teams, flight crews are asked to pitch in to help clean the aircraft after each trip.

RULE 12. USE TECHNOLOGY TO THE FULLEST

From the beginning, JetBlue's technology czar Jeff Cohen was given a clear mandate from Neeleman: Automate everything. From the cockpit to the airline's state-of-the-art reservations system, JetBlue uses technology unlike any other airline.

Pilots use laptop computers to figure out details from how much fuel to use to how long it will take to reach their destination. Every ticket on JetBlue is issued electronically. (As previously mentioned, Neeleman co-founded Open Skies, the company that created this technology.) JetBlue even uses technology for booking reservations—both through its friendly Web-based interface and by allowing reservations agents to work from home. These automated reservations systems make JetBlue's distribution costs the lowest in the industry, and eliminate the need for maintaining an expensive call center.

RULE 13. ATTRACT LOTS OF ATTENTION

For all his boyish affability, Neeleman is one of the most media-savvy executives around. Few are better at staying on message than he is. Neeleman has made himself available to speak before groups of all kinds and sizes, from Rotary Clubs to industry conventions. And the JetBlue publicity and marketing machine he put together is extremely effective at using guerrilla marketing techniques to spread the word about the airline through the media.

As testament to their abilities, before the first JetBlue plane took off—or was even delivered—the company and Neeleman were written-up in a variety of newspapers and magazines. Neeleman has since been featured on almost all of the major broadcast networks (including a profile on the CBS newsmagazine *60 Minutes II*), not to mention just about every newspaper and magazine around the country.

This savvy media relations strategy has given the company millions of dollars in free publicity and allowed it to keep marketing expenses to a minimum. In fact, almost everyone has heard of JetBlue today and the unique flying experience it offers. Yet chances are that little or none of this information was conveyed through the company's own advertising initiatives. Instead, the world has learned about JetBlue and what makes it unique largely through word of mouth and through the hundreds of free mentions it has garnered in the media.

RULE 14. STAY TRUE TO YOUR CORE VALUES

Neeleman's personal values were instilled at an early age. The strong Mormon faith he was raised in, which became even more deeply ingrained during his time as a missionary, gave him a solid grounding in humility and fraternity. That's why one of Neeleman's first orders of business at JetBlue was defining a list of core values for the company and its crewmembers. Neeleman is always quick to explain the added economic benefit of sticking to these altruistic-sounding values, though he maintains they go far beyond that. He truly believes that adhering to these values—and keeping them close to your heart—leads to happier customers, better employees, and greater overall business prosperity.

Under Neeleman's direction, JetBlue has profoundly changed the airline industry—and no doubt will continue to do so. By following these 14 principles, Neeleman has formed a series of phenomenally successful businesses in one of the world's most cutthroat industries, introduced innovations that have been adapted worldwide, and achieved some measure of his mission to bring humanity back to air travel. En route, Neeleman and JetBlue have altered the landscape for air travelers and provided a new paradigm for running a profitable and thriving organization. For a boy who couldn't figure out how he'd ever make a living, that's not a bad place to land.

JetBlue Timeline

February 1999	David Neeleman announces that he intends to start a new airline.
April 1999	JetBlue (then known as "New Air") places a $4 billion order with Airbus Industrie for up to 75 new A320 aircraft. At the same time, it commences leasing arrangements for another eight aircraft.
July 14, 1999	JetBlue unveils its launch plans to the public, announcing that it intends to fly Airbus A320 aircraft and offer 24 channels of live satellite television at every seat, a first for the airline industry.
September 16, 1999	JetBlue is granted an unprecedented exemption for 75 takeoff and landing slots at New York's John F. Kennedy International Airport (JFK).
December 4, 1999	JetBlue takes delivery of its first Airbus A320 aircraft.
February 3, 2000	The DOT issues a Certificate of Public Convenience and Necessity to JetBlue, representing the successful completion of

the airline's application process before both the DOT and the Federal Aviation Administration.

February 11, 2000   JetBlue launches operations with its first flight between JFK and Fort Lauderdale, Florida.

February 17, 2000   JetBlue starts service between JFK and Buffalo, New York.

March 16, 2000   JetBlue begins service between JFK and Tampa, Florida.

June 21, 2000   JetBlue launches flights between JFK and Orlando, Florida.

June 23, 2000   JetBlue receives its fifth Airbus A320 jet.

July 21, 2000   JetBlue begins flights between JFK and Ontario, California.

August 3, 2000   JetBlue launches service from JFK to Rochester, New York, and to Oakland, California.

September 7, 2000   JetBlue adds service between JFK and Burlington, Vermont.

October 18, 2000   JetBlue inaugurates flights between JFK and West Palm Beach, Florida.

November 10, 2000   JetBlue takes delivery of its 10th Airbus A320 aircraft.

November 17, 2000   JetBlue begins service between JFK and Salt Lake City, Utah.

November 18, 2000   JetBlue adds service between JFK and Fort Myers, Florida.

December 21, 2000	JetBlue flies its millionth customer and reports $100 million in flown revenue for 2000.
February 11, 2001	JetBlue celebrates its first birthday.
March 20, 2001	JetBlue is voted the number two domestic airline in the 2001 Zagat Airline Survey.
March 28, 2001	The utilitarian style of JetBlue's uniform is recognized by New York's Fashion Institute of Technology.
April 26, 2001	JetBlue welcomes aboard its 2 millionth customer.
May 1, 2001	JetBlue launches service between JFK and Seattle, Washington, along with a daytime flight to Oakland, California.
May 7, 2001	JetBlue launches service between JFK and Syracuse, New York.
May 14, 2001	JetBlue adopts a "roving" wireless check-in system, which is later scrapped.
May 17, 2001	JetBlue begins service between JFK and Denver, Colorado, and adds a daytime flight between JFK and Ontario, California.
June 18, 2001	JetBlue orders up to 48 more Airbus A320 aircraft in a deal valued at $2.5 billion.
June 30, 2001	JetBlue announces plans to take operational control of JFK's Terminal 6, doubling operational capacity at the airport.
July 26, 2001	JetBlue starts twice-daily service between JFK and New Orleans, Louisiana.

August 29, 2001	JetBlue launches service to Long Beach, California, with two daily flights to JFK, simultaneously establishing a West Coast base.
October 2001	JetBlue is named Best Domestic Airline in the *Condé Nast Traveler* Business Travel Awards.
November 1, 2001	JetBlue completes installation of bullet-proof, dead-bolted cockpit doors throughout its entire fleet.
November 5, 2001	JetBlue debuts as the number two domestic airline in the *Condé Nast Traveler* Readers' Choice Awards.
November 9, 2001	JetBlue takes delivery of its 20th Airbus A320 jet.
November 28, 2001	JetBlue begins twice-daily service between Washington, D.C. (Dulles) and Fort Lauderdale, Florida.
December 19, 2001	JetBlue expands service between JFK and Fort Lauderdale, Florida, to 10 daily flights.
January 14, 2002	JetBlue orders 10 Airbus A320 in a deal valued at more than $500 million.
January 23, 2002	JetBlue is recognized as "Best Overall Airline" for onboard service in the 16th annual Onboard Services Awards.
January 28, 2002	JetBlue wins *Air Transport World* magazine's 2002 Market Development Award.
February 11, 2002	JetBlue celebrates its second birthday.

March 7, 2002   JetBlue welcomes aboard its 5 millionth customer.

April 11, 2002   JetBlue announces the initial public offering of its common stock.

April 30, 2002   JetBlue buys two additional A320s.

May 1, 2002   JetBlue adds service from Washington, D.C., to the West Coast.

May 31, 2002   JetBlue begins service to San Juan, Puerto Rico.

June 13, 2002   JetBlue begins offering the TrueBlue frequent flyer program.

September 6, 2002   JetBlue starts service between Long Beach and Oakland, California.

September 24, 2002   JetBlue adds NBC and Telemundo to its DirecTV programming.

September 27, 2002   JetBlue acquires LiveTV, provider of the airline's in-flight satellite TV entertainment system.

October 10, 2002   JetBlue launches service between Long Beach, California, and Las Vegas, Nevada (the airline's 20th destination).

November 3, 2002   JetBlue is awarded Best Domestic Airline by *Condé Nast Traveler* readers.

November 15, 2002   JetBlue adds VH1 Classic, Nickelodeon/Nick at Night, and TV Land to its roster of DirecTV programming.

November 15, 2002   JetBlue launches service between JFK and Las Vegas, Nevada, with a 250-ticket giveaway promotion.

January 1, 2003   JetBlue welcomes aboard its 10 millionth customer.

January 31, 2003   JetBlue reports net income of $54.9 million for 2002.

February 11, 2003   JetBlue celebrates its third birthday.

April 24, 2003   JetBlue orders 65 additional Airbus A320 aircraft with options for 50 more.

May 8, 2003   JetBlue begins service between Long Beach, California, and Atlanta, Georgia.

June 10, 2003   JetBlue places order for 100 Embraer 190 jets with options for 100 more.

June 26, 2003   JetBlue launches service between JFK and San Diego, California.

August 6, 2003   JetBlue selects Orlando International Airport for its new training center and maintenance/LiveTV hangar.

August 8, 2003   JetBlue breaks ground on a new JFK hangar complex.

September 8, 2003   JetBlue begins service between Atlanta, Georgia, and Oakland, California.

September 10, 2003   JetBlue is named Best U.S. Airline by *Condé Nast Traveler* readers for the second year in a row.

September 22, 2003   JetBlue retains Deloitte & Touche to assist in the analysis of its privacy policy, after revelations surface that the company released customer data to an outside firm testing a system to screen for passengers who are potential security risks.

October 7, 2003	JetBlue announces three-for-two stock split.
November 12, 2003	JetBlue introduces free high-speed wireless service at JFK's Terminal 6.
November 13, 2003	JetBlue adds more legroom in some rows throughout its fleet.
January 7, 2004	JetBlue launches service to Boston, Massachusetts.
January 7, 2004	JetBlue announces plans to add Fox Video Entertainment System and debut XM Satellite Radio in-flight.
January 21, 2004	JetBlue applies for slot exemptions at New York's LaGuardia Airport.
March 3, 2004	JetBlue begins service from JFK to Sacramento, California.
April 1, 2004	JetBlue flies to 23 destinations with 54 Airbus A320 aircraft.

Acknowledgments

The author wishes to thank the many people who freely shared the thoughts, recollections, and insights that were so instrumental in telling the story of David Neeleman and JetBlue. Special thanks to Kirk Kazanjian of Literary Productions for his work in developing this project and seeing it through to completion. Much appreciation also to Janice Wood for her support, invaluable input, and helpful suggestions. Thanks as well go to Debra Englander at John Wiley & Sons for her enthusiasm for this book and her assistance in its creation.

Notes

CHAPTER 1   The Journey Begins

1. p. 8   *and they might (occasionally) give us a break."*   Tom Murphy, "U.S. Companies without U.S. Executives: Just as American and Even More Global," *Update Magazine*, October 2003.

2. p. 8   *and thinking outside the box all the time,"*   Gary Neeleman, interview by author.

3. p. 9   *where he takes an Otis elevator to his office"*   Murphy, "U.S. Companies." *Update Magazine*, October 2003.

4. p. 9   *because somebody is a local hire he's inferior."*   Gary Neeleman, interview.

5. p. 10   *spoke better Portuguese than they did English."*   Ibid.

6. p. 10   *thinking of something else."*   Alex Williams, "Super Fly," *New York Magazine*, January 31, 2000.

7. p. 10   *You don't know what you're talking about.'"*   David Neeleman with Julia Lawlor, "Rewards in Restlessness," *New York Times*, June 1, 2003.

8. p. 10   *he is throwing rocks in the pond."*   Chris Woodyard, "JetBlue soars on CEO's creativity," *USA Today*, October 8, 2002.

9. p. 11   *everything humanly possible to make it happen."* Neeleman with Lawlor, "Rewards in Restlessness."

10. p. 11   *to bring back the needed item."*   Fred Ball, "Fred Ball Speaking on Business," KSL Radio, November 6, 2001.

11. p. 11   *he didn't have what was needed."*   Ibid.

12. p. 11   *I think that was instilled in me."*   David Neeleman, interview by Willow Bay, *Pinnacle*, CNN, July 13, 2002.

13. p. 12   *selling 500 of those things a day."*   Ibid.

14. p. 12   *I felt like I was always behind"*   Willow Bay, interview.

15. p. 12   *'No, you're going to be okay.'"*   Gary Neeleman, interview.

16. p. 13   *everyone else was doing the right thing."*   Dennis Romboy, "JetBlue Chief a 'Utah Boy' Flying High," *Desert News*, September 29, 2002.

17. p. 13   *he'd get them more dessert."*   Ibid.

18. p. 13   *if I can't read and write?'"*   Neeleman with Lawlor, "Rewards in Restlessness."

19. p. 13   *I'm a deeply religious person."*   David Neeleman, speech at Rutgers, November 7, 2003.

20. p. 14   *"a life-changing experience"*   Ibid.

21. p. 15   *treat people the same [and] with respect."*   Ibid.

22. p. 15   *I felt like I had some talent"*   Wendy Zellner, "Bringing New Air to New York," *BusinessWeek*, May 3, 1999.

23. p. 15   *how much money do you need?"*   Willow Bay interview.

24. p. 16   *'Wow, this is a pretty good business.'"*   Ibid.

25. p. 18   *on the beach having a good time."*   Rebecca Reeder Hunt, interview by author.

26. p. 18   *at least one flight on The Hawaii Express."*   Ibid.

27. p. 19   *so we didn't discourage or encourage him."*   Gary Neeleman, interview.

28. p. 19   *I'm not ashamed that I don't have a degree."*   Julia

Lawlor, "A Driven Bunch Says No Degree, No Problem." *New York Times*, October 5, 2003.

29. p. 19   *He just had a lot of charm."*   Rick Frendt, interview by author.

30. p. 20   *I was devastated"*   Robert Carey, "Nothing but Blue Skies," *Business and Management Practices*, July 2002.

CHAPTER 2   Have I Got a Deal for You

1. p. 23   *give me his phone number.'"*   June Morris, interview by author.

2. p. 24   *I'm going back to work.'"*   Ibid.

3. p. 25   *what we saved them."*   Ibid.

4. p. 26   *to expand into the leisure market."*   Ibid.

5. p. 26   *so we specifically went after leisure business."*   Rick Frendt, interview by author.

6. p. 26   *the most creative person we'd seen."*   Ibid.

7. p. 27   *Stay away from me.'"*   David Neeleman, interview by Willow Bay, *Pinnacle*, CNN, July 13, 2002.

8. p. 27   *He had no interest."*   Morris, interview.

9. p. 27   *start a drapery business"*   Frendt, interview.

10. p. 28   *back to Honolulu for us"*   Ibid.

11. p. 29   *top this thing off, every week."*   Ibid.

12. p. 30   *a bunch of stupid kids."*   Ibid.

13. p. 31   *a funny operation."*   Morris, interview.

14. p. 31   *David was just this kid."*   David Evans, interview by author.

15. p. 32   *Los Angeles was a gold mine."*   Frendt, interview.

16. p. 32   *come and go pretty quickly."*   Evans, interview.

17. p. 33   *It was wild."*   Morris, interview.

18. p. 33   *half of everybody else's."* Frendt, interview.

19. p. 34   *every two minutes."* Ibid.

20. p. 35   *a very big inspiration to all of us."* Carla Meine, interview by author.

21. p. 37   *obey the airline rules,'"* *Evans says.* Evans, interview.

22. p. 38   *We've got to do it right'"* Frendt, interview.

CHAPTER 3   Morris Air Spreads Its Wings

1. p. 40   *here's some chocolate for you."* Carla Meine, interview by author.

2. p. 40   *every other week on Delta."* Ibid.

3. p. 42   *It was a great team of people."* Ibid.

4. p. 44   *we were doing it in record time."* Rick Frendt, interview by author.

5. p. 44   *going out of business again"* Robert Carey, "Nothing but Blue Skies," *Business and Management Practices,* July 2002.

6. p. 45   *just good or bad managers"* Ibid.

7. p. 46   *very profitable and beautifully run."* Ibid.

8. p. 47   *to really get our little airline set up."* David Evans, interview by author.

9. p. 48   *in three or four months?"* Ibid.

10. p. 49   *Why did we do the tickets at all?'"* Ibid.

11. p. 50   *to get these agencies to pay us."* Frendt, interview.

12. p. 50   *book the ticket, and be done."* Evans, interview.

13. p. 52   *no place else to put agents"* Meine, interview.

14. p. 53   *they have time to work."* Evans, interview.

15. p. 54   *buy [airplanes] rather than lease."* Frendt, interview.

CHAPTER 4   Off to Southwest

1. p. 55   *do it a little better."*   Arlyn Tobias Gajilan, "The Amazing JetBlue." *Fortune Small Business*, April 24, 2003.

2. p. 56   *as good as it was in California"*   James Ott and Raymond E. Neidl, *Airline Odyssey: The Airline Industry's Turbulent Flight into the Future* (New York: McGraw-Hill, 1995), p. 71.

3. p. 58   *picked up some ideas from them."*   June Morris, interview by author.

4. p. 59   *just like we encourage at Southwest."*   Colleen Barrett, interview by author.

5. p. 60   *"I don't think he was interested"*   Rick Frendt, interview by author.

6. p. 60   *core values and philosophies."*   Barrett, interview.

7. p. 60   *and surely considered him a protégé."*   Ibid.

8. p. 61   *The world was my oyster."*   Matthew Brelis, "Out of the Blue, High-Flying Start-Up Finds Its Niche in Not-So-Friendly Skies," *Boston Globe*, January 19, 2003.

9. p. 61   *we weren't going to have a job."*   Carla Meine, interview by author.

10. p. 61   *[few] of them took on jobs."*   David Evans, interview by author.

11. p. 62   *what they didn't have in services and frills."*   Ann Rhoades, interview by author.

12. p. 63   *it would be a love fest."*   Melanie Wells, "Lord of the Skies," *Forbes*, October 14, 2002.

13. p. 63   *the way you think it will be."*   Gajilan, "The Amazing JetBlue."

14. p. 63   *the people kind of resented that."*   Morris, interview.

15. p. 64   *trying to get his arms around what he was doing."*   Barrett, interview.

16. p. 64 *the old mainframe system they had inherited from Braniff."* Stephanie Overby, "JetBlue Skies Ahead," *CIO*, July 1, 2002.

17. p. 64 *all on the technology side."* Barrett, interview.

18. p. 64 *stepped on some toes."* Morris, interview.

19. p. 65 *things might have worked out differently."* Rhoades, interview.

20. p. 65 *'Can't we just decide and move on?'"* Wells, "Lord of the Skies."

21. p. 65 *they saw how much potential he had."* Ibid.

22. p. 65 *It was really being very destructive."* Rhoades, interview.

23. p. 66 *a behavior that was characteristic of who he was."* Barrett, interview.

24. p. 66 *driving myself crazy and them crazy."* David Neeleman, interview by Willow Bay, *Pinnacle*, CNN, July 13, 2002.

25. p. 67 *No, you're fired,' so I said 'OK,'"* he later joked. David Neeleman, speech to New York Harvard Club, September 10, 2003.

26. p. 67 *"a kind of oral hygiene assembly line."* Rhoades, interview.

27. p. 67 *with their particular operation."* Morris, interview.

28. p. 67 *not an entrepreneur"* Brelis, "Out of the Blue."

29. p. 67 *a little annoying back then."* Rhoades, interview.

30. p. 68 *a totally different reaction to us."* Barrett, interview.

31. p. 68 *do my own thing'"* Morris, interview.

32. p. 69 *something that needed to be addressed."* Neeleman, Willow Bay interview.

33. p. 69 *That's the downside."* Alex Williams, "Super Fly," *New York Magazine*, January 31, 2000.

34. p. 69   *They take more risks."* David Neeleman with Julia Lawlor, "Rewards in Restlessness," *New York Times*, June 1, 2003.

35. p. 70   *with ADD, comes creativity and hyper-focus."* Neeleman, Willow Bay interview.

36. p. 70   *then I'd be like the rest of you"* Neeleman with Lawlor, "Rewards in Restlessness."

37. p. 70   *a closet full of them."* Ibid.

38. p. 70   *from one day to the next," he admits.* Neeleman with Lawlor, Rewards in Restlessness."

39. p. 70   *"That was a problem."* Barrett, interview.

40. p. 71   *make sure that it's going the right direction.'"* David Neeleman, speech at Northwestern University, April 9, 2003.

41. p. 71   *upstairs doing something else.* Neeleman, Willow Bay interview.

42. p. 71   *'Do I do that?'"* Williams, "Super Fly."

43. p. 71   *mad at him all the time."* Chris Woodyard, "JetBlue Soars on CEO Creativity," *USA Today*, October 8, 2002.

CHAPTER 5   Opening Up New Skies

1. p. 73   *lost money on all of them"* David Evans, interview by author.

2. p. 73   *[being a venture capitalist]"* Michael Lazarus, interview by author.

3. p. 74   *the other was Morris Air."* Mark Hill, interview by author.

4. p. 78   *and one was David."* Ibid.

5. p. 78   *He got turned on to that."* Ibid.

6. p. 79   *But no one else was doing them."* Ibid.

7. p. 79 *So it was their idea now and they did it."* Evans, interview.

8. p. 80 *We can make this thing big."* Ibid.

9. p. 81 *dealing with other currencies."* Mary Nemeth, "Upstarts in the Air," *Maclean's*, March 11, 1996.

10. p. 81 *might not have traveled at all."* Ibid.

11. p. 82 *as much as we needed them."* Hill, interview.

12. p. 82 *you're going to want to go back for more."* Ted Larkin, interview by author.

13. p. 84 *It would have been interesting."* Hill, interview.

14. p. 84 *helped launch JetBlue."* Ibid.

CHAPTER 6 A Different Kind of Airline

1. p. 87 *He asked a lot of good questions."* Melanie Wells, "Lord of the Skies," *Forbes*, October 14, 2002.

2. p. 88 *Who needs an airline?"* Michael Lazarus, interview by author.

3. p. 89 *I thought he was out of his mind."* Ibid.

4. p. 89 *Now what do you think?"* Ibid.

5. p. 89 *build the best coach product in America with the lowest cost."* Robert Carey, "Nothing but Blue Skies," *Business and Management Practices*, July 2002.

6. p. 90 *'This is what this thing can become,'"* Alex Williams, "Super Fly," *New York Magazine*, January 31, 2000.

7. p. 90 *he knows the industry inside out."* Lazarus, interview.

8. p. 91 *"He has endless energy and is totally committed."* Ibid.

9. p. 91 *running a successful financial operation"* Sally B. Donnelly, "Blue Skies for JetBlue," *Time*, July 30, 2001.

10. p. 92   *"You want people to take some risk."* Lazarus, interview.

11. p. 92   *use humor to defuse a bad situation."* Ibid.

12. p. 93   *to have the balance in the management team"* Ann Rhoades, interview by author.

13. p. 93   *I didn't want to commute from Albuquerque."* Ibid.

14. p. 93   *he's very reflective in the way he listens."* Ibid.

15. p. 94   *the leader, and the process."* Lazarus, interview.

16. p. 96   *a big brand as well as the capitalization."* David Tait, interview by author.

17. p. 96   *similar to our Virgin Express all–Boeing 737 operation in Europe."* "One-on-One With Virgin Atlantic's Gareth Edmondson-Jones," World Airline News, July 24, 1998.

18. p. 96   *foreign ownership regulations in Congress."* Ibid.

19. p. 97   *they had their hands in all the pockets"* David Neeleman, speech to the New York Harvard Club, September 10, 2003.

20. p. 97   *noting that Branson "was very nice about it."* Lazarus, interview.

21. p. 98   *"I'll protect the brand, don't worry!"* Ibid.

22. p. 99   *"This was not without a lot of risk"* Ibid.

23. p. 100   *or not paying our staff enough."* Carole Shifrin, "Born to Be Blue," Reed Business Information UK, June 1, 2002.

24. p. 100   *We want to improve it."* Ibid.

25. p. 100   *coupled with the strength of the team, was staggering."* Eryn Brown, "A Smokeless Herb," Fortune, May 28, 2001.

26. p. 100   *He's also a natural born leader."* Lazarus, interview.

CHAPTER 7 Preparing for Departure

1. p. 104 *Try to create a little better company."* David Neeleman, speech at Rutgers, November 7, 2003, attended by author.

2. p. 105 *grew up in the Boeing culture and knew the planes."* Michael Lazarus, interview by author.

3. p. 105 *using them just as a foil."* Robert Carey, "Nothing but Blue Skies," *Business and Management Practices*, July 2002.

4. p. 105 *'Give me your pitch.'"* Ibid.

5. p. 106 *regardless of the cost."* Laurence Zuckerman, "New Low-Fare Airline to Buy Airbus Industrie Jets," *New York Times*, April 21, 1999.

6. p. 106 *The leverage we got was unbelievable."* Lazarus, interview.

7. p. 106 *"a blow" to Boeing's 737 program.* Zuckerman, "Airline to Buy Airbus Industrie Jets."

8. p. 106 *that Boeing walked away from."* Carey, "Nothing but Blue Skies."

9. p. 107 *the nirvana of all markets."* Alex Williams, "Super Fly," *New York Magazine*, January 31, 2000.

10. p. 107 *outside that 5 million [person] bubble."* David Neeleman, Willow Bay interview, *Pinnacle*, CNN, July 13, 2002.

11. p. 107 *"and the longest it's ever taken me is 25 minutes."* Ibid.

12. p. 108 *it's 42 minutes before you're airborne"* Williams, "Super Fly."

13. p. 108 *we'd like to put an airline here."* David Neeleman, speech at WCBS Business Conference, October 15, 2003, attended by author.

14. p. 109 *it was totally trash everywhere."* Ibid.

15. p. 110 *"This is going to be good for everybody"* Laurence Zuckerman, "Budget Airline Plans to Start from Kennedy," *New York Times*, February 7, 1999, p. 43.

16. p. 110 *but only if you fly to upstate New York."* Williams, "Super Fly."

17. p. 111 *during its first year of operation was "unrealistic."* Order to Show Cause Proposing Issuance of Certificate Authority, U.S. Department of Transportation, August 13, 1999.

18. p. 111 *at the time was only 7.39 cents.* Max Kj, "New Air Aims to Copy Southwest Method," *Flight International*, June 16, 1999, p. 17.

19. p. 111 *coming up with a name,"* Neeleman recalls. Neeleman, speech at WCBS Business Conference.

20. p. 111 *deliver on the promise every single day."* Ibid.

21. p. 112 *It just wouldn't sound right."* Williams, "Super Fly."

22. p. 112 *There was just no way it would work."* Ibid.

23. p. 112 *"'I'm going on The Competition.'"* Ibid.

24. p. 112 *without air conditioning"* Ibid.

25. p. 112 *fly at 39,000 feet on Chocolate"* Neeleman, speech at WCBS Business Conference.

26. p. 112 *crazy names they came up with."* Ibid.

27. p. 112 *everything's going to be yellow.'"* Ibid.

28. p. 113 *a good frequent flyer program,"* Ibid.

29. p. 114 *So how about "JetBlue"?'"* Williams, "Super Fly."

30. p. 114 *typed www.jetblue.com, and it wasn't taken."* Neeleman, speech at WCBS Business Conference.

31. p. 114 *we kept working down to center"* Lazarus, interview.

32. p. 115 *"I'll put up $5 million to get things going"* Ibid.

33. p. 115 *caring, fun, integrity, and passion.* Neeleman, speech at WCBS Business Conference.

34. p. 115   *let's figure out a way to do that.'"*   Ibid.

35. p. 115   *calls it the "key to the success"*   Ann Rhoades, interview by author.

36. p. 116   *important concepts that we started out with."*   David Neeleman, speech at Northwestern University, April 9, 2003.

37. p. 116   *to take care of our customers on a daily basis."* David Neeleman, speech at Rutgers, November 7, 2003, attended by author.

38. p. 117   *I'm sure we'll find some good people.'"*   Ibid.

39. p. 117   *it would cost you a buck."*   Neeleman, speech at Northwestern University.

40. p. 117   *attendants aren't necessarily what we're after."* Williams, "Super Fly."

41. p. 118   *'I know where you live, I get you.'"*   Mike Beirne, "NY Air Startup Mines City for Guerrilla Cues," *Brandweek*, June 21, 1999.

42. p. 118   *have working for us at JetBlue,"*   Anthony Cardinale, "JetBlue Founder Urges Grads to Serve Others," *Buffalo News*, May 5, 2003.

43. p. 118   *We wanted people who like people."*   David Neeleman, speech to the New York Harvard Club, September 10, 2003.

44. p. 118   *"I had them meet David."*   Rhoades, interview.

45. p. 119   *We thought a lot about it."*   Neeleman, speech at Northwestern University.

CHAPTER 8   JetBlue Takes Flight

1. p. 122   *New York's new low-fare hometown airline"*   JetBlue Airways, "The First 'Mega Start-Up' Unveils Launch Plans," press release, July 14, 1999.

2. p. 123   *pledges that may one day return to haunt him."*   Laurence Zuckerman, "Ambitious Low-Fare Carrier Names Itself JetBlue Airways," *New York Times*, July 15, 1999, p. 9.

3. p. 123   *"an end to the regimen of high fares."*   JetBlue Airways, "JetBlue Airways Receives Take-Off and Landing Rights at JFK," press release, September 16, 1999.

4. p. 124   *But it really made the difference."*   Author interview with Michael Lazarus.

5. p. 124   *pilot to buzz underneath the Verrazano bridge"*   Alex Williams, "Super Fly," *New York Magazine*, January 31, 2000.

6. p. 124   *"What's your vector, Victor?"*   Ibid.

7. p. 124   *he announced, straight-faced.*   Ibid.

8. p. 124   *before its first scheduled flight left the ground.*   Ibid.

9. p. 126   *it's great to be flying home with JetBlue."*   "Utahan CEO introduces his new airline to his hometown," JetBlue press release, JetBlue Airways, November 17, 2000.

10. p. 126   *our largest job is finding great people"*   Janice Wood, "JetBlue's Hiring Takes Off," AviationCareer.net, January 25, 2001.

11. p. 127   *but I try very hard not to waver."*   Robert Carey, "Nothing but Blue Skies," *Business and Management Practices*, July 2002.

12. p. 128   *will make a company successful."*   David Neeleman, speech at Rutgers University, November 7, 2003, attended by author.

13. p. 128   *every day. It's really fast-paced."*   Janice Wood, "Jet Who? Have You Got What It Takes to Work at JetBlue?" AviationCareer.net, June 20, 2001.

14. p. 129   *fit with us and do we fit with you?"*   Ibid.

15. p. 129   *This is the best of the best."*   Wood, "JetBlue's Hiring Takes Off."

16. p. 129   *It shows there are real people tied to these titles,"* Wood, "JetBlue's Hiring Takes Off."

17. p. 129   *That's not the kind of thinking we want."*   Ibid.

18. p. 130   *We said, 'You're hired!'"*   Jennifer Keeney, "JetBlue Flies High," *Fortune Small Business*, February 12, 2001.

19. p. 130   *somebody to experience the airline."*   Janice Wood, "Are the Skies Turning Blue? Upstart JetBlue Takes Off with a New Way to Hire Employees," Aviation Career.net, January 11, 2001.

20. p. 130   *we know as much about you as your mother."*   Ibid.

21. p. 131   *Their attention to detail is phenomenal."*   Wood, "Are the Skies Turning Blue?" AviationCareer.net, January 11, 2001.

22. p. 132   *not informing the other one of what's going on"*   Janice Wood, "Sharing Jobs and Working from Home: The New Face of the Airline Industry," AviationCareer.net, August 16, 2000.

23. p. 132   *It's a win-win situation"*   Ibid.

24. p. 132   *would have to be away from home so frequently."* Ibid.

25. p. 133   *kind of control thing with the employee."*   Keeney, "JetBlue Flies High."

26. p. 133   *we'll show you how to do it."*   David Neeleman, speech to New York Harvard Club, September 10, 2003.

27. p. 134   *because it costs money to train people."*   David Neeleman, speech at Northwestern University, April 9, 2003.

28. p. 134   *and the College of Customer Service."*   Neeleman, speech at Rutgers University.

29. p. 135 *because they took advantage of them."* Neeleman, speech at Northwestern University.

30. p. 135 *In essence it [is] a guaranteed contract."* Ibid.

31. p. 135 *We're in this thing together!'"* Ibid.

32. p. 136 *they will go anywhere with you."* Carey, "Nothing but Blue Skies."

33. p. 136 *[having to] constantly find new ones."* Ibid.

34. p. 136 *So we pay people really well."* David Neeleman, speech at WCBS Business Conference, October 15, 2003, attended by author.

35. p. 137 *doing very, very well as a workforce."* Neeleman, speech to New York Harvard Club.

36. p. 137 *the most valuable asset we have."* David Neeleman, interview by Charlie Rose, *The Charlie Rose Show*, PBS Radio, July 23, 2003.

37. p. 138 *from the very first day into the 401(k) program."* Neeleman, speech at Northwestern University.

38. p. 138 *but it's our company,"* Ibid.

39. p. 138 *maintain an appropriate level of professionalism."* Customer comments about JetBlue Airways from www.pricetool.com.

CHAPTER 9   Making Air Travel Entertaining

1. p. 141 *cost to put TV on Air Force One."* Glenn Latta, interview by author.

2. p. 142 *they didn't show you the movie"* Ibid.

3. p. 143 *somebody that I really need to talk to.'"* Ibid.

4. p. 143 *in-flight entertainment on any of our aircraft."* Ibid.

5. p. 144 *what they wanted—short-haul entertainment."* Ibid.

6. p. 144 *we'll call you back if we're interested."* Ibid.

7. p. 145   *nothing that's going to fix that experience.*"   Michael Lazarus, interview by author.

8. p. 145   *got it up and flying on an aircraft.*"   Latta, interview.

9. p. 147   *seats [watching television]; everybody's happy.*" Ibid.

10. p. 148   *and my gosh, has it paid off.*"   Lazarus, interview.

11. p. 148   *product paid for through customer revenue.*"   Latta, interview.

12. p. 149   *but it was a very positive relationship.*"   Ibid.

13. p. 150   *technology, so it's just been wonderful.*"   Ibid.

14. p. 150   *JetBlue made in buying the company?*"   Ibid.

CHAPTER 10   Keeping Customers Happy

1. p. 151   *It gets you up in the morning.*"   David Neeleman, interview by Lou Dobbs, *Lou Dobbs Moneyline*, CNN, May 15, 2002.

2. p. 152   *a great product, and service, service, service.*"   JetBlue Airways, "JetBlue Flies One Millionth Passenger and Announces More than $100 Million in Flown Revenue for the Year," press release, December 21, 2000.

3. p. 152   *treated are essential to achieving this goal.*"   From the www.jetblue.com web site.

4. p. 152   *'Wow, I love doing business with that company.'*" David Neeleman, speech at WCBS Business Conference, October 15, 2003, attended by author.

5. p. 153   *And they also don't want to hurt themselves.*" Kristin Zern, interview by author.

6. p. 154   *two hours later they're still there'*"   Carla Meine, interview by author.

7. p. 155   *collect a lot of business cards*"   Neeleman, speech at New York Harvard Club, September 10, 2003.

8. p. 155   *lead kind of an isolated existence"*   Jennifer Keenes, "JetBlue Flies High," *Fortune Small Business*, February 12, 2001.

9. p. 156   *as good an example as I possibly can."*   Ibid.

10. p. 156   *I kept buying more and more shirts,"*   Ibid.

11. p. 156   *I was really excited about it."*   Ibid.

12. p. 157   *like the way they feel about it."*   Ibid.

13. p. 157   *We try to follow these at JetBlue"*   David Neeleman, speech at Northwestern University, April 9, 2003.

14. p. 158   *they not had that experience in the first place,"*   Ibid.

15. p. 159   *they work, or be proud of it."*   David Neeleman, speech at New York Harvard Club.

16. p. 159   *they want to fly on JetBlue."*   Neeleman, speech at Northwestern University.

17. p. 160   *it's a good position to be in."*   Robert Carey, "Nothing but Blue Skies," *Business and Management Practices,* July 2002.

18. p. 160   *you can buy it for $119."*   Neeleman, speech at WCBS Business Conference.

19. p. 162   *capitalist cure known as competition."*   "JetBlue CEO David Neeleman Supports Hollings/McCain Bill to Give Smaller Carriers Access to Bigger Airports," *Business Wire*, March 13, 2001.

20. p. 162   *appreciated, like, 'I am a customer.'"*   David Neeleman, interview by Willow Bay, *Pinnacle*, CNN, July 27, 2002.

CHAPTER 11   The Technology Advantage

1. p. 163   *Let's keep pushing the envelope."*   Stephanie Overby, "JetBlue Skies Ahead," *CIO*, July 1, 2002.

2. p. 164   *'Is there a way we can improve this?'"*   Ibid.

3. p. 166   *learned from us and we learned from them."*   Ann Rhoades, interview by author.

4. p. 167   *improve our efficiency and customer service."*   "Jet-Blue Airways Books Windows XP Professional for Efficiency, Reliability, and Security," Microsoft web site, www.Microsoft.com/resources/casestudies/casestudy.asp?casestudyID=11102, March 7, 2002.

5. p. 167   *aligned with our business model."*   Overby, "JetBlue Skies Ahead."

6. p. 168   *make you efficient, it's not cool."*   Ibid.

7. p. 169   *they are ready to go straightaway."*   Insight Marketing and Communications, "JetBlue Airways Revolutionizes Its Cockpits with HP Notebook Computers," press release, April 25, 2001, www.insightmkt.com.

8. p. 169   *flight releases without leaving the cockpit."*   Ibid.

9. p. 169   *somebody hadn't done it sooner."*   Overby, "JetBlue Skies Ahead."

10. p. 172   *care of the people we do have."*   Ibid.

11. p. 176   *we have it baked into the system."*   Ibid.

CHAPTER 12   Getting the Word Out in Style

1. p. 181   *Cheap and cheerful"*   Arlyn Tobias Gajilan, "The Amazing JetBlue," *Fortune Small Business*, April 24, 2003.

2. p. 181   *I wanted cheap and chic"*   Ibid.

3. p. 181   *idea after idea until we get it right."*   Amy Curtis-McIntyre, speech at Forrester Consumer Forum, September 23, 2003.

4. p. 181   *they'll never come back.' "*   David Neeleman, speech at WCBS Business Conference, October 15, 2003, attended by author.

5. p. 182   *would initially serve was "absolutely nothing"*   Linda Tischler, "Marketing on $0 a Day," *Fast Company*, February 2003, p. 46.

6. p. 182   *on the same side of the fence"*   Ibid.

7. p. 182   *she doesn't have her fingers in the middle of"* Michael Lazarus, interview by author.

8. p. 183   *as one reporter called it, of "a Greene Street loft."* Alex Williams, "Super Fly," *New York Magazine*, January 31, 2000.

9. p. 183   *going to be the Starbucks of the sky."*   Ibid.

10. p. 183   *their on-time performance, and more."*   Amy C. Sims, "Looking Chic at 35,000 Feet," Fox News, September 2, 2003.

11. p. 184   *be stylish and distinctive as well."*   JetBlue Airways, "JetBlue's Utilitarian Style Recognized by New York's Fashion Institute of Technology," press release, March 28, 2001.

12. p. 184   *be as approachable as our flight attendants."*   Ina Paiva Cordle, "Airline Pilots Maneuver to Fly without Their Caps," *Miami Herald*, October 2, 2003.

13. p. 184   *and they have to put this thing on every day, too."* Sims, "Looking Chic at 35,000 Feet."

14. p. 184   *front line what they want to wear."*   Ibid.

15. p. 185   *airlines as much as all our other amenities."*   JetBlue Airways, "JetBlue's Utilitarian Style."

16. p. 185   *already a buzz about JetBlue,"*   Kristin Zern, interview by author.

17. p. 186   *[microphone], he just started to talk."*   Ibid.

18. p. 186   *something an airline had never done before."*   Ibid.

19. p. 186   *genuinely happy to have me onboard'"*   JetBlue Airways, "JetBlue Wants Travelers to Know 'Somebody Up There Likes You,'" press release, June 11, 2001.

20. p. 187   *We're in it to make a profit"*   Carole Shifrin, "Born to Be Blue," *Reed Business Information UK*, June 1, 2002.

21. p. 187   *better utilize your existing crewmembers."*   Ibid.

22. p. 189 *We have a big job to do here"* Chris Woodyard, "Jet-Blue Turns to Beatles, Beaches, Bars." *USA Today*, August 22, 2001.

23. p. 190 *let Amy and her team do it."* David Neeleman's acceptance remarks upon receiving the Marketer of the Year award for JetBlue by *Advertising Age* in 2002.

CHAPTER 13 Dealing with Disaster

1. p. 196 *hassled every time they go to do anything?"* David Neeleman, interview by Bill O'Reilly, *The O'Reilly Factor*, Fox News, November 26, 2001.

2. p. 196 *80-year-old ladies from the equation"* Neeleman said. Bill O'Reilly interview.

3. p. 196 *have a potential [to be a threat].* Ibid.

4. p. 198 *It was easier for us to do it."* Neeleman, speech at Rutgers Uninversity, November 7, 2003, attended by the author.

5. p. 198 *"And it was a very quick decision."* Glenn Latta, interview by author.

6. p. 198 *then give me the card."* Bill O'Reilly interview.

7. p. 198 *see the federal government get involved"* Bill O'Reilly interview.

8. p. 199 *this is just like a tough recession."* Mark Odell, "No-frills Flights of Opportunity," *Financial Times*, November 28, 2001.

9. p. 199 *only JetBlue didn't cut its payroll at all.* "Impact on Aviation," www.labournet.net/world/0110/aviatn1.html, October 2, 2001.

10. p. 199 *amongst a lot of these other airlines."* Neeleman, speech at WCBS Business Conference.

11. p. 200 *took some $20 million in federal aid.* "Impact on Aviation," www.labournet.net.

12. p. 201   *and entering attractive new markets,"*   From JetBlue's SEC filing dated February 12, 2002.

13. p. 201   *almost $125,000 of his own money in the airline.* Lawrence Zuckerman, "Private Sector: A Highflying Offering that Started as a Sleepover, *New York Times*, February 17, 2002.

14. p. 201   *so many of us have flown JetBlue."*   Steve Gelsi, "JetBlue IPO Taking Flight Friday," CBS.MarketWatch.com, April 8, 2002.

15. p. 202   *It's the hottest deal this year."*   "JetBlue IPO Soars," www.Money.com, April 12, 2002.

16. p. 204   *We're in the service business.'"*   Neeleman, speech at WCBS Business Conference.

17. p. 205   *we think is very, very important."*   David Neeleman, speech at New York Harvard Club, September 10, 2003.

18. p. 207   *We hate canceling flights"*   Neeleman, speech at WCBS Business Conference.

19. p. 208   *good company is how you handle adversity,"*   Ibid.

20. p. 209   *"was immediately apparent"*   Edward Hasbrouck, interview by author.

21. p. 210   *and then they slipped on it"*   Howard Rubenstein, interview by author.

22. p. 210   *government's efforts to improve security."*   David Neeleman, letter to JetBlue Airways customers, September 23, 2003.

23. p. 210   *the American people are pretty forgiving."*   Tom Incantalupo, "JetBlue Glides over Passenger Privacy Storm," *Newsday*, September 29, 2003.

24. p. 212   *do it with the best product and the lowest cost."* David Neeleman, speech at Northwestern University, April 9, 2003.

25. p. 212   *you're going to do well, even in bad times."*
              Ibid.

CHAPTER 14   Preserving the Culture

1. p. 214   *gone from JetBlue, that example will live on."*   David
             Neeleman speech at WCBS Business Conference, Octo-
             ber 15, 2003, attended by author.

2. p. 216   *will always succeed in any environment."*   Anthony
             Cardinal, "JetBlue Founder Urges Grads to Serve Oth-
             ers," *Buffalo News*, May 15, 2003.

3. p. 217   *go take care of the customers."*   Ibid.

4. p. 218   *who were in leadership in the company,"*   David Neele-
             man, speech at Northwestern University, April 9, 2003.

5. p. 218   *ask them to find another job."*   David Neeleman,
             speech to New York Harvard Club, September 10, 2003.

6. p. 219   *principles that they have around their necks"*   Neele-
             man, speech at WCBS Business Conference.

7. p. 219   *then that has an effect on the customers."*   Ibid.

8. p. 219   *because the foundation of JetBlue is our people,"*
             Neeleman, speech at New York Harvard Club.

9. p. 220   *have to have them go find another job."*   Neeleman,
             speech to New York Harvard Club.

10. p. 220   *what business you're in. It's essential."*   Neeleman,
             speech at Northwestern University.

11. p. 221   *any less important than our president of the com-
             pany."*   David Neeleman, interview by Charlie Rose,
             The Charlie Rose Show, PBS Radio, July 23, 2003.

12. p. 221   *there would be less for other people"*   Neeleman,
             speech at Northwestern University.

13. p. 221   *an officer's salary, whatever the officers get.'"*   Ibid.

14. p. 220   *help our crewmembers with their needs."*   Ibid.

15. p. 220   *health insurance or by any kind of insurance"*   Ibid.

16. p. 222   *funds so they can help their fellow crewmembers."*
Ibid.

17. p. 223   *out of business just like that."*   Ibid.

18. p. 223   *hard to do it every day. It's hard to make it happen."*
Ibid.

19. p. 223   *joy and happiness in life is serving other people."*
David Neeleman, commencement address to graduate
students at Canisius College, Buffalo, New York, May
14, 2003.

20. p. 224   *We can really make a huge difference.'"*   Neeleman,
speech at WCBS Business Conference.

21. p. 224   *Big Apple is "the greatest city in the world"*   Ibid.

22. p. 224   *not going to be a success over the long term"*   Ibid.

23. p. 224   *that's what we're trying to do at JetBlue."*   Ibid.

CHAPTER 15   Looking to the Future

1. p. 226   *at the gate area, and especially while on board."*
"Song in the Cities," press release from Song, March
27, 2003.

2. p. 226   *We're going to go and kick their butts."*   Steve Huet-
tel, "No Singing the Blues," *St. Petersburg Times*, February 10, 2003.

3. p. 228   *all this money, is less than zero."*   Warren Buffett,
Warren Buffett Talks Business, PBS Home Video.

4. p. 228   *one huge step backwards for capitalism."*   Ibid.

5. p. 229   *"a kind of a war between AirTran and Delta."*   Russell
Grantham, "JetBlue leaves Atlanta, opts out of West
Coast dogfight," *Salt Lake Tribune*, October 25, 2003.

6. p. 229   *"We're just into making money."*   Ibid.

7. p. 230   *"I applaud Delta for doing something,"*   "Twenty-
five Most Influential of the Business Travel Industry,

2003," *Business Travel News*, January 19, 2004, p. 19–20.

8. p. 230   *How does that motivate people?"*   David Neeleman, interview by Nick Pachetti, *Money*, February 2003.

9. p. 231   *2004 is "a very competitive year"*   Susan Carey, "JetBlue Flies Into High Pressure," the *Wall Street Journal*, January 30, 2004, p. B3.

10. p. 231   *"It could have a bigger impact"*   Ibid.

11. p. 233   *he found surprising, as "brilliant, but not riskless."* Comments from Robert Mann of R. W. Mann & Co. following JetBlue conference call with analysts, June 10, 2002.

12. p. 237   *against JetBlue and stay there very long," he says.* Stuart Klaskin, interview by author.

13. p. 238   *we're in a very difficult business."*   David Neeleman, speech at New York Harvard Club, September 10, 2003.

14. p. 238   *continue to dazzle and excite your customers?"* David Neeleman, speech at Northwestern University, April 9, 2003.

15. p. 239   *alter the prospects for the stock."*   Carey, "JetBlue Flies Into High Pressure."

16. p. 239   *important to your customers and to your crewmembers."*   Neeleman, speech at WCBS Business Conference, October 5, 2003, attended by author.

17. p. 241   *continue to grow in the future."*   David Neeleman, interview by Charlie Rose, *The Charlie Rose Show*, PBS Radio, July 23, 2003.

Index